D1572968

PROCTER & GAMBLE

The House that IVORY Built

PROCTER & GAMBLE

The House that
IVORY Built

By the Editors of *Advertising Age*

NTC Business Books
a division of National Textbook Company • Lincolnwood, Illinois U.S.A.

Published by NTC Business Books, an imprint of
National Textbook Company, 4255 West Touhy Avenue,
Lincolnwood (Chicago) Illinois 60646-1975 U.S.A.
Manufactured in the United States of America.
Library of Congress Catalog Number: 87-82613
890 RD 9 8 7 6 5 4 3 2 1

Contents

Preface

W HEN I WAS A YOUNG REPORTER FOR ADVERTISING AGE in New York back in the early '60s, I used to enjoy going to lunch with product managers at Colgate-Palmolive Co. to listen to how they were going to knock off Procter & Gamble Co. They never did, of course, although Colgate made some temporary gains at the time with its House of Ajax line of household-cleaning products.

Through the years, lots of companies have taken turns trying to knock off P&G. It hasn't happened yet. As P&G heads into its second 150 years, I fearlessly predict that the company's leadership will continue to survive the rigors of undiminished competition.

In the pages that follow you'll read how P&G, from its earliest days as a candle and soapmaker in what was then the bustling young port city of Cincinnati, has built and maintained a worldwide soap, food, drug and toiletries business during its first 150 years—and how it constructed its vaunted marketing organization to deliver those products to consumers.

We at ADVERTISING AGE feel we bring a special expertise to this assignment, because P&G people tell me that our publication probably devotes more space to their company than any single publication anywhere, including the hometown Cincinnati newspapers.

We're very proud that this traditionally taciturn company has provided us access to its four top executives—Chairman-CEO John Smale, President John Pepper and Vice Chairmen Thomas Laco and Edwin Artzt—as well as six other division or department heads in an unprecedented show of cooperation with an outside publication. We're also grateful that we've been able to draw from P&G's vast and voluminous archives for many of the advertisements and illustrations and early documents shown on these pages.

Our sincere thanks go to Ed Rider, P&G's corporate archivist. I'd also like personally to thank Bob Norrish, director of public relations at P&G, for alerting me to the company's 150th anniversary a couple of years ago over coffee at an American Advertising Federation conference and for facilitating our reporters' efforts during the year or so we've been working on this issue.

Many people who don't know how P&G works think the company's huge advertising budget forces its products into consumers' hands and assures their success. But P&G watchers—like

1

us—know that it's the company's commitment to product quality and consumer benefits that has provided it with an edge for 150 years.

John Smale, P&G's chairman since 1981, told Fred Danzig, our editor, Bob Goldsborough, executive editor for features, and me that he believes one of the major challenges of management "is to be able to communicate the value of the company, to be able to be sure that managers understand those values and live by them."

Interestingly, Mr. Smale sees some similarities between P&G and Japanese companies. "We've made that analogy from time to time," he told us, although P&G "is not a Japanese-like company" because the Japanese are much more of a homogeneous society than we are. "Still, if you go back into the last century, the principal characteristics of the company related to that feeling of identification. The employees' benefit and interest and the company's benefit and interest were identical.

"The foundation of our ability to be successful is to be able to embrace the talents of every person working in the company, to really get everything they've got to give, to contribute. We're not perfect at it, but we're very conscious of how important it is, and we spend a lot of time and effort trying to be sure that that's what's going on."

If you want to learn why P&G has been so productive over the years, you need look no further

than John Smale's last statement. It's no coincidence, I strongly believe, that American productivity and competitiveness declined in direct correlation to the increase in corporate deal making running rampant across our land.

Sadly, however, that lesson has been lost on vast segments of American business, and that helps to explain why we've lost so much of our competitive position over the last few years. Deal making has prevailed over product making.

When the wheeling and dealing become more important than the basic product, and the quality, endurance and technology of the basic product, when the quarterly bottom line becomes more important than the customer and the customer's needs, then you're forgetting the fundamental reason you're in business in the first place: to serve your customer. If you put the customer, the consumer first, above all else, the profits will follow.

Proctor & Gamble, in its 150 years of doing business, steadfastly has adhered to the "basic values of the institution," as Mr. Smale put it, and that's why, for my money, the company represents the best example of the American spirit of free enterprise.

Rance Crain
Editor in Chief
Advertising Age

I

THE
COMPANY

CHAPTER ONE

The House That Ivory Built

It began as a soap and candle company in Cincinnati 150 years ago. Guided through the years by people of vision, Procter & Gamble today has become the premier U.S. package-goods marketer.

W HEN JAMES GAMBLE AND WILLIAM Procter signed their now-famous partnership agreement on Oct. 31, 1837, neither could foresee that their newly formed candle and soapmaking company would be a $17 billion consumer package-goods giant 150 years later, as well as a household name in more than 100 countries worldwide.

However, these facts probably would not surprise them. From the very beginning, Messrs. Procter and Gamble built their business with an eye toward the future. Before signing their partnership contract, they bought land near the Miami-Erie Canal, close to the Cincinnati city limits. They knew they would need a good site for a soap and candle factory. This simple deed illustrates one of P&G's most enduring characteristics: a belief in careful planning for long-term growth, no matter what the specific problem or crisis.

That P&G has enjoyed tremendous growth and staying power is a tribute also to the founders' successors. By most accounts, P&G is the world's preeminent marketer; the leading U.S. advertiser; a leading supporter of basic research and product development; and the founder of the modern brand-management system. In almost every American bathroom, laundry room or kitchen, at least one P&G product is sure to be found. P&G is a phenomenal corporate overachiever, and the company's 150th anniversary slogan encapsulates its ongoing philosophy: "Excellence—Through Commitment & Innovation."

Last November, more than 10,000 Cincinnati-area P&G staffers gathered at Cincinnati Coliseum to hear several top managers discuss P&G's purpose and values. Chairman-CEO John Smale told the audience: "We are here today because two men 150 years ago had a vision. And we are here because, through the years, generations of men and women shared that vision. They nurtured it. They preserved it—through five wars, through three severe depressions, through fires and floods, and through many, many cultural changes." These countless individual efforts laid the foundation for "The House that Ivory Built."

The partnership

It was by chance that 36-year-old William Procter, a candlemaker, and James Gamble, a 34-year-old soapmaker, married into the same family. Both men were immigrants from the British Isles. Mr. Gamble's family came from Ireland in 1819 to escape that country's economic depression. The Gambles' original destination was Shawneetown, Ill., then considered the center of the Midwest. But when 16-year-old James became ill, the family ended their journey in Cincinnati, at that time a growing Ohio River port with a population of about 25,000. James recovered, and in 1821 apprenticed himself to soapmaker William Bell. By 1833, he did well enough financially to marry Elizabeth Ann Norris, the daughter of Cincinnati chandler Alexander Norris.

Just the year before, William Procter came to the U.S., after a fire and burglary of his newly opened woolens' shop in London left him penniless. With his wife, Martha Peat, he was heading for a new life in Louisville, Ky., when the first cholera epidemic swept through the U.S. As they traveled down the Ohio River, Martha came down with the disease and died in Cincinnati. Mr. Proctor decided to settle in the city. Having learned how to dip candles as a boy in England, he learned that candles were being shipped into Cincinnati, even though raw materials to make them were readily available.

Thus, he began a second career as a candlemaker, making, selling and delivering candles from a shop he rented on Cincinnati's Main Street. Within months of his soon-to-become business partner's wedding, Mr. Procter married Olive, another Norris daughter.

5

Alexander Norris believed his two sons-in-law would benefit by combining their efforts because their businesses used the same raw materials: animal fats and wood ashes needed for making lye. Messrs. Proctor and Gamble were reluctant to try a new business venture. In 1837, the U.S. was in its first financial depression. (Martin Van Buren was in the White House, and the last stand at the Alamo was front-page news.) Despite dismal economic prospects, the joint venture made enough sense that the two men each contributed $3,596.12 to form their candle and soapmaking partnership. While P&G does not sell candles today, in the early years, candles were the company's primary source of sales and income.

From the start, James Gamble supervised production while William Procter ran the office. Soap and candle production were primitive processes. Each morning, Mr. Gamble made the rounds of homes, hotels and riverboats, collecting raw materials, paying with small cakes of soap for the animal scraps and wood ashes needed to make lye. Eventually, the collection of materials had to be extended throughout Hamilton and Butler counties. The company's first employee, Barney Krieger, helped Mr. Gamble in the daily collection routine.

While Mr. Gamble made his rounds, at least 18 other Cincinnati soap and candlemakers were doing the same thing. Already, the fledgling company faced stiff competition, but the two partners quickly developed valuable buying skills. They seized every opportunity to store raw materials for the future.

By 1848, the railroads linked Cincinnati with Cleveland and the major East Coast cities. River traffic, especially to the port of New Orleans, picked up. P&G easily could expand its distribution outside Cincinnati. The partners' business acumen already was paying early dividends;

William Procter, Candlemaker   **James Gamble,** Soapmaker

P&G's corporate archives show the company was earning an annual profit of $26,000.

Because many Americans were illiterate, businesses relied on painted signs to distinguish their goods from others'. Dockworkers in the early 1850s began marking P&G's crates of candles with a crude cross, which was modified to a star, possibly to identify the contents as P&G Star candles. Still another version showed the stars enclosed by a circle, with a quarter-moon in the right-half of the circle. Alfred Lief writes in his 1958 corporate history "It Floats," the "man-in-the-moon" or "moon-and-stars" symbol was discontinued for an unspecified reason in the 1850s, but was hastily reinstated when a New Orleans retailer refused to accept a subsequent shipment of unmarked P&G goods, believing the goods were imitations. He wrote to the company, "We want Star brand candles and no other . . . the only kind we can sell."

Company records indicate William Procter suggested a refinement in the ad hoc symbol: The cluster of stars should number 13, for the original American colonies, and the man-in-the-moon should be more sharply delineated. The symbol came to represent more than product identification. It also stood for the "honesty and integrity of the company," records show. At a time when many manufacturers were enhancing profits by short-changing customers, P&G stood out as one of the few refusing to short-weight its products. In his diary, James Gamble wrote, "When you cannot make pure goods and full weight, go to something else that is honest, even if it is breaking stone."

Having realized the importance of its trademark, P&G in 1875 took steps to protect its emblem. The trademark eventually was registered with the U.S. Patent Office, when federal legislation in the 1880s enabled businesses to have legal protection against trademark infringement. By 1882, the company commissioned a sculptor to polish the details of the face and the general design, which was patented that year. By 1902, the trademark took on many of the "gingerbread" characteristics common to designs at the time. In the early 1930s, the trademark again was redesigned by Cincinnati sculptor Ernest Bruce Haswell, who designed the moon-and-stars trademark currently in use on all company collateral materials. (It recently has been removed from product packages, however, because of rumors linking the design to Satanism.)

About 1850, P&G's business outgrew the first combination factory and office on Main Street, and the decision was made to locate a new plant on Central Avenue, on land near the Miami-Erie Canal the partners had bought several years earlier. The factory was then separated from the downtown business offices. Mr. Procter continued handling the sales and finances, while Mr. Gamble ran the factory. Neither felt compelled to meddle in the other's affairs, believing their regular Saturday night meetings at Mr. Proctor's home were sufficient to discuss the business and make future plans.

Their weekly planning sessions evidently paid off. In 1859, a writer in Cincinnati described P&G as "probably engaged more extensively in manufacturing operations than any other establishment in our city," with sales "largely exceeding $1 million annually." Company records of the time list 80 employees, including several young Procters and Gambles who had joined the family business during the late 1850s. Of the five Procter sons, three joined the company: William A., George H., and Harley T. Of the six Gamble sons, three also joined: James N., David B., and William A.

By the 1880s, the second generation was firmly in command of the business, with their elders occasionally offering some advice. In 1883, a third-generation son, William Cooper Procter, was called back to Cincinnati to join the family business in a manufacturing capacity, a term short of receiving his degree from what now is Princeton University.

During the 1860s, George H. Procter particularly distinguished himself as one of the first traveling salesmen. A graduate of Ohio's Kenyon College, he spent most of his career on the road, establishing contacts with brokers and wholesalers in the large eastern cities. His brother, William Alexander Procter, meanwhile, was helping his uncle James Gamble in the factory, supervising lard oil production. (The second-generation also guided P&G to sales of about $10 million during the three fiscal years 1887–1890, and averaged a half-million dollars in annual net profit.)

The Civil War years

Although their business was doing well, the founding partners were not oblivious to events outside Cincinnati. In the 1850s, it became increasingly clear that the nation was on the brink of civil war.

The company's main concern was whether rosin supplies would be cut off. This key soap-making raw material was available mainly through Southern sources. Worries about rosin supplies prompted the partners in 1860 to send William Alexander Procter and James Norris Gamble, an analytical chemist, to New Orleans to buy rosin. They easily secured a vast reserve for $1 a barrel and shipped it back to Cincinnati. A competitor, watching the shipment of rosin being unloaded, is said to have commented, "There goes P&G's funeral."

Messrs. Proctor and Gamble's penchant for advance planning again proved prescient. When the Civil War broke out three months later, P&G was almost the only soapmaker with sufficient reserves to meet the soap and candle demands of the Union armies. To meet quotas, the company had to institute nighttime production. The only time the factory shut down was for the Sabbath, still religiously observed by the founding families.

Once the P&G crates were emptied of soap and candles, they served as impromptu chairs and tables for the field armies. It is quite possible that nearly every Union soldier was exposed to the P&G name. The company's reputation was spread further when the soldiers marched home carrying unused P&G products.

In James Norris Gamble's diary, he noted in 1863 that an ice shortage suspended oil and summer candle production, "while grease was increasingly scarce and high [priced]." The shortage proved beneficial several years later. Until the Civil War, P&G relied on lard stearin to produce the stearic acid for candlemaking. When lard prices skyrocketed during the war, tallow was substituted, and new processes were developed by P&G for making stearic acid without lard, a practice that continued after the war. Instead of being used for candles, the lard and lard stearin were refined into a kitchen cooking product. This technology eventually gave rise, in 1911, to the creation of Crisco, the first all-vegetable shortening for home cooking.

Despite the company's stockpiles of rosin, that raw material also was in short supply toward the end of the war. James Norris Gamble experimented with silicate of soda, which he soon rejected for not producing the quality soap synonymous with the P&G name. However, silicate of soda later played an important role in the development of modern soaps and detergents.

Shortly after the Civil War ended in April 1865, a young telegraph operator, Thomas Alva Edison, briefly joined the company. He told James Norris Gamble the company's horse-and-rider courier system was "inefficient" in sending messages between the downtown offices and the plant. Mr. Edison set up a primitive telegraph system but left the company before making needed improvements. P&G did not learn what happened to Mr. Edison until 1879, when it heard he had invented the incandescent electric light bulb. Although the light bulb eroded the candlemaking business, no one paid much attention: That was the same year P&G developed "the Ivory."

P&G and "the Ivory"

The years 1871 to 1890 marked the greatest period of industrial development in U.S. history. The transcontinental railway was completed in 1869, moving people and products from coast to coast. Public waterworks came into vogue, as did indoor plumbing. The demand grew for soap, both for laundering and personal hygiene.

Newspaperman Horace Greeley wrote in his book, "The Great Industries of the United States": "The population of Cincinnati has increased to over 200,000 persons. The city has built nearly a thousand steamboats, and shipped yearly nearly $80 million worth of produce, importing nearly $100 million worth of materials from abroad . . . the industrial enterprise of the city has built up a manufacturing interest which produced an aggregate of over $50 million worth of various articles. . . ."

P&G, like most companies of the time, used limited advertising. Small ads for P&G's candles and soaps had appeared as early as 1838, and ads also ran in religious journals and in newspapers in cities where P&G soaps like Town Talk, Mottled German, Princess, Queen and Duchess were distributed. By 1870, P&G's total annual ad budget was $1,500.

But more important than advertising for the company were the first results out of a makeshift research laboratory erected in the Central Avenue factory. James Norris Gamble was working with P&G's first full-time chemist, an Englishman named Gibson, to develop an inexpensive white soap equal in quality to expensive, imported castile soaps.

It was James Norris Gamble who initiated yet another enduring P&G practice, that of researching products and processes before acquiring outside technology. While searching for the correct formula, he purchased a white soap formula from another soap manufacturer and promptly made improvements. It took several years, but finally, in 1878, P&G's White Soap was declared ready for introduction and shipments began. Company records indicate that early the next year, a careless workman left his soap-mixing machine running during his lunch hour, causing more air than usual to be beaten into the soap. The workman's supervisor decided no harm had been done to the formula, and the soap was first shaped into cakes, then cut into bars and shipped. Within weeks P&G began receiving orders for more of "the floating soap," which puzzled the office. But the mystery soon was solved, and the "accident" has been repeated for more than 100 years.

The name, P&G White Soap, bothered Harley Thomas Procter. He instinctively knew the soap would sell better with a more descriptive name. Inspiration for the new name came to him during a Sunday church reading of Psalms 45:8: "All thy garments smell of myrrh and aloes and cassia, out of the ivory palaces whereby they have made thee glad." The word "ivory" stood out in Harley's mind; by July 18, 1879, P&G's White Soap officially was trademarked Ivory.

In "It Floats," Mr. Lief summed up the importance of Ivory to P&G's future: "After 40-odd years of sound and honest but humdrum trading in candles, lard oil, miscellaneous soaps and glycerin, the company was pitched into prominence by the new product, and by the imagination and vigor of Harley Procter. . . . In his hands it was not just another soap, but a newborn babe with a great future."

Harley Procter's marketing prowess was evident. He was the first to recognize the importance of the independent chemist's analytical report of the 56/100% impurities in the bar; the first to recognize that the floating quality would allow consumers to find the bar in the wash water; and the first to persuade the company's board to advertise the soap with the then unprecedented budget of $11,000.

In a 1977 speech, Edward G. Harness, then chairman-CEO of P&G, discussed Ivory's legacy: "To the housewife of the year 1879, Ivory soap was a remarkable innovation in many ways. . . . Most of the soap was yellow or brown and much of it could irritate the skin and could damage washable surfaces and fabrics. Compared to other soaps of the time, Ivory was mild and gentle. It came in attractively wrapped cakes of uniform size and quality. It had a brand name so consumers could ask for it by name and thus know what they were getting each time they shopped. Finally, the product was advertised, which gave the consumer further assurance that the manufacturer stood behind the product. . . .

"Outside observers of our business frequently attribute marketing successes such as Ivory to our advertising and selling skills," Mr. Harness said. "They conclude that the success of a product . . . is the result of a high level of consumer demand which we have somehow pumped up through large-scale advertising and promotion campaigns. While advertising and selling are terribly important, we have never been able to build a successful brand through these skills alone. Advertising and selling skills can get consumers to try the product, but after that the health of the brand depends entirely on satisfaction with its performance."

In 1882, when Harley Procter first persuaded his colleagues to allocate funds for national advertising, they did it with great reluctance. Although it had been running small ads since 1838, the idea of investing a large sum of money in advertising was a radical idea for a company that historically tried to put every available penny back in the capital assets of the business.

The first Ivory ad appeared in a religious weekly, *The Independent*, on Dec. 21, 1882. It was targeted to the consumer at a time when most ads were aimed at dealers. The copy read, in part, "The Ivory is a Laundry Soap, with all the fine qualities of a choice Toilet Soap, and it is 99 and 44-100% pure." The "99 and 44-100% pure" claim stemmed from one of P&G's first product-oriented independent analyses. Harley Procter, ever searching for ways to make Ivory different from other soaps, asked a New York chemist to analyze the three leading brands of castile soap, then asked that same chemist to evaluate Ivory. By the chemist's own definition of purity, Ivory was purer than the castiles, with only 0.56% impurities.

Emphasis on scientific confirmation became a cornerstone of early Ivory ads. In ensuing years, P&G continued its reliance on scientific testimony to endorse products, everything from Crest toothpaste (the American Dental Association's Seal of Acceptance in 1960 for fluoride content), to Ultra Pampers disposable diapers (last year's National Association of Pediatric Nurse Associates & Practitioners' seal of approval for prevention of diaper rash). Surprisingly, Ivory's "floating quality" was slow to dominate the product's advertising. It was not used as a principal feature until 1891.

Harley Procter, who exhibited many of the forward-thinking traits of his father and uncle, was convinced the new national magazines coming into prominence, including *Good Housekeeping, Harper's Monthly* and *Ladies' Home Journal*, were the best way to "post the public" about Ivory. His practice of using new advertising vehicles to promote P&G's Ivory translated in later years to the company's early support of radio, TV and cable TV. This desire to be first in any new advertising and promotional development continues to the present day. P&G in 1987 is helping develop CheckRobot, a supermarket check-out system that places an interactive video screen and automatic coupon dispenser at the point-of-purchase.

For Harley Procter, buying ad space in the new magazines still was not enough. He also had definite ideas about where his ads should be placed. According to "It Floats," he was known to say, "How often, when you come into a home, do you see the back cover is ripped off. Then the first thing you notice is the Ivory ad." Although P&G was not the first company to use premiums and promotions to sell soap (the honor goes to a rival, Schultz Soap Co. in Zanesville, O.), the company quickly recognized their value. Ivory's first premium offer was a "miniature facsimile of a cake of Ivory Soap with a gold-plated ring to attach it to the watch chain . . ." for 12 soap wrappers.

Ads for Ivory began appearing on storefronts and fences. With the advent of trolley cars, P&G bought space on those early mass-transit vehicles.

Harley Procter not only was serving as one of the company's traveling salesmen, he also was responsible for all Ivory advertising. Not until 1900 did P&G hire its first advertising agency. The company contracted with Procter & Collier Co., run by Allen C. Collier, a Cincinnati printer who did advertising as a sideline, to produce Ivory's increasingly sophisticated four-color ads. Those ads boasted illustrations from many of the best-known illustrators of the time. According to Harley Procter's notes, he bought works for as much as $1,000 from Maxfield Parrish, W. Granville Smith and Alice Barber Stephens.

The artists' Ivory babies were a substantial improvement over the company's first baby, which looked more like a wrinkled old man than an infant. P&G archivist Ed Rider says the origin of the Ivory baby in ads was to represent "gentleness and mildness in a simple and memorable visual con-

cept." The new color ads pushed the Ivory ad budget to $300,000 annually by 1897.

According to the 1981 P&G corporate history, "Eyes on Tomorrow," written by Oscar Schisgall, once when Harley Procter ran out of ideas he appealed to the public to come up with "new, unusual and improved methods of using Ivory soap." He received so many suggestions the company eventually published a booklet, "Unusual Uses of Ivory Soap."

In the midst of P&G's Ivory boom, the company's Central Avenue plant burned down. The decision was made to rebuild on a 55-acre site near the Bee Line Railroad in Mill Creek Valley, about seven miles north of downtown Cincinnati. A $1 million loan was secured from the Mercantile Bank of New York, and Ivorydale, as the new factory was to be named, opened for business in 1886. Designed by the noted industrial architect Solon Beman, the new production facility was sorely needed. Capacity for soap at the old Central Avenue plant was 200,000 bars per day; Ivorydale could produce more than double that amount. Harley Procter's advertising had created a steady market for Ivory, as well as Lenox soap, a yellow laundry bar containing tallow and rosin created by James Norris Gamble. Lenox soap was advertised primarily to grocers.

In 1887, James Norris Gamble hired chemist Harley James Morrison, a distant relative, who built P&G's first modern analytical laboratory at Ivorydale. The mission then was to study and improve the soapmaking process. P&G's Mr. Rider says the Ivorydale Technical Center is one of the earliest U.S. industrial research laboratories and probably one of the first to employ women. The laboratory firmly established P&G as an innovative, technology-driven company committed to providing "added-value" to the consumer.

By 1889, P&G employed 600 people, and annual sales topped $3 million. The company with two top-selling brands even then demonstrated a willingness to market new products, even if those new brands took business away from existing ones. The seeds had been planted for the modern brand-management system, and it truly marked the beginning of the company's longstanding tradition of responding to consumers' needs.

Labor relations

By the turn of the century, the company had to weather its own version of the growing national labor unrest of the decade.

At Ivorydale, there is a marble statue memorializing William Cooper Procter, grandson of the founder. William Cooper believed the company should provide for the well-being of its employees. His beliefs were grounded in his days as a soapmaker. A 1919 issue of "Moonbeams," P&G's in-house employee magazine (which debuted that year), included a co-worker's description of William Cooper's activities: "He was dead set on learnin' the business from the ground up. I remember how he set up (sic) all night with his first kettle of soap. When it came noon he used to squat on the floor with the rest of us, in his overalls and smock, and eat the cold lunch he had brought from home."

William Cooper's close association with the factory workers gave him a unique insight into the current labor unrest. He knew what was being said by the Knights of Labor, a national labor group, as well as the newly formed Federation of Organized Labor Trades and Labor Unions (the forerunner of the AFL-CIO).

In 1884, he told his father, William Alexander Procter, and his uncle, James Norris Gamble, that the work week was too long; workers deserved Saturday afternoons off. This was a radical departure for American business at the time. The half-holiday was put into effect in 1885, setting a precedent for the rest of the nation's industry.

However, it became apparent the half-day was not enough. Ivorydale workers began a series of work stoppages to underscore their point, with 14 different strikes during the next two years. Additionally, there was a 50% turnover in factory workers during the course of the year. This prompted Cooper Procter, as he was known, to come up with satisfactory solutions.

The answer, he believed, was a form of profit-sharing, a European concept that was considered suspect in the U.S. because it originated overseas. But Cooper Procter believed profit-sharing would give workers an incentive to improve production efficiency. He wrote in his diary that "any worthwhile change in the conduct of a business must first and last have the element of lessening cost . . . the main claim of the employer is that the root of existing trouble lies in the fact that the employee takes no interest in his work and has no consideration for his employer's property or welfare." Sharing profits would supply the motive "which is now admitted to be sadly lacking," he continued.

Persuaded by his logic, the company introduced the plan on April 12, 1887, in a letter to all employees. It explained how the plan would divide net profits between the employees and company in the "proportion that total wages bore to the total cost of manufacturing and marketing." Each employee would receive a twice-a-year cash dividend based on the ratio of his wages to total wages. Although they greeted profit-sharing at first with skepticism, P&G factory workers quickly warmed to the plan at the company's first Dividend Day that October. Checks ranging from $14 to $280 were distributed to 193 employees (those who had been employed for the previous six consecutive months). In all, a total of $9,026.66 was given out to employees.

Despite the general acceptance of this first profit-sharing plan, Cooper Procter noted that there was no considerable productivity increase on the part of the factory workers. Mr. Procter concluded that workers who showed indifference should not receive their share of profits, which could be turned over to other workers who put out greater effort. Four classifications of workers were created, with dividends handed out according to merit. The modified profit-sharing plan helped somewhat, but failed to produce the desired production results. It took the incorporation of the company to add the much-needed final element.

Incorporation

By 1889, P&G was experiencing growing pains. To finance capital expenditures for additional plants, new equipment, and new product development, a new funding source was needed. The answer was incorporation. In 1890, "The Procter & Gamble Company" was organized under the laws of New Jersey, "only because that state had more liberal incorporation statutes than Ohio," writes Mr. Schisgall in "Eyes on Tomorrow." "There was never any thought of P&G leaving its hometown of Cincinnati."

The newly incorporated company was headed by William Alexander Procter, president; James Norris Gamble, VP; Harley T. Procter, second VP; William Cooper Procter, general manager; and David B. Gamble, secretary and treasurer. The incorporation made the company's shares more widely available, and in 1892, special provisions were made for employee stock purchase.

By 1903, Cooper Procter implemented the final phase of his profit-sharing plan. He proposed that profit-sharing should be tied directly to employee ownership of P&G common stock. In his words, the plan would "place a premium on thrift by requiring our people to save a certain fraction of their wages if they are to receive any extra money from the firm."

According to P&G's records, to be eligible for profit-sharing an employee had to buy stock equivalent at current value to his annual wage, "but could spread payment over several years with a minimum payment of 4% of his/her annual wage. At the same time, the company contributed 12% of the employee's annual wage toward purchase of that stock." The company's stock purchase and profit-sharing plans became so popular that, by 1915, 735 out of 1,200 eligible employees were participating.

Noted muckraker Ida M. Tarbell, in her 1917 book "New Ideals in Business," included interviews she conducted with workers at P&G's Ivorydale factory about the company's employee-benefits programs: "One of the reports which interested me most was that of a prominent union workman to whom I asked an introduction. . . . 'What do you think of it?' I asked. 'Think of it? It's the greatest thing ever, you can't believe it. It's too good to be true.' He figured it out (his dividends and profits of $725) in my notebook with satisfaction. It was evident that he often went over the figures trying to convince himself of their reality. 'You can't believe it,' he said. 'I never heard of such a thing before.' "

She continued, "I doubt very much if their profit-sharing could succeed as it is doing if employes (sic) did not realize not only that they were being given a chance to acquire an interest in the business but that the door is always open to higher positions. . . . I would not give the impression that it is a simple matter to acquire stock or reach the top in this business. It is no automatic machine by which men and women are pushed ahead by virtue of so many years of service. . . . You earn all you get at Procter & Gamble's. . . . The aim is development of individuals, not the creating of an industrial bureaucracy."

P&G also led the nation in its implementation in 1915 of a comprehensive sickness-disability-retirement-life insurance plan to protect its employees and their families against loss of income. Three years later, the eight-hour workday was introduced, followed in 1933 by the five-day work-week. Cooper Procter said, "This action is taken because of the company's desire to participate in the nationwide movement for the spreading of employment. The change will result in the employment of additional people and will provide greater security for our employees at work."

By the turn of the century, P&G was expanding through the development of new products and the application of new processes and inventions. Ms. Tarbell wrote, "The prompt sense which had led the early firm to see that candles were to fall before kerosene and to develop its soap market, had never been dulled in the business. It [the company] did not rest itself on soap alone. It had added glycerin-making when the process for extracting glycerin from what had been a waste of a soap factory was discovered and is one of their leading products.

"When it was discovered that cottonseed oil could be used for soapmaking instead of tallows and greases they began to manufacture the oil from the seed itself. They crush 4 million pounds a day now in the season. . . . It has developed enormous business in different lard compounds— a natural outgrowth of their other products." Indeed, P&G's sales were growing along with the U.S. population. Harley Procter's ad campaigns were running smoothly, with full-page Ivory illustrations prominently placed in leading magazines. While the company's net income exceeded $1 million in 1900, by 1904 profits reached $1.5 million. With the research laboratories constantly refining and exploring new products, it seemed nothing could keep P&G from doubling its profits again within 10 years.

More change

By the beginning of the 20th century, P&G's labor relations were relatively stable, but the company was being primed for a fundamental shift in its business. Candle production was rapidly declining. Taking precedent was the growing demand for soap and glycerin. The pressure was on to produce. Ivory and Lenox were being challenged by a number of new toilet and laundry soaps, which promised results "as good as P&G's Ivory," competitors' ads said. P&G's response to these newcomers was to improve its soaps and increase ad expenditures.

Meanwhile, laundry habits were changing. Where home washing once involved boiling and scrubbing clothes on corrugated washboards, a new yellow soap called Fels-Naphtha was helping eliminate much of the scrubbing. By 1902, P&G began producing its own White Naphtha, backed with substantial advertising. By 1920, it had become the largest-selling brand of soap in the world, according to company records.

By 1904, P&G was selling soap faster than its Ivorydale plant could produce it. To keep pace with demand, the company opened its second production plant in Kansas City, followed three years later by the opening of Port Ivory on New York's Staten Island. The new plants were needed for Ivory bar-soap production as well as for P&G's newly acquired laundry soap flakes brands. In 1903, Schultz Soap Co., Zanesville, Ohio, (Star bar and powder soaps) was offered for sale. P&G, eager to sell a similar laundry product, saw a chance to enter the field with an established brand. P&G bought the company for $425,000, promptly changed the formula to include naphtha, renaming it Star soap Star Naphtha washing powder and advertising it as useful for "all manner of rough cleansing, pots, pans, wood floors, etc."

Around the time naphtha soaps became popular, P&G found itself fighting for an ever-dwindling supply of cottonseed oil, a key ingredient in its soaps that also had potential for edible foods. Turn-of-the-century meat packers were buying much of the available cottonseed crop for use in lard compounds. Rather than continue bidding against the meat industry, P&G instead decided to ensure its own present and future needs by producing its own oils. In 1901, the Buckeye Cotton Oil Co. was created as a wholly owned P&G subsidiary. Its one production site, a leased mill in Greenwood, Miss., rapidly expanded to eight additional mills.

The new oil was good for salads, but some company managers opposed selling the oil to consumers. According to "Eyes on Tomorrow," they "felt the household market for salad oil might not be big enough to justify the cost of new installations, equipment, advertising, sampling and all the other expenses involved in introducing a new product." James N. Gable also was hesitant to sell the new oil directly to the public until further laboratory tests were completed. He did not object to sales to institutions because "their buyers were experts who could rely on their own tests and judgment," according to "Eyes on Tomorrow."

In 1907, 44-year-old William Cooper Procter was named president and CEO, following the suicide of his father, William Alexander Procter. In addition to his pioneering work in labor relations, Cooper Procter also presided over P&G's transformation from a soap and candle company to a modern-day soap and food company. Company records show he pushed for a broad research program. A chemical division was established in 1915, and two years later, four new recruits with chemistry degrees were hired.

One recruit, F. W. "Wes" Blair, later helped set up P&G's first pilot plant. In a recent P&G publication, "Memorable Years in P&G History," it was noted that the pilot plant was "a small-scale version of equipment in which the laboratory hoped to duplicate the final results that could be achieved in the regular industrial-size operation. In this case, the pilot plant was a miniature soap kettle, about 4 feet across and 5 feet deep. Up to this time, new soap formulas and processes had been tried in regular soap kettles, requiring full measure of raw materials. Now the laboratory could try out its preliminary findings at less cost and without tying up regular soap production."

Shortly after Cooper Procter assumed the presidency, research continued at Ivorydale for a way to develop very thin, quick-dissolving soap flakes for use in commercial laundries that now had washing machines.

P&G also was looking to develop an all-vegetable shortening, based on its winter-oil technology, which would compete against lard, butter and other cooking products. The answer was found in the hydrogenation process, which turns liquid oil into a solid. However, P&G was stalemated in its research until a German chemist, E.C. Kayser, visited Ivorydale. He showed Cooper Procter how hydrogenation worked and P&G's chemists eagerly adopted his methods.

While a hydrogenation plant was under construction at Ivorydale, Wallace E. McCaw, owner of McCaw Manufacturing Co., Macon, Ga., approached P&G with an offer to sell his business. Mr. McCaw's main product was a shortening called Flake White. Cooper Procter viewed Mr. McCaw's facilities as an opportunity to acquire a pilot plant for further experiments with P&G's hydrogenation formula. P&G's final formula combined liquid cottonseed oil with hardened cottonseed oil. After a series of failures, P&G filed for a U.S. patent on Nov. 10, 1910, for its new vegetable shortening "consisting of a vegetable oil, preferably cottonseed oil, partially hydrogenized, and hardened to a homogeneous white or yellowish semi-solid closely resembling lard . . . to provide a new food product for a shortening in cooking."

At a meeting in Cooper Procter's office, two product names, Kripso and Cryst, were combined to make Crisco. In one of its first ads, which appeared in the January 1912 issue of *Ladies' Home Journal,* Crisco was introduced as "An absolutely new product. A scientific discovery which will affect every kitchen in America."

The fledgling advertising department had to come up with ways to prove to the consumer that Crisco was different and better than lard or butter. According to "It Floats," a Cincinnati bakery was used for on-site taste tests. Bakers fried 400 dozen doughnuts in Crisco. The pastries were handed out to passersby. Out of that test came the idea for an experimental bakery in Ivorydale for product testing and recipe creation. P&G also helped sponsor national cooking schools as part of the company's Crisco introduction.

Mr. Lief writes in "It Floats": "Under newspaper sponsorship, and with advertisers of stoves, refrigerators, cooking utensils, etc., a well-known lecturer on domestic science served as instructor. The stage was turned into a kitchen . . . as eager audiences watched the performance, the instructor did not have to recite a commercial for Crisco. The can was in plain view."

Four-color ads including recipes were created by J. Walter Thompson Co., New York, on a fee basis. This marked the first time any P&G advertising had been handled outside Cincinnati's Procter & Collier Co. In late 1922, P&G gave the Crisco and Ivory accounts to Blackman Co., a New York ad agency. Years later, Blackman Co. became Compton Advertising.

Direct to retailers

By the turn of the century, retail trade relations were changing, beginning with a 1910 U.S. Supreme Court decision. It invalidated specific types of selling contracts, especially price fixing. Before this, P&G had bound wholesalers to sell at the list price to retailers and refused to deal with wholesalers who undercut prices.

New York wholesalers began harassing P&G's salespeople (as well as competitors Lever Bros.

and Colgate Co.) with demands for preferential prices. Cooper Procter recognized that "the only way to maintain a decent public respect for our prices and products is for us to take over the job of dealing with the retailers. Once these retailers become convinced that we insist on quoting the same price to every store, that we will not haggle or play favorites, then common sense may return to the New York market. They'll stop trying to cut our throat—and each others'."

When P&G announced its new direct-to-retailers policy in 1913, the wholesale grocers called a boycott of P&G products. The boycott did not last long; P&G's beefed-up sales force ably supplied area stores. Although company executives discussed extending its direct-to-retailers policy beyond New York, those plans were put on hold with the start of World War I in 1914. Before the war, P&G took steps to guard its Canadian markets against Lever Bros., and built its first international factory in 1915 at Hamilton, Ontario. The plant, with 75 employees, concentrated on producing Ivory soap and Crisco.

War again

The country's entry into World War I in 1917 strained P&G's manufacturing capabilities. Factories ran day and night to meet wartime needs. Yet the company was able to function. P&G again had taken measures to ensure its raw materials and manufacturing processes would not be disrupted, similar to the rosin stockpiling before the Civil War.

In a letter Cooper Procter wrote in April 1917 to his niece, Mary E. Johnston, then doing relief work in France, he noted, "Procter & Gamble are (sic) very fortunate and have (sic) enough raw material to last them a year and could make a great deal of money from their position, but I am going to try not to do so. . . . I don't want to make any money out of the war and I don't want the company to do so. I am afraid we will have trouble holding our prices down as our orders will be more than we can fill. . . ." P&G sales that year totaled $128.5 million, according to company records.

During the war, Cooper Procter spent much of his time fund raising and was considered to be the best speaker on the fund-raising circuit. (The Cincinnati Community Chest, organized in 1919, was an outgrowth of wartime fund raising, with Cooper Procter serving on the board. The Chest became a focus of community service for P&G executives as part of an ongoing company tradition of giving back to its hometown.) P&G also aided WWI recruiting efforts by giving employees paid time off to register for the draft and guaranteeing enlistees jobs with the company when they returned home. The patriotic themes carried over to advertising. Ralph F. Rogan, advertising manager since 1914, supervised P&G's wartime ads. "The Government says: Use No Butter in Cooking," read one Crisco headline. And Ivory bar soap was popular with doughboys. Back home, however, the new soap flakes were gaining popularity.

P&G's competitors in the soap industry developed new products threatening Ivory, White Naphtha and Lenox's market shares. Lever Bros. had invaded the U.S. with Lux Flakes and later, Lux soap. Colgate Co. also was active, with Cashmere Bouquet and Palmolive soaps. By 1919, Ivory soap in flaked form was introduced. Capitalizing on Ivory's fame, flakes were mentioned in Ivory's ads: "Now you can buy genuine Ivory Soap, ready shaved into snow-like flakes that warm water melts into 'Safe Suds in a Second.' " In 1921, Chipso soap flakes were introduced as the first P&G soap specifically designed for use in washing machines. P&G once again was giving the public what it wanted.

When the war ended, Cooper Procter turned the company's attention back to selling direct to retailers. During the planning stages, it became evi-

dent that Richard Redwood Deupree, general sales manager, was becoming Cooper Procter's right-hand man. Mr. Deupree suggested the direct-selling practice used in New York be extended nationally, starting in the New England area. Although the company again faced resistance from wholesalers, P&G implemented the plan by opening district sales offices in 19 cities, from Philadelphia to Chicago, from Minneapolis to Baltimore, and hiring and training 450 salesmen.

Another boycott of P&G products failed, but not before company profits declined sharply, coinciding with the recession in the early 1920s. But by 1923, the shift to direct selling paid off and retail orders were stabilized, thus allowing Cooper Procter to implement yet another labor relations coup. By maintaining an even flow of business, P&G was able to stabilize production and offer year-round employment. The guarantee of at least 48 weeks of employment attracted national attention. Mr. Deupree was asked whether it would truly work. He replied, "Guaranteed employment forces you to know your business. Anything that does that forces a better control and direction of the business. . . . We like to try the impractical and impossible and prove it to be both practical and possible—if it's the right thing to do in the first place."

On the air

While the switch to direct selling to retailers was taking place, P&G was attracted to radio as a direct advertising medium to reach consumers. Crisco recipe shows were first broadcast in 1923 over WEAF in New York, and P&G products were promoted through a variety of daytime programs: Emily Post's etiquette chats and Helen Chase's "Beauty Forums" for Camay, and "Mrs. Reilly's" discussions of the uses of Ivory soap. George, the singing Lava Soap Man, was the first

P&G-sponsored radio entertainer. Still not satisfied that this kind of programming was the most effective way to reach consumers, ten years later the company's product-oriented shows made way for a new type of entertainment, the daytime serial or "soap opera."

Although 1933 was not the best time to make risky business decisions, Mr. Deupree, by now company president (he would become chairman in 1948), knew people still were buying essential household products. Some shareholders argued that P&G should cut back on its advertising expenses, but Mr. Deupree insisted that P&G would continue its advertising despite economic conditions.

Soon too busy guiding the company through the Depression and then World War II, Mr. Deupree left P&G's radio programs in the hands of Ralph Rogan and Neil McElroy, then in advertising. They in turn relied on William Ramsey, who was named director of radio advertising.

Daytime serials began in earnest with "Ma Perkins," sponsored by Oxydol. It was a tremendous success. Satisfied daytime radio could indeed sell, P&G had serials developed for Crisco ("Vic and Sade," a comedy team); Ivory (" 'O'Neills''); Camay ("Forever Young"). Writes Mr. Lief, "P&G virtually built daytime radio for the networks and became the leading radio advertiser by the yardstick of number of periods of time on the air. . . . From a little over $2 million spent for network radio in 1935, the amount came close to $4.5 million in 1937, while general magazine and newspaper advertising remained static at $2 million."

At the same time, Oxydol was helping to create a new format for ads, the "slice of life" situation. A husband, talking to his wife over dinner, says, "A big meal like this on wash day? And we're going to the movies? Say, where's that old backache?"; His wife responds with a smile, "I've found a new soap called Oxydol, dear. No more backaches for me."

By 1939, P&G's radio staff was working on 21 programs. Network radio advertising cost almost $8.8 million that year; $1.8 million went to magazines and $3 million to newspapers. But that media schedule changed forever that same year, when Red Barber talked up Ivory's virtues on the first TV broadcast—a baseball game between the Cincinnati Reds and the Brooklyn Dodgers. TV's future as an advertising medium was established during that historic broadcast.

Satisfying consumers

In its desire to understand consumers' needs, P&G in 1923 devised a system to study finished products and determine whether they satisfied consumers. Wes Blair, of pilot plant fame, was the first to go with the advertising and sales crews into the field, where he distributed product samples and talked to consumers. His early market research led to the formation of an economic research department, where another associate, D. Paul Smelser, began in-depth studies of consumer habits. In "Eyes on Tomorrow," Mr. Schisgall writes: "His market research did not confine itself to products. It tested even the effectiveness of advertising—especially that of radio broadcasts. By such devices as offering 'Ma Perkins' flower seeds for an Oxydol box top plus 10¢, he was able to gauge the extent of public attention to a program. In the early days, probably no one in P&G's advertising departments or in its agencies did more to ascertain an advertisement's CPM [cost-per-thousand] as a guide for the efficient use of company funds. . . . Smelser and his associates, 34 by 1934, produced the basic data on which production, advertising and other operating decisions were made."

New P&G products were tested regionally before they were distributed nationally. Mr. Schisgall suggests such testing methods saved

P&G millions of dollars in "what could have been futile promotions." As Ed Harness noted in 1977: "In our business we are forever trying to see what lies around the corner. We study the ever-changing consumer and try to identify new trends in tastes, needs, environment and living habits. The successful company is the one which is the first to identify emerging consumer needs and offer product improvements which satisfy those needs."

P&G's records of the early 1920s note that for years there had been a laundry at the Ivorydale plant for employees' uniforms. In 1923, it became a research laboratory for studying laundry methods and products. P&G hired its first full-time professional home economist to run a home-economics kitchen and laundry. Her duties were to study "home washing and the home use of fats and oils in cooking and baking." Later a professional baker was employed to run a commercial bakery set up within a working research laboratory.

Despite soap flakes' success in improving on bar soaps for home laundering, the product occasionally would clump. To improve the soap flake, a P&G chemist in 1924 experimented with a bar of soap, scraping it with a comb. He let the particles fall onto a hotplate, where they puffed up into irregularly shaped granules. Although they were slow to dissolve in water, it was believed soap granules would be more effective than flakes. The first soap granules to be sold were branded Selox in 1927, but the "puffiness" of the product wasn't popular with consumers because the product contained too much air.

Beginning with Oxydol, a brand purchased in 1927 from the William Waltke Co., St. Louis (along with Lava, a soap based on vegetable oils and pumice), P&G succeeded in producing a soap with greater density.

During World War I, German scientists had developed a substitute cleaning agent called surface active agents or surfactants. Before long, P&G researchers were working on surfactants. In 1933, P&G introduced Dreft, the first synthetic detergent for all-around household use. Its only drawback was its inability to remove heavy dirt. Research continued for a heavy-duty synthetic detergent.

Another spinoff from early synthetic detergent research was the development of Drene liquid shampoo to replace soap. It quickly became apparent that Drene, introduced to retail drugstores in 1934, cleaned hair too well, stripping it of natural oils. A conditioning agent was added to overcome that problem. Problems with Drene led P&G to develop a new kind of research facility. It was a beauty parlor where employees could receive free shampoos and hair waves—if they were willing to have one side of their head washed with one shampoo and the other side with another brand. A new sales department was created to sell Drene; it was later expanded to sell other toiletries. (One of the first new brands, Teel dentifrice, another spinoff from the synthetic technology, was discontinued when the product turned teeth brown.)

A new regime

By the late 1920s, Mr. Deupree was the obvious heir apparent to the P&G presidency. He shared many of Cooper Procter's ideas. For example, an early memo he wrote to Cooper Procter argued for the necessity of giving sales employees greater responsibilities—a proposal that Cooper Procter found hard to turn down. Mr. Deupree probably did not realize he was formulating another P&G policy, that of exposing people to as many responsibilities as they could handle. His suggestion led to the promotion-from-within policy, whereby future executives would be well-trained in P&G's methods, problems and objectives. Mr. Deupree also insisted that executives keep their memoranda to no more than one typewritten page. In "Eyes on Tomorrow," Mr. Schisgall notes that the CEO often would return a lengthy memo with a warning: "Boil it down to something I can grasp."

The one-page memo remains ingrained in P&G's corporate culture. The company's numerous and far-flung alumni often recount their experiences with "the memo" with a mixture of pride and chagrin. According to Gordon Wade, a former brand manager who now runs his own firm, the Cincinnati Consulting Group, the P&G memo "performs the function of removing individual ego from a business decision. Because when thing gets discussed, you're never there, it's the memo and its contents that are discussed."

Cooper Procter decided in 1927 to give Mr. Deupree the title of general manager. A year later, the board elected him VP and he began assuming more of the duties of the CEO. It was a significant turning point. When Cooper Procter became the company's first chairman on Oct. 14, 1930 (a newly created position), Mr. Deupree became president. Four years later, on May 2, 1934, Cooper Procter died at the age of 71.

Under Mr. Deupree, the new president-CEO, P&G quickly moved to acquire a number of rival soapmaking companies, primarily for their equipment and manufacturing facilities. And it was to Mr. Deupree, in 1931, that Neil McElroy proposed the now-famous brand management system.

Brand management

Mr. Deupree had convinced Cooper Procter that consumer preferences for hard-milled, perfumed soaps would continue to grow. He pointed out that competitors' Lux, Palmolive and Cashmere Bouquet brands were making steady inroads on Ivory. P&G had to compete. The answer was Camay. In 1925, Neil McElroy joined the company

as an advertising department mail clerk. In 1929, he became manager of the promotion department, helping to introduce a new soap, Camay, and keeping an eye on its ad schedules.

Company executives decided Camay was being held back "by too much Ivory thinking," particularly in the ad agency handling both brands—Blackman Co., New York. Advertising VP Ralph Rogan suggested a new agency be appointed. Following his advice, Pedlar & Ryan, New York, was chosen as Camay's new agency, thus ensuring that Camay and Ivory could compete without restrictions. Mr. McElroy was appointed the soap's brand supervisor.

He had to leave Camay in 1930 when the company needed a marketing executive to run P&G's first overseas subsidiary, Thomas Hedley & Co., Newcastle-on-Tyne, England. While in England, Mr. McElroy was able to study Unilever at close range, "giving him an early understanding of the requirements of the business apart from those of advertising promotion," Mr. Lief writes in "It Floats."

When he returned to Cincinnati a year later, Mr. McElroy determined that a single brand man could not keep up with all of the details of running a brand. He outlined the responsibilities of his "one man-one brand" idea. It involved creating a new position, assistant brand manager. The assistant "would follow through on office work laid out by the brand manager; make field studies as directed by the latter; stay in close touch with the advertising and field plans. . . . Finally, he'd be able to step into the shoes of his superior at a moment's notice," wrote Mr. McElroy in a three-page memo (this one wasn't kicked back for being too long).

Out of this memo grew the brand-management system: Brand-group supervisors would report to the head of a brand division, each of which oversaw the work of a brand manager. Brand managers would be aided by brand assistants. Writes

Mr. Schisgall, "The basic principle of brand management—to operate each brand as a separate business—has, of course, become so fundamental a part of P&G operations that few people can imagine the company had ever operated in any other fashion."

At the time, there were a few P&G executives who thought it "suicidal" to pit one brand against another. *Time* magazine noted, "Eventually McElroy won his point. He persuaded his elders that the way to keep fast-growing P&G from becoming too clumsy was indeed to have it compete with itself." As the company states in a recent recruiting brochure: "P&G is organized with the Brand Group at the very center of things—deeply involved in every aspect of our consumer and industrial businesses. P&G invented brand management over 50 years ago to assure us that each brand has behind it the single-minded drive and personal commitment from talented managers it needs to succeed. This brand independence lets us market vigorously a number of different products, many of them competitive with one another."

Indeed, the brand-against-brand competition did not seem to hurt Ivory or the company's sales. In 1937, P&G celebrated its centennial with sales reaching $230 million. Mr. Schisgall notes, "The company also owned 11 manufacturing plants in the U.S. and five in four other countries— Canada, England, Cuba and the Philippines. It was operating 12 mills for the crushing of cottonseed. Also, for the processing of cellulose, it had in Memphis what was described as 'the largest such mill in the world.' The founders would have been astounded."

Military contractor

By the time P&G held its annual shareholders meeting in October 1939, Europe once again was at war. Although this country had not yet become involved, Mr. Deupree, P&G's president, told employees, "The company must be ready at all times to meet sudden wartime emergencies. . . . No one can foresee what the future may hold, but we have the satisfaction that we have built wisely in preparation for the future and . . . are prepared to meet conditions as they develop."

In the fall of 1940, the U.S. Army Ordnance Department asked P&G to construct and then provide the trained manpower for a new plant to load shells near Milan, Tenn. P&G was chosen for its experience in applying scientific and technical methods to large-scale, high-speed manufacturing processes and the Army saw "no reason why P&G's expertise in putting powdered and granulated soaps into paper packages could not be applied to putting powdered and granulated explosives into steel packages," notes "Eyes on Tomorrow." Procter & Gamble Defense Corp. became P&G's newest subsidiary. Harvey C. Knowles, general manufacturing manager, was put in charge of the new Wolf Creek Ordnance Plant.

In August 1941, three months ahead of schedule, the first production line went into action producing 60mm trench mortar shells. Soon, the Wolf Creek plant was producing more than the contract specified. The Army was so impressed with P&G's performance that early in 1942 it asked the company to construct and run a second shell-loading facility, which became the Gulf Ordnance Plant at Aberdeen, Miss.

At peak production in 1944, both the Milan and Gulf operations employed about 14,500 workers, about the total number of people Procter & Gamble employed at all its other plants in the U.S. and overseas. Shell-filling at the two ordnance sites was halted when the war ended in 1945.

(P&G reactivated in the Milan Ordnance Center during the Korean War, and for about five years during the 1950s, P&G also managed an ordnance plant in Amarillo, Tex., for the Atomic

Energy Commission. The plant and its work, kept secret, was noted in P&G's files only as "a manufacturing center for important components of atomic and hydrogen bombs.")

Other wartime efforts

Glycerin, a substance P&G had been producing for 80 years, also was in great demand during WWII. The company, considered to be the world's largest glycerin processor, provided the military with large quantities of refined glycerin, a key ingredient of nitroglycerin, dynamite and smokeless powder, and sulfa drugs.

Rationing of tires, gasoline, canned goods, sugar, coffee, meats, cheese and fats became routine by 1943. However, government rationing of soap was prevented by a salvage campaign. Homemakers took used fats to butchers, who gave them to renderers to be made into soap. About 940 million pounds of used fats were collected and consumer soap rationing was avoided.

P&G's plants in England survived numerous air raids, but its facilities in the Philippines were commandeered by the Japanese to make soap. When the American forces stormed the Philippines, most of the Manila plant was destroyed. Another plant believed to be demolished in Surabaja, Java, was only slightly damaged. Both plant sites were quickly restored after V-J day, marking P&G's continued commitment to expand its markets outside the U.S.

In 1946, two unconnected events also prepared the company for its post-war boom years. Neil McElroy was elected VP and general manager of the company on Oct. 9, 1946, and Mr. Harness rejoined the company after serving in the Air Force during the war.

P&G continued its advertising and promotion campaigns during wartime, especially on radio. By 1945, the company was spending $15 million on radio, about twice as much as it did for all other media. P&G's TV advertising plans were put on hold for the duration of the war. P&G sponsored a number of new radio shows during WWII including "Perry Mason," "Queen for a Day" and "Professor Quiz," some of which later became TV shows.

Although P&G in 1945 purchased a Saginaw, Mich.-based family-owned business that sold Spic & Span wall-cleaning powder—a brand P&G thought would make a good all-purpose cleaner—the purchase was barely noticed because of the war.

Post-war juggernaut

By the time Japan surrendered, P&G had become a vastly different company from the one founded by Messrs. Procter and Gamble. No longer was a direct descendant of the founders in charge of what in 1945 was a $352 million company, although Richard Deupree (elected chairman in 1948, allowing Neil McElroy to become president) in many ways continued Cooper Procter's leadership style.

The war wrought even greater changes. In 1945, P&G essentially was a soap and laundry products company, with interests in edible oils and toiletries. After the war, P&G, already geared for growth with its brand-management system, national selling force, dedication to advertising and ongoing research program, was ready to meet pent-up consumer demand. "Yet the amazing thing is, you can trace each of these developments all the way back to candles and soaps," says archivist Ed Rider.

"Technologies learned from crushing cottonseed for soap led to foods, to paper, to coffee. Each new business somehow tied in to an already established business."

Washday miracle

In 1947, Ivorydale underwent major expansion to further its experiments to improve soaps and detergents. It also was the year P&G nationally introduced Tide, the "washing wonder" heavy-duty synthetic detergent that set the detergent-industry standard. Although P&G had created Tide in its laboratories during the war, shortages of key materials held up test marketing. P&G was working with a new kind of phosphate compound—sodium tripolyphosphate (STPP)—that cleaned without leaving harsh mineral deposits in institutional dishwashing machines. When STPP was added to detergent, it improved its washing abilities.

P&G executives knew the new detergent would cut into Dreft and Duz sales, but Neil McElroy is credited with saying, "If we don't [use this technology], someone else will."

By 1946, P&G had created a new brand-management team to market Tide, which was tested in six cities: Springfield, Mass., and Albany, N.Y., for soft water; Evansville, Ind., and Lima, O., for medium water; Wichita, Kan., and Sioux Falls, S.D., for hard water. (Benton & Bowles, New York, was assigned the advertising account; in 1961, P&G yanked it out of B&B to give to Compton Advertising, New York, now Saatchi & Saatchi DFS Compton.)

Samples of the new detergent and an initial retail stock of Tide were readied for the test. P&G, however, was unprepared for the sales success of its "modern washday miracle." Tide, patented in 1946, had no immediate competition, although Lever Bros. soon brought out Surf and Colgate-Palmolive introduced Fab. Mr. Lief notes in "It Floats" that by 1948 the industry volume of synthetic detergents "amounted to nearly one-fifth of the total of all other household laundry products." Aiding Tide's estimated $21 million advertising and sales promotion introduction was the expanded presence of home automatic washing machines. Washing machines increased from 3% to 33% of U.S. households in the decade following the end of WWII.

New machines and new fabrics like nylons demanded detergent changes. P&G researchers continued tinkering with the Tide formula and worked on new detergents as well. Tide, touted as P&G's "revolutionary detergent," received the best of the new technologies. Fabric brighteners, new perfumes and a switch from coconut oil to tallow gave Tide richer suds and lowered the price. By 1949, Tide was the No. 1 detergent, outselling P&G's own Oxydol and Duz. P&G could barely produce enough to meet demand. That same year, P&G introduced Joy, its first light-duty liquid detergent specifically formulated to cut grease while washing dishes. (At the same time, regular detergents were being used for dishwashing.)

Because every soap company was trying to produce as good a detergent as Tide, P&G executives decided they should be the one to grab the No. 2 market position. In 1950, P&G introduced Cheer detergent into test markets. ADVERTISING AGE reported that the brand was supported "by a concentrated merchandising and advertising campaign, using newspapers, comic supplements, radio and outdoor media" (AA, Apr. 17, 1950).

Known in its early, top-secret stage as Product J, Cheer was assigned to Young & Rubicam, New York. However, sales languished until someone thought to add blueing to Cheer. Many housewives at the time were adding a blueing agent to the white wash for the slightly blue tint it gave clothes. Y&R's TV campaign announced to the nation, "It's New! It's Blue!" (Cheer still is blue, with advertising handled by Leo Burnett USA, Chicago.)

Based on consumer research, P&G realized detergents could be tailored to meet specific laundry requirements: Cheer was formulated to clean in cooler water; Oxydol contained a color-safe oxy-gen bleach; Dash was P&G's first low-sudsing concentrated detergent; Bold 3 had brighteners and fabric softener; and Era, a heavy-duty liquid detergent, was effective against oily and greasy soils.

Tide has remained the leading detergent brand, despite tough competition. In 1984, the company introduced Liquid Tide, backed by an AA-estimated $100 million advertising campaign. The heavy-duty liquid laundry detergent contains 12 cleaning ingredients—two to three times the number in other liquid detergents.

Health and beauty

In the midst of the detergent surge, P&G in 1948–49 made three key organizational changes. Neil McElroy became president; Howard J. Morgens was named VP-advertising and also had responsibility for what were then called drug products; and Walter Lingle became VP-overseas operations. P&G's drug products group was started before World War II with the introduction of Drene. It was the first time synthetic-detergent technology was applied to a shampoo. In 1946, P&G introduced Prell, a concentrated shampoo in a tube. An early radio spot by Benton & Bowles, New York, brought the shampoo fame the company would rather have avoided. The spot ended with the tagline, "I'm Tallulah the Tube, take me home and squeeze me!" Tallulah Bankhead, a well-known actress, sued P&G for $1 million for the unauthorized use of her name. The story was national news—but it gave P&G an esti-mated $10 million of free advertising. The actress settled her suit for $5,000 (AA, Sept. 11, 1950).

Prell and Drene in the late 1940s were sold by a national sales force of fewer than 20, although company executives agreed such health and beauty aids were "natural companions of the company's basic soap line. Certainly the care and cleaning of hair and teeth were closely allied to the care and cleaning of skin and clothes," notes "Eyes on Tomorrow."

Mr. Morgens, allowed to treat the drug prod-ucts business as a separate company, appointed managers of advertising, product development manufacturing and sales, thereby pushing P&G further into the beauty, health and personal care business. Early work with shampoos gave P&G a knowledge of hair, which led to the development of Lilt home permanent. It is considered P&G's first strictly cosmetic toilet goods product.

With an AA-estimated budget of $14 million to $19 million to introduce Gleem in 1953, P&G began its attempt to squeeze money from the toothpaste business in the same manner as in the soap business. Ad managers of the time told AA "the only other time a new product received such intense promotion was when P&G launched Tide—and the Gleem push is bigger" (AA, Feb. 8, 1954). By yearend, AA reported that Gleem, po-sitioned by its then-agency Compton Advertising as the toothpaste "for the people who can't brush their teeth after every meal," had grabbed 20% of the $135 million category, a close second to Colgate-Palmolive Co.'s Colgate, with 37%.

P&G continued its toothpaste research, with cavity prevention being a priority. One estimate was that Americans developed 700 million cavi-ties annually. Fluoridation of local drinking water was believed to help prevent decay, and the direct application of fluoride to tooth enamel rendered it more resistant to acids produced in the mouth. P&G in 1950 began working with Joseph Muhler, an Indiana University researcher, on anti-tooth decay ingredients for toothpaste.

At P&G's new Miami Valley Laboratories near Cincinnati, the combined P&G-Indiana Univer-sity research staff found the combination of ingre-dients necessary for making an anti-decay tooth-paste. Crest, a toothpaste containing Fluoristan, a

P&G trade name for stannous fluoride with a polishing agent, went into test market in 1955 in Columbus, Ohio, and sections of New York and Oregon (AA, Feb. 21, 1955). Sales, however, were lackluster. Early Crest ads from Benton & Bowles announced "milestones in modern medicine," the latest being Crest's "triumph over tooth decay" (AA, Jan. 23, 1956). But the public did not immediately see the results of using the toothpaste. The brand group soon realized that if an outside authority were to promote Crest's antidecay abilities, the brand would get the validation—and market push—it needed.

The American Dental Association had set up a formal review panel for evaluating the therapeutic benefits of oral hygiene products, both to guide the dental profession and help keep advertising claims truthful. In 1954, the brand group, led by P&G Associate Advertising Manager John Smale, began submitting to the ADA the results of P&G's extensive clinical tests. Although the organization never before endorsed a toothpaste, the ensuing five-year review paid off. The ADA's staff in 1959 felt it had gathered enough data to submit to the ADA's Council on Dental Therapeutics. Within a few months, the Journal of the American Dental Association reported "Crest has been shown to be an effective anticaries [decay preventative] that can be of significant value when used in conscientiously applied program of oral hygiene and regular professional care" (AA, Aug. 1, 1960).

It was the first time the ADA had allowed its name to be used in consumer product advertising. And P&G quickly made the most of that endorsement: TV spots created by Benton & Bowles stressed "25 to 49% fewer cavities with Crest" and a specially trained group of "detailers" was formed to inform dentists around the country about Crest's benefits. According to "Eyes on Tomorrow," Crest sales by 1962 had nearly tripled from $127.6 million in 1956, pushing it ahead of Colgate as the best-selling toothpaste in the U.S.

In 1981, New Advanced Formula Crest with an improved fluoride system doubled the cavity-fighting ability of original Crest. In mid-1985, Tartar Control Crest helped restore Crest as the No. 1 brand, after almost allowing Colgate to take the lead in the early 1980s (AA, March 14, 1984).

Although later product developments included Sure and Secret deodorants, Scope mouthwash and Head & Shoulders shampoo, Crest set the stage for P&G's future as a major player in healthcare products. This eventually led to the company's 1982 acquisition of Norwich-Eaton Pharmaceuticals (Chloraseptic, Head & Chest, Pepto-Bismol) and the 1985 acquisitions of Richardson-Vicks and the Metamucil, Dramamine and Icy Hot brands from Monsanto Co., which earlier had acquired them from G.D. Searle & Co. These latest acquisitions, directed by current Chairman-CEO John Smale (who once worked for Richardson-Vicks), made P&G the largest marketer of over-the-counter drugs in the U.S. (AA, July 14, 1986).

Paper breakthrough

The tremendous success of Crest and experience with other toiletries increasingly led P&G into industrial chemical technologies. This industrial chemistry, in turn, was put to use by P&G's Buckeye Cellulose division in a giant paper mill at Foley, Fla. It opened in 1951 to meet the growing need for cellulose in synthetic fibers, film and plastics. The cellulose produced in Foley was not directly applicable to the soft tissue products P&G wanted to develop. In 1957, P&G bought the Charmin Paper Mills, Green Bay, Wis., a regional paper manufacturer that had been in business since 1892. Charmin already had a consumer following in the Midwest for its toilet and facial tissues, paper towels and napkins. It also had three plants in operation.

In "Eyes on Tomorrow," Mr. Schisgall writes, "Howard Morgens, who spearheaded the effort for this start in the industry, described Charmin as a 'pilot plant and a little pilot marketing area with which to learn the business.' "

Hercules Segalas, senior VP-household products analyst with Drexel Burnham Lambert, New York, was in P&G manufacturing when the company entered the paper business. "In the mid-1950s, P&G's long-range planning had analyzed [trends in] non-woven fabrics and decided that by the mid-1980s, [consumers] would be using disposable sheets and shorts, which of course would mean a crisis for the laundry business. P&G had been working on paper processing in the Miami Valley Laboratories but needed a [pilot] plant to make sure it worked."

P&G's intent from the start was to improve the quality of Charmin tissue and create new products. A new way to dry pulp created White Cloud bathroom tissue, Puffs facial tissue and an improved Charmin toilet tissue. To maintain market growth, P&G needed to build more production capacity. The original Green Bay and Cheboygan, Mich., plants were expanded. In April 1965, the company announced it would build a huge, 52-acre paper plant in Mehoopany, Pa.

By the mid-1960s, P&G had created Pampers and a new product category, disposable baby diapers. Pampers' story began in 1956, when Vic Mills, P&G's director of exploratory development, spent some time caring for his newborn grandchild. He decided there had to be some way to eliminate the chore of cleaning cloth diapers.

After much research and experimentation, three years later the staff had assembled 37,000 then-unnamed diapers for a test in Rochester, N.Y. Parents liked the diaper, and manufacturing had to come up with machinery to produce the new product. For some time, the new diaper didn't have a name, but by the time it was brought into test market (in 1961 in Peoria, Ill.), it was named Pampers. Handled by Benton & Bowles, New York, Pampers were promoted "as flushable through modern plumbing facilities," therefore "providing a highly sanitary diapering method" (AA, Dec. 18, 1961).

However, the Peoria test was considered a failure by P&G. Mothers liked the new diaper, but balked at the 10¢ per diaper price. P&G determined that a sharply lower price was needed to obtain broad acceptance, and a sales plan was implemented based on a 6¢ per diaper price. The combination of superior-to-cloth performance and reasonable pricing worked. Parents liked the new diapers so much that by the mid-1980s, nearly 98% of all U.S. households with infants were using disposable diapers (AA, Feb. 14, 1985).

Edward Harness, VP-group executive (he became chairman-CEO in 1974), in the late 1960s told shareholders, "Pampers is a beautiful example of P&G's ability to look into the future and recognize tremendous opportunity. Disposable diapers had been sold [before] yet when . . . Pampers were launched, less than 1% of the billions of diaper changes which take place in America were being made with disposables. Existing products were not good, their prices too high and retail distribution was minuscule. . . ."

After much additional research, P&G developed a diaper with "elastic leg gathers." It was introduced as a second brand, Luvs, in 1980. Luvs was positioned as a premium-quality diaper. It also led to Attends disposable briefs for incontinent adults. In 1984, both Pampers and Luvs added refastenable tapes, double-elastic leg gathers and improved absorbency (AA, Dec. 23, 1985). In 1985, P&G poured $500 million into new technologies and equipment to design two new versions of Pampers: New Pampers, with a thicker core and softer topsheet, and Ultra Pampers, with a "lockaway core" that is about half as thick as other disposable diapers, but more absorbent.

In "Memorable Years in P&G History," the company said it would increase its "world leadership in disposable diapers [by] continual development of even better products. The company is committed to producing future diaper innovations that will give babies the best quality and parents the best value available anywhere in the world."

Government calls

In 1957, the government once again requested a small favor from P&G. U.S. President Dwight D. Eisenhower asked to "borrow" P&G's president, Neil McElroy, 52, to serve as Secretary of Defense. In accepting the appointment, Mr. McElroy resigned as president of P&G, although he later returned to the company as chairman when Richard Deupree retired (AA, Dec. 7, 1959). On Mr. McElroy's confirmation by the Senate, P&G's board elected Howard J. Morgens to be the new president.

AA noted, "When P&G had to pick a new president, they went back to the place where they got the old one—the advertising department" (AA, Aug. 26, 1957). Although Mr. Morgens "was never regarded as a protege of Mr. McElroy, observers think the principal difference between the two men as administrators . . . is personality," AA reported. "Mr. McElroy is less deliberate in his decisions than is Mr. Morgens."

Acquisition appetite

Mr. Morgens supervised P&G's growth by acquisition in the late 1950s and early 1960s.

In August 1955, P&G widened its product lines by acquiring W.T. Young Foods, Lexington, Ky., producer of peanut butter and salted nuts marketed under the brand name Big Top. Compton Advertising was appointed to handle the new subsidiary's advertising. In 1956, P&G entered the baking mix field with the acquisition of the Duncan Hines operations of Nebraska Consolidated Mills Co., Omaha. AD AGE reported, "Indirectly, P&G also bought its way into a host of other business, ranging from major appliances to salad dressings by acquiring Hines-Park Foods and the Duncan Hines Institute, both in Ithaca, N.Y. . . . [which] license companies to make products under the Duncan Hines name" (AA, Aug. 20, 1956).

In announcing these purchases, Mr. Morgens (then exec VP) said, "Procter & Gamble has naturally been interested for some time in the growth of household cake mixes and other baking mix products. Through our shortening products, we have been deeply involved in the home-baking field for more than 40 years. Since housewives are showing an increasing interest in buying shortening already mixed with flour, sugar and other ingredients, it seems quite logical for P&G to extend its interest to prepared mix products as a companion line to Crisco and Fluffo," another P&G shortening, since discontinued (AA, Aug. 20, 1956).

P&G entered the coffee business with its 1963 purchase of the 113-year-old J.A. Folger & Co., San Francisco and Kansas City (AA, Sept. 2, 1963). At the time, Folger was said to be the second-largest coffee company and the largest independent one in the U.S. AA reported that the company was the "leading seller of ground coffee west of the Rockies." As might be expected, P&G revamped advertising for Folgers with agency Cunningham & Walsh, New York, which had handled the brand's campaigns east of the Rockies. The campaign featured a fictional Mrs. Olsen, played by actress Virginia Christine, who delivered testimonials as though she was talking to members of her family.

Concurrent with its food company acquisitions, P&G also acquired Clorox Chemical Co., Oakland, Calif., as a wholly owned subsidiary

(AA, April 24, 1957). Immediately after purchasing Clorox, P&G moved in its own marketing veterans and upgraded advertising to P&G standards.

Operating structure

In June 1955, P&G reported record sales of $966 million and net earnings of more than $57 million. It became clear that to sustain P&G's remarkable growth some changes were needed in the organizational structure. A company approaching the $1 billion mark could "hardly be run with the simple methods of a small, single-interest soap company," writes Mr. Schisgall in "Eyes on Tomorrow."

Ever since the company created the drug products group in 1943, P&G had been moving toward establishing separate operating divisions. At an annual meeting of managers in 1955, Howard Morgens, then exec VP, said, "The company expects to grow naturally and soundly by building on its present foundations in those areas where we already have much background and experience." To do so, Mr. Morgens divided P&G's "three major areas of U.S. business—soaps, foods and drug products—through three separate operating divisions," each responsible for its own operations (volume, growth and profits) and with its own general management.

As outlined by Mr. Morgens, the plan included "staff or corporate functions" to allow the company to coordinate the activities of its separate divisions. These P&G staff responsibilities included basic research, relations with advertising agencies, broadcasting networks, radio and TV talent, general supervision of sampling and couponing activities and engineering.

In 1965, P&G further divided its household soap products business into two separate divisions and began trying out two separate sales forces to handle the new setup. P&G's U.S. detergent, soaps and other household cleaning products now would be handled by the packaged soap and detergent division with responsibility for packaged soap and detergents for laundry and dishwashing. The bar soap and household cleaning products division would handle bar soaps, fabric softeners, cleaners, cleansers and other household cleaning products.

By the late 1970s, Chairman-CEO Edward Harness would be overseeing 10 operating divisions worldwide for consumer products and five for industrial products. Many U.S. companies then were expanding by means of mergers and acquisitions. Some, like General Foods Corp. with its ill-fated Burger Chef restaurant chain purchase, diversified into unfamiliar categories.

P&G aware that growth without planning and "a unifying product concept" could be disastrous, chose to focus on household products that had certain common characteristics. Mr. Schisgall quotes one company executive: "These are products which move through grocery stores and drugstores primarily for use in the home. They are small-unit, low-priced, packaged products which are purchased frequently and are used up in a relatively short time." It's a policy P&G has not deviated from over the years.

Modern advertising

In the years following World War II, TV began coming into its own. City dwellers began buying sets by the thousands. P&G, which earlier recognized radio's ability to reach a large number of consumers, quickly jumped on the TV bandwagon. At the same time, P&G's stable of advertising agencies increased rapidly to keep pace with the company's TV activity and brand proliferation.

By 1961, P&G's roster listed nine agencies. Compton Advertising, New York, handled the flagship Tide detergent brand, Ivory soap and nine other products; Dancer Fitzgerald Sample, New York, had Oxydol, Dreft, Gain, Dash, White Cloud and Puffs; Benton & Bowles, New York, had seven, including Charmin paper products and Crest; Leo Burnett Co., Chicago, listed five—Camay, Joy, Salvo, Lava and Secret; Gardner Advertising, St. Louis, was responsible for Jif peanut butter and Duncan Hines cake mixes; Grey Advertising had Duz, Downy, Big Top peanut butter and Lilt; Tatham-Laird, Chicago, had Mr. Clean and American Family flakes/detergent; Honig-Cooper & Harrington, San Francisco, had Clorox; Young & Rubicam, New York, handled Cheer and Spic & Span.

P&G's ties with some agencies have lasted decades. The main reason why, says Norton O'Meara, a former P&G account manager at what is now Tatham-Laird & Kudner, Chicago, and now VP-management supervisor at Campbell-Mithun, Chicago, is that P&G considers its agencies to be its "creative and marketing partners." He says he doesn't believe there is any other company that "can outdistance the value they place on their agencies. We were hired to think. It was traditional for them to bring a new product, one not named yet, and ask the agency what it could do with it. P&G looks to their agencies not to reinforce their preconceptions but to either offer alternatives or reinforce the product's going-in objectives. All clients should expect that of agencies and should be open to that kind of response from agencies."

Many of the demands P&G places on its ad agencies also apply to the various outside package design companies that work closely with P&G's own art and package design unit. Don Baker, formerly P&G manager of art and package design and now a Cincinnati-based package-design consultant, says P&G for years talked about moving its design work in-house, but "P&G doesn't want to do its design inside just as the company doesn't have its ad agencies inside. When they're [agen-

cies] outside, you're getting a lot better creativity [by not] controlling them. You're buying them for their creativity—and they better stay creative and competitive. Too often, internal agencies have a stultifying affect; you don't get the creativity you want."

In essence, P&G's art and package design unit "acts like art directors. They set the direction and direct the design process," says Mr. Baker.

Libby Perszyk Kathman, a Cincinnati-based package design company, has created new looks for a number of P&G brands, including Folgers instant coffee, Prell and Pringle's. Jerome Kathman, VP of LPK, says P&G is the most demanding of the agency's clients. "They're in communication with us sometimes three times a day; there's constant communication," he says. "What has happened is package design has become a strategic communication tool for companies, and P&G has been in the vanguard of recognizing that value at the point-of-purchase." Like its ad agencies, P&G's package design companies act as creative resources. "The day we start to assume they require a certain look or a certain attitude, is the day we're less valuable to them," Mr. Kathman says.

Global marketer

Not only did Tide ease the "burden of washday drudgery" in the U.S., but it also fueled P&G's postwar international expansion. Before World War II, P&G's primary foreign business had been in the U.K. and Canada, with lesser operations in Cuba (sold in 1960), the Philippines and Indonesia. Under the leadership of Walter Lingle, VP-overseas operations, P&G after the war moved into new foreign markets, including Mexico, Venezuela and France. However, products successful in the U.S. would not necessarily be as successful abroad. In the U.K., for example, a high percentage of housewives boiled their white wash to enhance whitening and tea stain removal. To be successful in the U.K., a detergent would have to include a bleaching agent.

To meet the needs of an international market, P&G researchers changed the Tide formula. In the early 1950s, brands such as Daz—a blue detergent with bleach—and Ace (pronounced ah-say) were introduced in the U.K. and Mexico, respectively. By 1955, Mr. Lingle supervised foreign operations with total net earnings of $8 million. Within 25 years, earnings jumped to $149 million, with more than 200 brands sold in 24 nations.

While the 1950s and 1960s were the "decades of detergents" for P&G's international interests, by 1970 the attention had shifted to Pampers. With Pampers sold in 75 countries within nine years, P&G had full-fledged operations, including manufacturing facilities, in 22 countries, and products were being exported to more than 100 nations.

Environment pressures

In the 1960s and early 1970s, concerns over environmental pollution sparked controversy, especially on both sides of the Great Lakes. In Canada and in the U.S., there was little question that the quality of the Great Lakes was deteriorating because of agricultural waste and improperly treated sewage emptying into the waters.

Phosphates, a major ingredient in detergents, were named as a prime pollutant, eventually forcing detergent marketers to change their soap formulations. But P&G did not reformulate its detergents without first arguing that phosphates were only part of the pollution problem. Mr. Morgens, then P&G president, described the widespread fear as "a case history of how confusion and misunderstanding can sweep across the country."

The company argued that phosphate was not the primary pollutant; rather, improperly treated city sewage and waterfront manufacturing wastes were behind the "accelerated eutrophication" (over-fertilized algae growing rapidly, using up oxygen needed to sustain fish and marine life).

P&G in 1970 told a Senate subcommittee that it had replaced 25% of the phosphates in one-third of its package detergents with a substitute agent called NTA (sodium nitrilotriacetate) and was experimenting with a 50% replacement level. At the same hearing, representatives of all three big U.S. soap companies—Colgate-Palmolive Co., Lever Bros. and P&G—told the subcommittee that "phosphates are necessary and safe, and it is difficult to find a suitable replacement; NTA alone will not do the job. More effective sewage treatment would be a much better way to fight pollution than cutting phosphates from detergent" (AA, June 1, 1970).

However, the government claimed it detected a possible health hazard in NTA, especially for pregnant women. The U.S. Surgeon General asked the three marketers to voluntarily cease using NTA, which caused P&G scientists to scramble for a replacement for both phosphate and NTA.

After months of waiting for attacks on soap products to subside, the soap companies began introducing new marketing programs, new formulations and new label information on their detergents (AA, June 12, 1972). By October 1972, P&G was selling its detergents without phosphates in Chicago, Miami and Buffalo, cities where phosphates were first banned, and reduced by half the phosphorus content in detergents in other areas. The company also identified all major ingredients by their chemical names, while minor components are identified by their function, "instituted in response to consumer interest in ingredients."

Mr. Morgens—by then P&G chairman—

speaking at the company's annual meeting that year, said that the zero phosphate products "fall short of providing housewives with what we feel is the proper level of cleaning effectiveness" (AA, Oct. 16, 1972). He noted that P&G spent more than $85 million to find a lower phosphate product that is both safe and effective.

Rely

By the end of the 1970s, P&G had another crisis on its hands. Rely, a superabsorbent tampon introduced in 1974, was suspected of increasing women's chances of contracting a rare disease called toxic shock syndrome (TSS). The link between Rely and TSS prompted P&G in September 1980 to withdraw Rely voluntarily and suspend production and sale of the product. P&G's action followed the release of a government report concluding that the use of Rely might increase the risk of acquiring the serious disease (AA, Sept. 29, 1980). "We are taking this action . . . despite the fact that we know of no defect in the Rely tampon and despite evidence that the withdrawal of Rely will not eliminate the occurrence of TSS," said P&G's then-Chairman-CEO Mr. Harness.

The product withdrawal cost P&G about $75 million and sparked a number of lawsuits. At the 1980 shareholders' meeting, Mr. Harness said the write-off "doesn't mean we have given up on the tampon or, alternatively, the sanitary napkin business. . . . Developments in coming months and years will be closely studied for opportunities to put us back in the [feminine hygiene] business, where we believe we have much to offer in superior technology" (AA, Oct. 20, 1980). Within four years, P&G made good on its promise to re-enter the $1 billion market, with the national intoduction of the Always sanitary napkin brand (AA, May 7, 1984).

Regulatory tremors

A week after Mr. Morgens was named P&G president in March 1957, the Federal Trade Commission charged that the company had violated Section 7 of the Clayton Act when it purchased Clorox Chemical Co. The FTC said P&G should not be allowed to keep Clorox because it "leaves other bleach makers at a severe disadvantage and gives P&G more power in its competition against other marketers of soaps and cleansers" (AA, Oct. 14, 1957). The complaint was based on the argument that P&G had such tremendous promotional resources it was able to "grab the leadership for any product it decides to promote . . . and through the addition of Clorox to its line of cleansing and laundry products, it will be in even a better position to demand the best shelf positions for its full line," ADVERTISING AGE reported.

In challenging P&G's right to own Clorox, the FTC pointed out that the product already dominated the household bleach market, accounting for 48% of sales in 1957 while the No. 2 Purex had only 16% (AA, Oct. 14, 1957). P&G replied to the FTC that the complaint had "no judicial basis for proceeding." Mr. Morgens said, "The basic ground for the complaint is that P&G advertises widely, is successful and has gained broad acceptance for its products among housewives and other consumers . . . the inference is that this case of competence—which is basic to success of American business, large and small—may possibly result in some future violation of the law."

Nearly three years later, the FTC ruled that P&G "has so much merchandising know-how and advertising power" that it should be required to dispose of Clorox. In handing down the ruling, Examiner Everett F. Haycraft said "Clorox already had increased its market share under P&G management . . . more importantly, the entry of P&G into the household bleach field with the largest selling brand is forcing consolidations among the smaller competitors and is creating a trend toward concentration" (AA, July 11, 1960). The examiner's opinion, agreed to in 1963 by the commission, rested primarily on P&G's power in the soap and food businesses, with its "sales force skilled in getting valuable ad space and supermarket display space," AA reported.

P&G appealed the decision, and the case went to the U.S. Supreme Court. At a meeting of the New York Society of Security Analysts, Mr. Morgens said P&G "isn't planning on any more acquisitions of grocery products, at least in this country." He said the Clorox and Folger acquisitions (the FTC began reviewing the Folger acquisition in 1966) were done "with the rules of legal advice" but "the rules of the game are far from clear, and even the most careful and competent legal advice does not prevent difficulties" (AA, Nov. 7, 1966).

In April 1967, the Supreme Court upheld the FTC order requiring P&G to divest itself of Clorox, finding that "P&G's advertising and promotional resources represented a decisive threat to Clorox competitors." Two months earlier, P&G had made an agreement with the FTC that allowed the company to retain the Folger coffee company. P&G agreed that it would not enter into any additional grocery product areas via acquisitions in the next seven years without government approval. Nor would it try to acquire any coffee business for the next 10 years.

The 1970s and beyond

The FTC's decision, upheld by the High Court, effectively put a freeze on P&G's acquisition frenzy of the late 1950s and 1960s. During the 1970s, when many consumer-goods companies diversified through acquisitions, P&G, for the most part, waited on the sidelines. Prohibited from growing by acquisition, the company instead turned its attention inward, developing new products for the consumer market. Also, the industrial and institutional divisions developed food and chemical products marketed in bulk to restaurants, hotels and institutions. By the late 1970s, the two divisions were marketing more than 20 products, according to "Eyes on Tomorrow."

At the same time, P&G also began to take an interest in the then $130 billion-plus healthcare industry, one of the few industries growing faster than the general economy (AA, Dec. 26, 1977). Its interests then were twofold—hospital supplies and prescription drugs. Although P&G appeared to be devoting much of its attention to those areas, the company continued working on ways to apply medical knowledge to new consumer products. But P&G did not come up with the much-desired "breakthrough" products during this period.

In the late 1960s, it had lavished a tremendous amount of time, energy and money figuring out how to make potato chips uniformly shaped so they would stack up in a damage-resistant canister. The buying public initially was impressed with Pringle's, the "newfangled" potato chip. But this attraction faded over time.

Noted Charles Eberle, formerly a P&G VP-manufacturing and now the founder and principal of CEE Enterprises, a business consultancy in Cincinnati, "There's been a tendency at times to create overly elaborate technologies. P&G gets caught up in it and it becomes hard to change." Added a former P&G brand manager: "The bottom line was P&G got fooled by their early-market test data [on Pringle's]. The product was so novel that it attracted a lot of sales. P&G just overreacted when the product started going crazy and didn't anticipate taste fatigue. They thought they had a jillion-dollar success on their hands and started building manufacturing capacity to match that early success. About nine months after its national introduction, taste fatigue set in, and Pringle's [market share] deteriorated."

Indeed, many former P&G brand managers label the '70s decade as P&G's "period of diversion," when the company was distracted from doing business as usual in its three core categories: detergents, diapers and toothpaste. The distractions were for good reason. During the 1970s, oil prices surged and the price of chemicals used in soaps and detergents quadrupled. Inflation not only raised manufacturing costs but consumers reacted by shying away from premium-price brand names, like P&G's, and buying generic versions of nearly every product. P&G was trying to meet each challenge as it arose.

Pressure also came to bear on P&G's Crest brand. It was facing increased competition from the new sweeter-tasting gels introduced in 1969 by Lever Bros. and in 1979 by Beecham Products. P&G finally responded by nationally introducing Crest gel, backing it with a $45 million campaign that successfully stemmed the brand's share erosion (AA, Sept. 9, 1982).

A hugely successful new product, Rely, was on its way to being the blockbuster of the 1970s, until fears that it was contributing to toxic shock syndrome caused the company to withdraw the tampon from stores. This was a great blow to P&G's corporate self-esteem. The disappointments with Rely and Pringle's forced a reassessment of the company's direction.

"P&G is the manifestation of the philosophy that there must be a unique strategic difference for the product in the consumer's mind that distinguishes it from competitors' products. They don't put products out unless they have that unique strategic difference. They want and need to create something that's unique," says Joseph Kornick, a principal of Chicago-based package-design company Kornick Lindsay, who worked in P&G's art department in the 1970s.

By 1981, under the leadership of John Smale, the new chief executive, P&G began to pursue new avenues to return to its traditional 7%

growth rate. Despite the absence of the "blockbuster" product, P&G had 14 new products in test market worldwide, more than at any time in its history. Jack Henry, a former P&G market research department manager who now heads his own Cincinnati-based consulting company, says the reason for the flurry of activity is that P&G reaffirmed its belief that all new products begin in research and development and product development. "The company feels that new products are the lifeblood of its business. Although many companies are doing line extensions rather than new brands, P&G is not doing that to the exclusion of the other. Once the door opened to line extensions, it didn't dissuade P&G from an aggressive new products program. It's more an evolution of what the company's been thinking about in terms of meeting consumer needs."

Perhaps more important, the company was nearing the end of its no-acquisition agreement with the FTC. Mr. Smale began preparing P&G once again for growth. It purchased Crush International soft drinks in 1980 and the Ben Hill Griffin citrus processing operation in 1981, and in early 1982, the company made its long anticipated buy into the healthcare industry by acquiring Morton-Norwich Products' $216 million pharmaceutical business, Norwich-Eaton, for $371 million (AA, Sept. 9, 1982). At the time, ADVERTISING AGE reported that Norwich-Eaton "gave P&G a vehicle by which to learn the pharmaceutical business, a practice it developed with its earlier acquisitions." It also gave P&G over-the-counter products in areas that complemented its product lineup. One product, Pepto Bismol, made P&G the leader in stomach remedies.

P&G's return to an aggressive acquisition strategy was the result of several years of careful planning, spurred by the end of P&G's acquisition ban and Mr. Smale's position as heir-apparent to P&G's top executive office, chairman-CEO. Margaret Wyant, former manager of market development at P&G and now a Cincinnati-based marketing consultant, served on a task force created by Mr. Smale to formulate plans to put P&G back on the acquisition track.

"We had to get the company back to the business of growing," she says. "It had been [almost] 20 years, a whole generation, since P&G had bought a company. We had not opened up any new avenues for growth. John was about to take over as chief executive, and he recognized that his most important contribution would be to open the doors so the company could have another 25 years of growth. But nobody knew how to do that because nobody had helped do that. That's what the task force's mission was to lay the groundwork for future growth."

Perhaps influenced by Mr. Smale's long-time interest in healthcare (his first big success was his work in winning the American Dental Association Seal of Acceptance for Crest's fluoride preventative capabilities), the task force firmly pointed P&G in the direction of drug products and healthcare for its future growth—"which is not so unusual considering that P&G first and foremost always has been a health company. What is the biggest single contributor to health and well-being? Soap! Because if you're not clean, you can't be healthy. Now that P&G has taken care of the outside, it's time to take care of the inside," says Ms. Wyant.

In 1981, Drexel Burnham Lambert analyst Hercules Segalas, who diligently tracks P&G's new product patents, and Leo J. Shapiro, principal of a Chicago-based market research company bearing his name, both predicted a slew of health-related products: a margarine that could reduce blood cholesterol; a dental product that would help eliminate plaque; and a possible cure for male baldness. Their predictions proved correct. One turned into Tartar Control Crest, a toothpaste that helps remove cosmetic tartar above the gum line; the fake-fat, cholesterol-reducing compound,

olestra, is pending Food & Drug Administration approval as a food ingredient; and P&G in 1987 began working with a group of Scottish scientists on a remedy for balding pates.

"It's clear to me, through all this activity, that P&G has gone through their low point and they're on the way up," says Mr. Segalas. That low point not only applied to a lack of new-product successes and market share erosion along all product lines, but also to the company's bottom line. In fiscal 1985, earnings dropped 29% to $635 million, the biggest one-year decline in 33 years.

True to form, P&G quickly rebounded financially and in market share superiority, with across-the-board market-share gains in its traditional categories. Instead of chasing the competition with me-too products, P&G returned to new-product introductions with superior points of difference. Although the new products came with familiar brand names—Ultra Pampers, Tartar Control Crest and Liquid Tide detergent—they rescued P&G's market share in all three basic businesses from the lows of 1984 and 1985.

"The key here is P&G believes first that any product it's going to produce has to be shown to give added-value to the end result user, the consumer. P&G doesn't like gimmicky products," says Hoyt Chaloud, who retired from P&G in 1981 after 35 years in soap and detergent research and development.

In October 1985, P&G further added to its medicine chest by acquiring Richardson-Vicks and several G.D. Searle & Co. brands. In a letter to shareholders, P&G Chairman-CEO John Smale said the purchases made P&G the leading otc (over the counter) pharmaceutical marketer (AA, Sept. 1, 1986). Including the purchase of Norwich-Eaton in 1982, P&G has spent nearly $2 billion buying into the market, and may still be interested in another prescription drug company.

Backed by its tremendous research and development program, P&G has a good shot at significantly affecting consumers' diets and health, much as it altered the country's washday habits after World War II.

Wall Street analysts say both the otc and prescription drug emphasis are good markets for P&G. While the company's core businesses are mature, otc and prescription drugs are growing at annual rates of 10%, industry studies show. P&G needs such an infusion to supplement the food and beverage products (Citrus Hill orange juice brand was introduced in 1982; Duncan Hines ready-to-eat cookies were introduced in 1983) that were supposed to be the company's primary growth center.

The company in early June, 1987, announced it would undertake a consolidation of its production facilities, the overcapacity of which was a result of previous acquisitions. The company said it would take an $800 million pretax write-off in fiscal 1987. A big portion of the write-off is related to the sharp reduction in capacity for baking Duncan Hines cookies, a decision "related directly to the infringements of P&G's patented technology by three major U.S. manufacturers" (AA, June 15, 1987). Three years ago, P&G filed suit against Nabisco Brands (marketer of Chewy Chips Ahoy and Almost Home cookies), Frito-Lays (Grandma's cookies) and Keebler Co. (Soft Batch) in U.S. District Court in Wilmington, Del. (AA, June 25, 1984). The case still is pending.

Although the pretax charge will hurt 1987 fiscal-year income, an estimated $17 billion, it will "set the stage for more vigorous earnings growth" in fiscal 1988 and beyond, Mr. Smale says. That P&G would be willing to take a loss of earnings demonstrates the lengths it will go to be a market leader, not a follower. P&G "expects to be the leader, they want to be the leader, and they'll pay the price to be the leader—meaning they have the willingness to invest extremely heavily in product

research and the technical side of the business," says Gordon Wade, a former brand manager and now president of the Cincinnati Consulting Group. "It means a willingness to hire large numbers of good people and expend a lot of money in establishing a brand franchise via advertising. Most companies want to get by on the cheap. They'll spend a few dollars and hope that the product sticks in consumers' minds. P&G, though, will pay the price to go the extra mile to attain leadership," he says.

P&G also is demonstrating it can keep up with the faster new-products pace, as evidenced by the national introduction of Tartar Control Crest after brief testing.

P&G watchers say the company is re-examining its Kremlin-like centralized and insular structure, which may have held the company back from maintaining its traditional rates of growth and profitability. At the same time, President John Pepper is said to be reviewing the company's venerable brand-management system. In some of the big divisions, like detergent and paper, the ad manager's job has been divided among several group product managers.

True to the founders' principles, P&G continues making major strategic decisions for the long-term, not on current market conditions. Mr. Smale, in his speech to employees last year at the Cincinnati Coliseum, said P&G's competitive advantage is its heritage. "When times are tough, and it would be easy to follow the expedient route to achieve immediate results, our heritage directs us to the alternate course—the one that leads to the right decision for the long term."

It's a statement that James Gamble and William Procter, the immigrant soap and candlemakers, would agree characterizes the company they founded 150 years ago, and it certainly describes the giant consumer products company it is now. Not a bad return on a $7,192.24 investment.

150 years of P&G
People and events that shaped a great company

1837

■ William Procter, candlemaker, and James Gamble, soapmaker, pooled their resources and formed a partnership Aug. 22, 1837. They signed a formal partnership agreement on Oct. 31, 1837.

■ The first combination plant and office was located at Sixth and Main.

1838

■ P&G occasionally placed local newspaper ads for its candles and soaps under the name of Procter, Gamble & Company, offering for sale "No. 1 Palm Soap, No. 2 Rosin Soap, Toilet and Shaving Soap; also Pure Tallow Candles, mould and dipped."

SOAP AND CANDLE FACTORY,
Main street, second house north of Sixth street.
THE subscribers offer their manufactures, warranted full weight, correct tare, and marked as the late city Ordinance directs—
        No 1 Palm Soap,
        " 2 Rosin do,
     Toilet and Shaving Soap,
     Pure Tallow Candles, mould and dipped.
                        PROCTER, GAMBLE & Co.
oct 26   99tf

1850–51

■ P&G began marking its Star candles packages with a cross, which by 1859 had been altered to the "moon and stars," symbolizing the 13 original American colonies.

1853

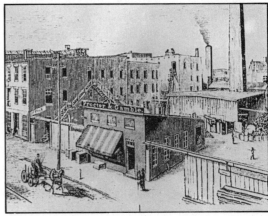

■ The factory outgrew the Sixth and Main Street building. A new plant was built on Central Avenue next to the Miami-Erie Canal to facilitate the growing business.

1854

■ Moved offices to Second Street from Main Street.

1859

■ Sales reached $1 million. The company had 80 employees.

1860

■ On the eve of the Civil War, P&G stockpiled rosin, a key ingredient in soapmaking. This enabled P&G to supply the Union armies with soap and candles.

1863

■ A major shortage of "grease" (lard stearin) for candles forced P&G to use tallow to make stearic acid. The lard stearin instead was refined into a kitchen cooking product, which led to the development of Crisco in 1911. To replace the hard-to-

get rosin, James Gamble began using silicate of soda (researched by James N. Gamble), which later played an important role in soap and detergent technology.

James N. Gamble, son of founder

1865

■ Thomas Alva Edison, a Western Union employee, set up a telegraph line to facilitate communications between the company's downtown office and the factory.

1875

■ P&G hired its first full-time chemist, Mr. Gibson.

1878

■ P&G White Soap was formulated.

1879

■ White Soap was renamed Ivory by Harley Procter.

1881

PROCTER & GAMBLE'S SOAPS. PURITY.

■ Harley Procter began promoting Ivory soap via print ads ". . . to post the public by letting them know of the superior quality of the genuine article." The first ad budget of $11,000 was used for newspaper advertising, storefront and fence signs, as well as streetcar cards. A miniature booklet titled "Poetical Selections" interspersed with ads for P&G products, was printed for grocers to give to customers—a forerunner of point-of-purchase promotions.

■ Through the 1880s, P&G is said to have been one of the first industrial advertisers to have used large outdoor board posters. Crews began distributing Ivory door-to-door in the company's first sampling program.

1882

■ P&G patented its moon-and-stars trademark. The design originally was developed by wharf hands to mark boxes of P&G Star candles.

P&G's first national consumer magazine ad ran in *The Independent*, a religious weekly. It introduced one of the most famous of all ad slogans, "Ivory . . . is 99-44/100% pure." The ad also stated "the Ivory Soap will float." Harley Procter pushed for scientific confirmation of Ivory's purity; the scientifically tested "purity" claim ran in full-page magazine ads carrying the testimonials of the chemists who had examined Ivory.

The first Ivory ad appeared Dec. 21, 1882.

THE "IVORY" is a Laundry Soap, with all the fine qualities of a choice Toilet Soap, and is 99 44-100 **per cent. pure.**

Ladies will find this Soap especially adapted for washing laces, infants' clothing, silk hose, cleaning gloves and all articles of fine texture and delicate color, and for the varied uses about the house that daily arise, requiring the use of soap that is above the ordinary in quality.

For the Bath, Toilet, or Nursery it is preferred to most of the Soaps sold for toilet use, being purer and much more pleasant and effective and possessing all the desirable properties of the finest unadultered White Castile Soap. The Ivory Soap will " **float.**"

The cakes are so shaped that they may be used entire for general purposes or divided with a stout thread (as illustrated) into two perfectly formed cakes, of convenient size for toilet use.

The price, compared to the quality and the size of the cakes, makes it the cheapest Soap for everybody for every want. TRY IT.

SOLD EVERYWHERE.

1883

■ William Cooper Procter, 24, grandson of William Procter, joined the company, leaving the College of New Jersey (now Princeton) a month before graduation. He began by working in the Central Avenue production facility and helping with construction of Ivorydale.

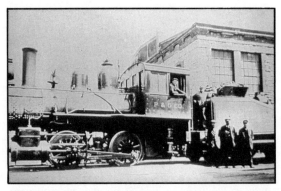

The Ivorydale train

1885

■ P&G pioneered Saturday afternoons off with pay for its employees.

1886

■ Ivorydale was opened.

1887

■ Oldest continuing U.S. profit-sharing plan

was instituted. The first Dividend Day was celebrated in October.

■ Harley Morrison joined the company, beginning to refine glycerin and fatty acid, and improve distilling and cottonseed oil refining.

1890

■ P&G incorporated to raise money for expansion. William Alexander Procter, son of the founder, was the first president.

■ A central analytical laboratory was established at Ivorydale to improve the soapmaking process.

1892

■ The employee stock purchase program was inaugurated.

1896

FOR 10 IVORY SOAP Wrappers

"A BUSY DAY"
by Maud Humphrey

■ Drawings of Ivory babies and children by well-known artists such as Jessie Wilcox Smith and Fanny Cory captured the public's interest. This Maude Humphrey drawing was one of the first color print ads done by a soap company.

1900

■ Net earnings reached $1 million.

■ P&G began making soap chips and flakes for commercial laundries.

1902

■ P&G White Naphtha laundry soap was introduced.

1903

■ Profit-sharing plan was tied directly to employee ownership of P&G common stock.

1904

■ A second plant opened in Kansas City, Mo., to supply products to the West.

1907

■ Labor relations pioneer William Cooper Procter named P&G president.

1911

■ Crisco shortening, the first all-vegetable short-

Rhubarb Pie at Its Best

RHUBARB pie is the first of the fresh fruit desserts of the spring that come to whet appetites jaded by winter's want of variety. It is especially delicious when made with Crisco. The crust is as tasteful and wholesome as the juicy pie-plant it encloses. You'll marvel at the tenderness of the undercrust. All pastry properly made with Crisco is light, dry, and unusually sweet as well as digestible.

CRISCO

Crisco is the solid cream of vegetable oil, having neither taste nor odor. Its delicate richness is an aid to better cooking. Natural food flavors in all their appetizing realities are brought out by its use. Try Crisco and you will understand why so many housewives use it exclusively.

Send for this Valuable Book

ening, was introduced. The first color ad (1917) ran in *Woman's Home Companion*.

1915

■ A comprehensive sickness/disability-retirement-life insurance plan went into effect.

■ The company opened its first international plant in Hamilton, Ontario, for production of Ivory and Crisco.

1918

■ P&G instituted an eight-hour workday.

1919–20

■ Ivory Flakes was introduced as the first P&G flaked soap.

■ P&G pioneered direct selling to retailers; 450 salesmen were hired. This move led wholesale grocery companies to call a boycott of P&G products.

1921

■ P&G introduced Chipso, the first P&G soap specifically designed for use in washing machines.

1923

■ Trying out a new medium: P&G became interested in radio's potential to reach consumers. The company started advertising with Crisco-sponsored cooking shows.

Crisco cooking shows were first broadcast over WEAF in New York.

"Vic and Sade," an early Crisco-sponsored radio show

1924

■ P&G established its market research department to study consumer buying habits.

1926

■ P&G competed against itself for the first time when it introduced Camay soap, a competitor to Ivory.

1930

■ Ivory Snow was introduced.

■ The company established its first overseas subsidiary by purchasing Thomas Hedley & Co. in England.

1931

■ Neil McElroy began refining the idea of a brand management system in a 3-page memo to President Richard Deupree, violating Mr. Deupree's one-page memo rule.

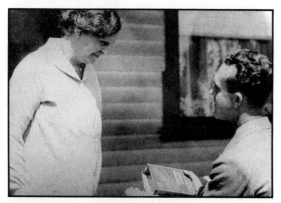

Selling Chipso door-to-door in the '30s

1933

■ P&G initiated a five-day work week.
■ Dreft, the first synthetic detergent—it contained a "miracle molecule"—was introduced.

1937

■ P&G celebrated its first 100 years.

1939

■ Ivory soap was pitched by Red Barber on TV, an event that marked two firsts: The telecast of a major league baseball game (Cincinnati Reds vs. Brooklyn Dodgers), and P&G's use of TV to advertise a consumer product.

1940

■ P&G President Richard Deupree told shareholders and employees that "the company must be ready at all times to meet sudden wartime emergencies. No one can possibly foresee what the future may hold, but we have the satisfaction that we have built wisely in preparation. . . ."

■ At the request of the U.S. Army Ordnance Department, P&G began construction of a shell-loading plant near Milan, Tenn. It went into production August 1941—3 months ahead of schedule.

P&G defense plants produced 25% of all the shells, fuses and bombs used by U.S. forces in World War II. Production lines stopped in August 1945.

P&G's shell-loading plant began production in 1941.

1945

■ Spic & Span, originally a wall-cleaning powder, was acquired.

1946

■ Tide, the first heavy-duty synthetic detergent, was test marketed. A year later, it was introduced nationally.

■ Prell concentrate shampoo was introduced.

1947

■ A new plant for the new drug products division's brands—including Drene and Prell shampoos—opened in Cincinnati.

1949

■ Lilt home permanent was introduced.

1950

■ Joy dishwashing detergent was introduced.

1952

■ White-formula Cheer, a brand introduced two years earlier, was reformulated as Blue Cheer, satisfying housewives' fondness for adding a blue tint to white clothes.

■ The Miami Valley laboratory was opened in Cincinnati.

1954

■ A pulp mill in Foley, Fla., was opened to meet the demand for cellulose in synthetic fibers, film and plastics.

1955

■ P&G introduced Dash, its first low-sudsing detergent. Sales were good, but didn't match Tide's introduction.

■ Crest, the first toothpaste to incorporate fluoride, was introduced.

■ Howard Morgens (CEO, 1957–1971) reorganized the company along divisional lines to "support a larger and stronger P&G business."

■ Cascade automatic dishwashing detergent was introduced.

■ W. T. Young Foods, the manufacturer of Big Top peanut butter, was acquired.

1956

- Sales reached $1 billion.
- Jif peanut spread was introduced.
- Comet, the first household cleanser with chlorine bleach, was introduced.
- P&G entered the deodorant category by introducing Secret cream deodorant. It also entered the baking mix field by acquiring Nebraska Consolidated Mills Co. and the Duncan Hines name.

1957

- President-CEO Neil McElroy was "borrowed" by U.S. President Dwight D. Eisenhower to serve as secretary of defense.
- The company entered the consumer paper products category when it acquired Charmin Paper Mills.
- Ivory Liquid dishwashing detergent was introduced.

1959

- Winton Hill Technical Center was opened in Cincinnati.

1960

- The American Dental Association issued a report that Crest toothpaste was effective in preventing cavities.

1961

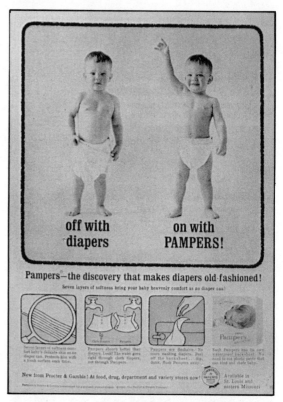

- P&G created a new product category, disposable diapers, with Pampers.

1963

- P&G entered the coffee business by acquiring J.A. Folger & Co.

1965

- Mehoopany (Pa.) paper plant was built at a cost of $150 million—the company's largest construction project to date.

■ Scope mouthwash and Bounty paper towels were introduced.

Actress Nancy Walker portrayed Rosie the waitress in Bounty TV spots.

1968

■ Pringle's potato chips were introduced.

1972

■ Bounce fabric softener and anti-static agent was introduced.

1973

■ Sharon Woods Technical Center was opened

in Cincinnati to provide research space for bar soap and household cleaning products.

1974

■ Rely tampons were introduced in test market. (The brand was discontinued in 1980.)

1976

■ Luvs disposable diapers were introduced.

1980–82

■ Sales reached $10 billion.

■ The company entered the soft drink, orange juice and pharmaceutical businesses by acquiring Crush International, marketer of the Crush and Hires soft drink brands; Ben Hill Griffin Citrus; and Norwich-Eaton. The Norwich-Eaton

acquisition (1982) added to P&G's roster such products as Pepto-Bismol, Chloraseptic oral antiseptic/anesthetic, Head & Chest cold remedy and Norwich aspirin.

1984

■ Liquid Tide, with 12 active cleaning ingredients, was introduced.

1985

■ P&G expanded its over-the-counter healthcare business with the acquisition of Richardson-Vicks. It also acquired the Metamucil, Dramamine and Icy Hot brands from G.D. Searle & Co., making it the largest manufacturer of over-the-counter drugs.

■ Crest Tartar Control Formula was introduced—the first toothpaste clinically proven to prevent tartar buildup.

Michael A. Marcotte

■ The new General Offices Tower building opened in Cincinnati.

1986

■ John Smale was named P&G chairman in April, while continuing as CEO.
■ Ultra Pampers brand was introduced.

1987

■ P&G celebrates its 150th anniversary.
■ The company seeks Food & Drug Administration approval for olestra, a low-calorie, cholesterol-free fat substitute.

CHAPTER TWO

Good Citizen of Cincinnati

Community needs, charities, education, politics and fine arts are all addressed in a well-rounded program of participation. Indeed, of 117 members in the local United Way, 112 had P&G people on their boards.

Attractive landscaping and flower beds front the Central Building (left) and the New General Offices (background).

W AS IT COINCIDENCE, OR WAS IT IRONY? On July 9, 1986, a Mercedes-Benz fell through Broad Street in Columbus, Ohio. The giant cave-in, only a few hundred feet from the state capitol, was caused by the collapse of a brick-lined sewer installed in 1872 when Ulysses S. Grant was president. Reverberations of the crash were heard in Cincinnati's city hall. On July 28, 1986, Cincinnati Mayor Charles Luken asked Procter & Gamble Co. Chairman-CEO John G. Smale to form an independent commission to assess the needs of Cincinnati's infrastructure—the sewers, streets, bridges, parks and all other physical facilities owned or operated by the city.

Exactly two weeks later, Cincinnati experienced a sewer cave-in at a major intersection just east of downtown. A brick sewer, installed in 1866 when Andrew Johnson was president, had collapsed. These prize potholes punctuated the urgency of the infrastructure commission's task in a city that turns 200 years old in 1988, Mr. Smale later told a meeting of the Greater Cincinnati Chamber of Commerce.

The Smale commission is perhaps the most visible recent example of P&G's role as Cincinnati's leading corporate citizen. Immersing himself deeply in the task, Mr. Smale recruited a small army of business, community and civic leaders to study a variety of intractable problems from aging infrastructure to future waste-disposal sites. A comprehensive report on their findings is expected sometime this year.

Such volunteerism is not unusual for P&G as a company, or for its individual officers and employees. The reason is that few companies are so completely identified with their headquarters cities as P&G and Cincinnati. The extent of that involvement is difficult to assess. It may well be impossible to find a single community activity—from charitable causes to education, politics and fine arts—that has not been influenced by the company or its employees. "With Procter & Gamble, it's easier to say what kind of project they are not involved in," says Robert A. Taft II, one of three Hamilton County commissioners (and grandson of the late U.S. Senate Republican leader of the same name).

"In my experience, every time that we've had to go after the community for support or assistance, Procter & Gamble has been there. And they've often been a leading participant." For example, several years ago, county commissioners proposed a tax levy to establish a facility for abused and neglected children. The commissioners planned to raise $70,000 to fund an advertising campaign to explain the idea to the voters. "The first place we went was Procter & Gamble," Mr. Taft says. "The reason is that when it comes to contributing to a campaign for a tax levy, most other companies in town wanted to know whether Procter & Gamble had participated." P&G gave the initial $20,000, which enabled the commissioners to raise the additional money for the full campaign. "If a project is going to succeed, it has to have the support of Procter & Gamble," says Mr. Taft.

A similar situation occurred with a successful tax levy for Drake Hospital, a county-operated long-term rehabilitation facility for the terminally ill and disabled, he adds. "Procter & Gamble was willing to invest in that campaign," Mr. Taft says.

P&G also has taken the lead in an effort to reform Hamilton County government, which represents 40 municipalities and 12 townships. James W. Nethercott, a senior VP at the company, heads a business committee now investigating creation of a new county charter that potentially would streamline county government, establish the office of a chief executive officer, increase the number of commissioners and give the county home-rule powers.

But P&G also contributes in small, often overlooked ways. The company recently offered the use of a van to county jail probationers to clean up city streets and parks, Mr. Taft says. "These are just a few examples of a very concrete, tangible contribution that Procter & Gamble makes," Mr. Taft says. "Beyond that, the company encourages its employees to become involved. . . Procter & Gamble is the leading corporate citizen both of Cincinnati and of Hamilton County," he says.

This is true despite the fact that P&G is not the largest local employer; that status belongs to General Electric Co., which is headquartered in Fairfield, Conn. But P&G has a sense of responsibility to the community where it was founded in 1837 and where it is still the largest locally based company. "This being our worldwide headquarters puts a special responsibility on us to become involved in the community," says W. Wallace Abbott, senior VP in charge of external affairs.

And yet, the company typically downplays its efforts. "In the midst of trying to be recognized for what we do in the community, we try to maintain a sense of balance in not having people feel that we dwarf everyone else's [contribution]. We don't try to force ourselves on the community, but it is the nature of our people to become involved," Mr. Abbott says. "This city works well because a lot of other companies—large, medium and small—also are willing to volunteer their time and effort. If any one company overshadowed all the others, it would tend to discourage this involvement."

Says Gerald S. Gendell, P&G's manager of public affairs, "We try to be sensitive to [appearances] because you could very easily thwart the efforts of others if they see P&G as getting too big. The attitude would become, 'Let Procter to it. We don't have to get involved.' But we do recognize our responsibilities," Mr. Abbott adds. "In any fundraising campaign we're probably the first door that gets knocked on. We're constantly being told, 'As you go, so goes the community.' Well, that isn't always true; a lot of projects have succeeded without us. But we feel a special responsibility because we usually are asked first."

Of course, P&G has an element of self-interest in its corporate giving. As a result of mushrooming requests over the years, P&G developed guidelines for corporate contributions, gifts and grants, which totaled $27.9 million for the 12 months ending in June 1986. The guidelines follow general company objectives, which channel the bulk of P&G's contributions into three main areas, Mr. Abbott says. First, P&G invests in communities where it has large concentrations of people. An example is the Cincinnati area, where 13,000 of its 45,600 U.S. employees live. Corporate charitable donations in Cincinnati during fiscal 1986 totaled more than $3.3 million. A good portion of these funds was divided among health and social service programs, the United Way and cultural, civic and environmental organizations.

P&G also invests heavily in other communities where it has plant facilities. An example is Mehoopany, Pa., where P&G in 1966 built the world's largest paper mill. Over the years, P&G has helped Mehoopany buy a building for its public library, fire engines, ambulances and even athletic uniforms for the local high-school teams. Many of the newer P&G plants are located in communities surrounded by rural areas, including Mehoopany, Augusta, Ga., and Alexandria, La. In some cases, even small grants can make an important difference. In Gallatin County, Ky., for example, a 1983 grant to the county life-saving squad for special equipment proved valuable when a fatal bus accident occurred shortly after the donation. The new equipment allowed paramedics to treat a seriously injured woman. "In communities such as these, you quickly become a major factor, and we have a very special responsibility there," Mr. Abbott says.

There is a strong self-interest in P&G's concern about the quality of life in communities where it has a large presence, Mr. Abbott adds. The reason is that P&G fosters an attitude of career employment. "We don't hire management from outside," Mr. Abbott says. "All of us at the senior level have literally spent our entire careers here. "For many of us, if we are located in Cincinnati, we expect to move here, raise a family . . . and ultimately retire in the community. Therefore, the community has to be an attractive place in order to get people to want to come here and spend a lifetime," he says.

Education is the second major area of contributions by P&G, totaling more than $7.5 million in fiscal 1986. Grants, gifts and contributions to higher education each year represent the largest expenditures by the Procter & Gamble Fund, the charitable arm of the company. "Indirectly, our contribution to education also is in our self-interest," Mr. Abbott says. "The thing that sets this country apart from much of the world, and certainly provides for the kind of standard of living we have, has been the quality of our educational system. Keeping that healthy and vital and keeping an educated public is very valuable to us because it improves the standard of living. And that, in turn, directly affects the products we can sell."

Promotional opportunities are the third major area of P&G's charitable spending, accounting for more than $3 million in fiscal 1986 contributions. The best example is P&G's $2.4 million in support of the Special Olympics through promotions involving nearly all divisions and many different brands. "Our support of the Special Olympics helps to build our business, but at the same time it supports a worthwhile cause," Mr. Abbott says.

On this solid foundation of financial support, P&G has added two pillars. The first is that the volunteer approach works best in getting things done, Mr. Abbott says. "The volunteer movement in this country is virtually unique around the world. In most countries, there are no volunteer groups; someone either gets paid to do something or it doesn't get done. In the U.S., the volunteer movement encourages individuals to do something because it's good for their company, the community or their country," he says. The second pillar is the belief that problems are best addressed on a local basis.

"This may be a huge company, but it's also one that is composed of many individual brands. We try to break things down to the smallest level," Mr. Abbott says. "The same thing applies to solving problems. By far, we would rather see them solved on the local level with the smallest group. That encourages the involvement of people who live in the community and who can tackle the problem. Philosophically, volunteerism and solving problems on the local level are things we believe in as individuals and as a company," Mr. Abbott says.

There is plenty of evidence that this philosophy starts at the top levels of the company. Chairman-CEO John Smale, who retired in May as national chairman of United Negro College Fund, is chairman of the board of trustees at Kenyon College and a governor on the national United Way board, among numerous other activities.

Mr. Abbott, a former chairman of the United Appeal's general campaign, is a trustee of the United Appeal of Greater Cincinnati and chairman of the board of trustees of the Joint Council on Economic Education, among other activities. "Volunteerism starts from example," Mr. Abbott says. "If we we took a profile of all of our senior officers,

you'll see one or more volunteer activities that they're involved in either locally or nationally."

Mr. Abbott wonders whether there is a board of trustees of a community group in the Cincinnati area that doesn't currently have or hasn't recently had somebody from P&G. A few years ago, the company did such a head count when it was setting up a local Volunteer Support Center. Of the 117 member organizations of the local United Way, 112 had P&G people on their boards.

Despite the widespread volunteer effort, Mr. Abbott stresses that the company does not pressure employees to donate their time. "We don't evaluate their job performance based on whether they're involved in the local United Way, but we certainly encourage them to become involved and we give recognition to people who are doing that sort of thing," Mr. Abbott says.

The biggest current community effort is Mr. Smale's infrastructure commission, a project undertaken at the request of the mayor and the city council. It is a model of business, community, state and national cooperation, says Ohio Gov. Richard Celeste. "There is no question that what's being done here in Cincinnati in mapping the infrastructure program and in setting priorities is a model that we should encourage other communities to follow," he says. "We're tremendously proud to have a company like Procter & Gamble headquartered in Ohio, and it makes a big difference in a community such as Cincinnati to have P&G's commitment. . . . A good example is John Smale's leadership on this very tough issue of the infrastructure needs of the city of Cincinnati."

As a result of lobbying by the infrastructure commission, Gov. Celeste recently approved an $890,000 grant to beautify land along Cincinnati's expressways in preparation for the 1988 National Governors' Conference and the city's bicentennial. Mayor Luken says the grant resulted from a recent visit he paid the governor, accompanied by Mr.

Smale. "If I had gone by myself, we wouldn't have gotten a nickel. But together with the head of one of the nation's largest corporations, we made a pretty strong statement about what Cincinnati thinks is important," Mayor Luken says.

Although Cincinnati's infrastructure is in reasonably good condition, the mayor says it has suffered over the years from a loss of federal funds. But more damaging has been an attitude that infrastructure improvements provide little political gain, because they are essentially invisible to voters. "A former Ohio governor once said, 'Never build anything under the street because you won't get any credit for it,' " Mayor Luken says. "If you want immediate credit for something, build a public swimming pool, but don't set up a fund to maintain it," he says.

Cincinnati is setting aside $18 million in 1987 for capital improvements out of an operating budget of $160 million. Assessing the best way to approach and pay for repairs and setting the spending priorities is the job of the infrastructure commission. "It is a monumental task," says James A.D. Geier, chairman-CEO of Cincinnati Milacron, one of the city's largest industrial companies. "John [Smale] took this on and he's got the business community really scurrying to pull this report together. But a lot of valuable information is going to come out about improvements the city will need in the future."

Hamilton County is involved because it owns, sets the rates for and makes policy decisions for the metropolitan sewer district, although the city manages the system. The sewer district, which has 4,500 miles of drainage, is the biggest challenge facing the commission. A typical sewer system has a lifespan of 50 to 75 years, and much of Cincinnati's system is well over 100 years old, says Thomas Saygers, district director. The old sewer system creates chronic pollution problems by today's standards, says Mr. Saygers. For example, nearly 80% of the system's sanitary-and-storm systems are combined, causing effluents to spill into the Ohio River after large rainstorms, he says.

Mr. Smale's leadership will be critical in resolving problems with the system because an executive understands how to find solutions to long-term problems, Mr. Saygers says. "We need someone who . . . understands the importance of planning, resource management and people," he says. And because certain issues, such as the sanitary sewer system, affect every community up and down the river, it is important to examine the problem from the largest perspective possible, Mr. Saygers says. "A firm like Procter & Gamble has a global view. We need that if we are going to manage this environment and maintain the Ohio River for future generations. That is something that is difficult for local politicians to grasp."

Perhaps most impressive about the infrastructure commission is that members chose not to narrow their focus only to today's problems but to expand it to include potential problems of the future, such as transportation and waste disposal, Mr. Saygers adds. "Typical of the way Procter & Gamble does things, they are looking at the big picture to find comprehensive solutions to long-term, communitywide problems, rather than conducting a quick and dirty study that focuses on a narrow set of issues," he says.

If there is a credo that sums up P&G's corporate citizenship, Mr. Abbott believes it was stated best by former Chairman-CEO Howard J. Morgens, who said: "We do not and must not mistake business for an end in itself. It is only a means to an end, and the end is a constantly improving society. That is something we believe in very strongly," Mr. Abbott says. "We have a role that goes beyond simply returning value to our shareholders, employment to our employees, and being good customers to our suppliers," Mr. Abbott says. "That role is to try to help society. It's something we believe in as individuals and it's something we believe in as a company."

A reprieve for nature

CRITICS OFTEN COMPLAIN THAT PUBLIC CORporations are less concerned about the environment than quarterly profits. But that can't be said of Procter & Gamble Co. As a corporate citizen, P&G is something of a quiet environmentalist. A good example is P&G's recent involvement in a drive to conserve one of the nation's largest remaining stretches of undeveloped coastland.

In a Dec. 31, 1986, transaction, P&G's Memphis, Tenn.-based Buckeye Cellulose subsidiary sold a 65,000-acre tract along the Gulf Coast of Florida for less than $20 million to The Nature Conservancy, a Washington, D.C.-based group devoted to preserving ecologically significant natural areas. The land was valued around $30 million, with the balance being donated.

The sale transfers 60 miles of coastline to the non-profit organization for permanent protection. The Nature Conservancy plans to resell the tract to Florida later this year. The state already has allocated funds from its Save Our Coasts Program to purchase the tract at cost. The move represents the largest state acquisition ever made east of the Mississippi, says Butch Horn, senior bureau of land acquisition agent with the Florida Natural Resources Department, Tallahassee.

After the transfer, the Big Bend area will be used exclusively for conservation and recreation. More important, however, the acquisition will help link more than 200 miles of protected public lands known as Florida's Big Bend Coastal Project. Encompassing more than 100 square miles, the protected area, bounded on the west by Apalachicola Bay and on the south by Chassahowitzka Na-

tional Wildlife Refuge, is nearly five times the size of the island of Manhattan.

The habitat is home to many threatened and endangered species, such as bald eagles, ospreys, manatees, Florida black bears, Ridley's sea turtles, peregrine falcons and the rare salt marsh mink. It also is an important stopping place for migratory birds. "This is conservation at its finest," says William D. Blair Jr., president of the Nature Conservancy. "An extremely rich and productive coastal ecosystem will be saved because Procter & Gamble, an environmentally conscious state government and a private, non-profit organization joined forces in conservation.

The Big Bend tract has been owned since 1951 by Buckeye Cellulose, says Robert E. Cannon, P&G group VP. "This transfer of the largest existing privately owned stretch of the U.S. coastline continues P&G's tradition of nurturing and protecting the environment. We will manage our substantial remaining forest lands in the area in the same responsible way we have in the past," he adds.

Projects such as Florida's Big Bend signal a change in the state's attitude toward aggressive land conservation, says Mr. Horn. In previous years, the state was more interested in economic development. "We used to drain the swamps, or dredge them up. We don't do that anymore," he says. For example, placing the newly acquired land under state protection eliminates the possibility of a barge canal being dug through the heart of the Big Bend area from Carrabelle, Fla., to Tarpon Springs, a federally authorized project that has lain dormant for several years.

P&G was anxious to close on the sale of its Big Bend property before the new tax code took effect on Jan. 1, says Dick Ludington, who heads Nature Conservancy's Chapel Hill, N.C., office. Mr. Ludington and Mr. Horn negotiated the sale of the property with Buckeye Cellulose. Mr. Ludington estimates P&G gained an additional $1 million in tax benefits by selling the property in 1986, as opposed to waiting until 1987. "Money isn't the sole motivator of everything," Mr. Horn says. "Procter & Gamble and Buckeye wanted this area preserved. That's to the good of the state of Florida, the federal government and most of all, the people."

Self-help program offers a way out

AT 21, BARBARA TRAMMELL LEARNED A hard lesson. Black and a high school dropout living in a housing development, she had no luck breaking into Cincinnati's job market, even with a high-school graduate equivalency diploma and college courses in computer programming and accounting. "They looked at my GED and at the area where I lived, and they pitched my applications," she says.

The year was 1982, and Ms. Trammell joined a pilot 12-week Youth Employment Program sponsored by Procter & Gamble and administered by the Cincinnati Metropolitan Housing Authority. The program features morning technical school sessions where students learn plumbing, wiring, carpentry and other skills. In the afternoon they work for CMHA.

For Ms. Trammell, it led to a job with the housing authority and a ticket out. Now 26, she is a maintenance clerk [grade] 2, drives a Grand Prix and rents an apartment on the city's west side. "The program really opened opportunities for me. There were no decent jobs available that would allow me to rent an apartment, buy furniture, acquire a car and live above the poverty level," she says.

The program also is having a positive impact on Cincinnati's 11 major housing developments, 80% black, where 17,541 residents—10,000 under age 20—live in 7,282 housing units. The 125 youth-program participants this year are building three large playgrounds under the supervision of Adventure Playgrounds, an affiliate of the University of Cincinnati. "You can see their pride," John Nelson, the housing authority's executive director, says of the participants. "They wear their hard hats everywhere like baseball caps."

One effect since the program's inception has been fewer incidents of vandalism, Mr. Nelson says. "The kids say, 'I helped put that window in, so don't throw rocks at it.'" The program also builds bonds between youths and older people in the developments, who see them painting, plastering, and fixing their refrigerators.

"It's another example of P&G leveraging its corporate contributions for the maximum benefit," says Gerald S. Gendell, P&G's manager of public affairs. P&G is spending $165,000 on the program in 1987. "Rather than just give money, we try to apply the funds in imaginative and thoughtful ways that will create more good than just might occur if we turned money over to people," Mr. Gendell says.

CHAPTER THREE

Through the Eyes of Wall Street

"The days of putting together decades of up quarters and up years are over" and analysts now speak in terms of patience, long-term, methodical. While some insist P&G must come up with a major new business each decade, others seem optimistic about margin improvement.

DEALING WITH PROCTER & GAMBLE CO. requires a lot of patience. Because the company is painstakingly thorough in the development of everything from a cookie to a disposable diaper, this often long, drawn-out attempt to achieve superiority in the marketplace demands a different kind of analysis by Wall Street. The company's long-term approach to business is reflected in the package-goods giant's usually steady but not spectacular quarterly and yearly figures. Wall Street investors and analysts appreciate a quicker return.

"Even though I've been following this company for six years, I feel like I'm looking at a snapshot because it has such a long time horizon," says Hugh S. Zurkuhlen, VP at Salomon Brothers, New York. Analysts have begun to take a much less critical view of the Cincinnati marketer's extremely long-term outlook.

Still, Wall Street no longer places P&G on a pedestal, as it did before the last round of marketplace difficulties that began in the late 1970s and early 1980s. "Procter in a class by itself is over," says Daniel J. Meade, managing director, First Boston Corp. "The days of putting together decades of 'up' quarters and 'up' years are over. They are much more like other companies that have quarters and sometimes years when earnings are going to be down. That doesn't mean that there will be periods of time when the company's stock is not going to be attractive, but you no longer put Procter & Gamble in a separate class to buy it and own it forever." Says Brenda Lee Landry, principal at Morgan Stanley & Co., "They certainly have lost their superstar status. The company's patina has gotten a little cloudy."

Other analysts maintain P&G always has been successful at accomplishing what it has set out to do. "The investment community is very short-term oriented. In that regard, P&G's management gets beat up for having a time horizon that is longer than Wall Street's," notes Jay H. Freed-man, VP at Kidder, Peabody & Co. Because the company's employees own 20% of its stock in one form or another, "it's naive to believe that no one at the company has any interest in where the share price is," Mr. Freedman says.

But Mr. Zurkuhlen still thinks "P&G's growth horizons demand a lot of patience on the part of investors. They are so long-term in nature. I used to say that's wrong, but now I don't criticize the company. I simply say it's a stock investors shouldn't own [if they feel that way]. Remember, investors buy stock, not companies. It's a pretty simple philosophy.

Comments analyst Jack Salzman, VP-investment research at Goldman, Sachs & Co., "There's no question that P&G wants to be methodical. But the bottom line for an analyst is, 'Can you translate it into outperforming the market?'" It's on this point that Mr. Salzman gives P&G a poor grade.

Over the past 20 years, the company has outperformed the Standard & Poor's 500 index only 13 times, which means the company has underperformed the index seven times—which is certainly not an outstanding record, Mr. Salzman notes.

"The $64,000 question for Wall Street is, will there ever be a change in [P&G's] operating philosophy?" muses Emma W. Hill, associate managing director, Wertheim Schroder & Co.

According to the New York Stock Exchange, as of Dec. 31, 1986, P&G had issued 169.3 million listed shares with a market value of $12.93 billion. It ranked 25th in market value on a list led by IBM Corp., with a $74.12 billion value. Just ahead of P&G in 24th position is American Home Products, with a market value of $12.99 billion; immediately behind it in the 26th slot is GTE, worth $12.88 billion. Other advertisers ahead of P&G in market value include Merck & Co., Philip Morris Cos., Coca-Cola Co., Sears, Roebuck & Co. and Ford Motor Co.

Many analysts have become somewhat philosophical in their suggestions of how P&G can improve its standing on Wall Street. Mr. Meade would like to see the company rethink its "business-as-usual" philosophy of relying on research to supply real growth. He says he "has a hard time" coming up with much more than 3% compound real sales growth on a sustainable basis for P&G, despite the company's adherence to its longtime goal of a 7% growth rate in real terms. This analyst notes that P&G's two primary management beliefs—that the company can grow at 7% in real terms and that R&D is almost sacred—need to be reexamined. "We question the value of a half billion dollars of per annum research & development spending. The last product discovery that significantly influenced P&G results was Pampers disposable diapers a generation ago."

Alice Beebe Longley, VP-Donaldson, Lufkin & Jenrette, asserts that P&G must come up with a major new business each decade in order to compensate for less profitability. Detergents and dentifrices carried the company into more recent decades, and in the 1970s, it was disposable diapers. But in the 1980s what P&G has done has not been as successful. The game plan has been to go into existing categories—cookies, juice, liquid detergents, sanitary napkins—without much innovation. So the company has not achieved high market shares beginning in this decade, and has not been able to achieve the high profitability levels it previously enjoyed. The answer to this, she notes, is sucrose polyester or olestra, as P&G now calls this low-calorie fat substitute that has the potential of reducing cholesterol and fat levels absorbed by the body in a variety of foods. "If it works it would be great," she says. But the problems are many. To name two, the possible delays in obtaining FDA approval and other competitors. As optimistic as she is about sucrose polyester for the long term, Ms. Longley questions where the momentum is going to come from until the payoff hits for olestra.

Brenda J. Gall, VP at Merrill Lynch, Pierce, Fenner & Smith, observes, "One important trend is P&G's increased willingness to acquire as an avenue of growth. Management realizes that although it might have to pay a premium, the higher cost of establishing new brands today is so expensive, it could be in the company's best interests to acquire." This kind of discussion leads to the debate of whether P&G's future is tied more closely to traditional top-line growth (through greater sales) or bottom line (through margin improvement).

Certainly, P&G's decisive action in June 1987 consolidating much of its manufacturing operations, with the resulting cost cutting, supports the position of the proponents of bottom-line improvement. While that action resulted in a negative effect on the 1987 fiscal year's income, it will produce positive long-term financial effects. It's the kind of action analysts like Ms. Longley want to see. She feels that P&G can no longer rely simply on unit growth. "P&G is strapped with the problem of its gargantuan size, so that a mere average 3% growth rate is tough for it to sustain. Its efforts to grow have been directed toward mature and increasingly competitive market segments. As a result, its marketing costs as a percentage of sales, while abating from extremely high launch levels in fiscal 1985, will almost certainly remain higher than former normal levels," she says. (Estimated fiscal 1987 sales were $17 billion; earnings figures were not available as of this writing.)

Similarly, Mr. Freedman maintains that most people aren't giving P&G enough credit for its ability to improve margins. "The company's real potential is in improving margins," he says. The analyst notes that the way P&G has to be analyzed has changed over the years. Traditionally, the company had huge profit margins, both in terms of return on assets and percentage of sales, so historically analysts focused on the top line because that was the only way P&G could grow. Now, however, the focus should be on what's below the company's top line, Mr. Freedman says. In fact, he believes P&G is doing many of the things other companies are trying to improve margins, but P&G—unlike others—isn't out there "beating their chests" about it, he says.

Hercules A. Segalas, senior VP, Drexel Burnham Lambert, also is optimistic about margin improvement. "We believe that the major element that will propel P&G's profits within the next 18 to 24 months will be continued margin expansion," he noted in early 1987.

Ms. Gall indicates that this last fiscal year was one of improved operating margins as management achieved cost reduction at its Richardson-Vicks subsidiary by consolidating certain functions with P&G's already established ones, among other moves.

Mr. Salzman says management has indicated that it plans to return to historic rates of growth within the next few years, meaning 9% to 11% (taking into account 2% to 4% annual inflation). One business opportunity that may enable this kind of growth rate is the entry into the drug business, where rates are higher than those in P&G's traditional lines.

While there has been much discussion of asset restructuring among the financial community—of creating, for example, a Tide Soap Co., a Folgers Foods, Charmin Paper Co., etc.—most analysts don't really buy those theories. Mr. Salzman, for one, believes little restructuring of P&G is likely to occur in the near future.

Wrote Mr. Meade in a December 1986 report, "We don't see how P&G can restructure in the classical sense. The major improvements that are taking place at Unilever and Colgate were possibly made by divesting loss operations, upgrading manufacturing and slimming down overstaffed companies. P&G does not really have large cancerous operations that can be cut out." He notes that while the food business has so far been un-

profitable for P&G, that is because of the unprofitable Duncan Hines ready-to-eat cookies line; it has nothing to do with any problems with established businesses. Dividing the company into four pieces—foods, soaps, paper and toiletries—is "probably pie in the sky," he writes.

"My problem with them," says Ms. Landry, "is that their philosophy was very clear cut when I began to follow them in 1970." The company believed in having the most efficacious product in each category. Once it had that superior product, P&G had to get that message across to the consumer, she says. But what happened in the early '80s and through today is that for a number of reasons, they don't have the most efficacious product, and they have lost market share. In addition, they are not sticking to that same philosophy. Their products didn't remain superior." Detergents and diapers are just two examples she cites.

In one instance, P&G not only is not in the vanguard, but it also is trying to catch up. Colgate-Palmolive came out with the first liquid automatic dishwasher detergent and gained 19% of the market within months, much of it taken away from P&G's category leader, Cascade.

Mr. Salzman believes P&G is still committed to its philosophy of being the best. "It's a philosophical viewpoint that says 'we don't care [how many times] we restage.' They are willing to suffer for the residual value. It's not stupid. It's a philosophical viewpoint. No other company will tolerate such operating losses," he says. Mr. Salzman cites Pringle's potato chips as a classic example. No other company could justify the losses from Pringle's. With Encaprin, an encapsulated aspirin, the company missed the market altogether, because it was introduced at a time when the ibuprofens were coming on strong. And P&G "blew $40 million," he says.

Mr. Zurkuhlen, who shares Mr. Salzman's assessment that P&G will work with brand names much longer than other package-goods marketers, maintains that the "successful accomplishments of P&G's growth goals are totally irrelevant to the investor; the negative near-term can be disaster." He cites as examples cookies and orange juice, both of which Mr. Zurkuhlen says he thought were poor ideas.

"You could throw that back at Procter now and say [the products are] failures. But they'll say, 'No, they're not. Someday we'll be No. 1.' " And who knows, says Mr. Zurkuhlen. "Maybe they will be No. 1 in cookies one day. It might take 30 years, but P&G will wait it out."

Ms. Gall notes, "Their historic pattern is to work on something until they get it right. In a much faster changing market, I'm not sure that strategy will work."

Regardless of their outlook for the future of P&G stock, the top Wall Street analysts following the company offer words of high regard and respect for the way the company deals with the financial community and for sticking to a philosophy in which it believes.

In years past, P&G had earned the reputation of being uncommunicative, uncooperative and downright secretive with the financial community. In fact, in 1903, the New York Stock Exchange withdrew the company's listing after 12 years on the Big Board. That occurred after the P&G board decided not to issue detailed reports to stockholders because of some unclarified "indiscreet use" of information. The policy of secrecy continued for 10 years, but the stock was not reinstated on the exchange until 1929.

As far as the New York Stock Exchange is concerned, P&G's history with the exchange began on Sept. 12, 1929. And the company has successfully put to rest any negative image of its relationship with Wall Street. "The comments you hear about P&G being secretive and uncooperative go back a long time," Mr. Meade says. "The company is in the mainstream in terms of investor relations."

Despite his more negative view of the company's prospects, Mr. Salzman says he has always enjoyed following the company. And Mr. Freedman says his experience has been that management is always more than willing to help anyone with any meaningful question they have to understand the company better.

"I enjoy following them because the people there are terrific," says Ms. Landry.

Mr. Segalas believes he has an advantage over everyone else on the street, because of his background, which included a 10-year stint at P&G in manufacturing and engineering. "Maybe it sounds arrogant, but I feel I have a point of difference," he says.

Even when these experts differ on their advice to investors on whether to buy, sell or hold, they would all give the same enthusiastic advice to an upcoming analyst that P&G is one of the best learning experiences in the business. And they wouldn't trade that experience for any other.

Towering Tradition
P&G Builds for the Future

P&G's new headquarters builds a bridge between the past, present and the future.

THE VIEW FROM CINCINNATI'S MOUNT ADams at sunrise is breathtaking. As the sun clears the seven hills of the Queen City, deep shadows and the morning mist from the Ohio River begin to recede beneath the cover of heavily forested slopes. The view overlooks the east side of downtown Cincinnati. On a clear morning, the golden tones bring the city's limestone, granite, red brick and marble facades into sharp relief. The lookout site is appropriately named Eden Park. It is the best place to ponder the significance of Procter & Gamble Co.'s new headquarters complex.

Even from a distance of several miles, the complex is imposing, dominating the eastern edge of downtown Cincinnati like a fortress. Twin 17-story octagonal towers topped with pyramidal roofs form a symbolic gateway to the city, and conversely a city boundary. The locals jest that the towers resemble somewhat the physical endowments of a female country music singer. But a building such as this could not be more serious in its attempt to define P&G's new identity on Cincinnati's skyline. As such, it is the culmination of

P&G's ever expanding physical presence there.

Despite the fact that P&G is an international giant, one of the nation's largest advertisers and the 14th largest U.S. company, it has always kept a low profile in its hometown. P&G has a history of placing greater emphasis on the interior needs of a building and the company than on its exterior facade. From the first offices in a three-story brick storefront until 1956 when it moved from the Gwynne Building, its home since 1914, P&G has found the need continually to improve operations to meet changing consumer needs.

Over the years, P&G has moved five times to larger headquarters, but encountered the same limitations in each—a lack of office flexibility. Until P&G build a home designed for its own use in 1956, the company was at the mercy of 19th century design. The 1956 headquarters, now called the Central Building, was built to accommodate change. It was the first structure to incorporate a design strategy that is common in P&G structures today, says David Crafts, manager of P&G's corporate buildings division. Movable partitions and convenient access to wiring gave the building flex-

The scenic view of Cincinnati at sunrise from Mount Adams. P&G provides the anchor on the east side of downtown.

ibility to change with growth in the organization, reconfiguration of marketing, research and office personnel and new office technology.

But the Central Building's facade epitomized P&G's conservative posture in the community, which was reinforced by the carbon-copy 1972 addition designed by the Chicago-based architectural firm Skidmore Owings & Merrill. As P&G neared capacity in the 591,000-square-foot building, the overflow was housed in P&G's 77-year-old Duttenhofer Building, now called the Sycamore Building.

By January 1979, P&G had leased floors of the Central Trust Center, relocating about 500 people, and occupied smaller spaces in the Dixie Terminal and Gwynne Building, Mr. Crafts says. Meanwhile, P&G began buying parcels of land around the headquarters site, laying the foundation for expansion. In the late 1970s, when P&G began planning construction of its newest headquarters, the decision was made to build both internal flexibility and architectural style into the design. "We wanted to construct something that was functional and would represent the real char-

acter of Procter & Gamble. We wanted to make a statement about what Procter & Gamble is and yet design a building that would blend well with what existed then." Mr. Crafts says.

P&G began with a list of about 30 architectural firms. After selecting three finalists—SOM-New York, I.M. Pei & Partners and Kohn Pedersen Fox—P&G asked for presentations, including details on architects who would be assigned to the project. "Our experience is that it is the people who are assigned to a project that are critical to its success," Mr. Crafts says. Eyebrows were raised in April 1982 when P&G announced the selection of New York-based KPF as architects for the new headquarters. At the time, KPF was a 4-year-old company with few projects either completed or under construction. "They were hungry, aggressive and, we felt, extremely creative and responsive to the project needs," Mr. Crafts says. "Because they were young, they were anxious to do an outstanding job for us and they gave us their top people," he adds.

The original master plan called for an 800,000-square-foot, 30-story tower in the center of the square-block site. KPF's clay models of the tower were rejected because large departments such as purchasing and market research needed more space than a single floor of a tower could provide. Then-Chairman O.B. "Brad" Butler and President John Smale were not convinced a tower was the solution, says A. Eugene Kohn, principal with KPF. "The tower concept never really caught their fancy. What did appeal was a lower building, where you can create atriums, high lobbies and parks, and where people can have a sense of family," he says.

"The challenge was to come up with a unified complex," Mr. Crafts says. "While the Central Building was not an architectural edifice we were proud of, we were not going to tear it down because it was still very functional. And the decision had already been made not to move the executive

offices and board room from the building," he says. The twin-tower concept evolved because it opened a view corridor from the east into downtown. Second, it anchored the east side of the downtown area, Mr. Crafts says.

KPF favored a building that represented a link between P&G's past; the architectural style of downtown Cincinnati; and the fact that the headquarters complex was no ordinary office building, but instead an international headquarters. With full creative license, the present form of the building evolved, including two towers and a plaza that stretches the full length of the site, which is instrumental in bringing the new headquarters and Central Building together. In addition, many themes echo between the two buildings, including setbacks on the 10th floor; building widths; and the use of marble, limestone and granite.

KPF also redid the facade of the Central Building, adding dummy columns redone in the same granite-and-limestone configurations as the new building. P&G even persuaded the city to allow it to repave the street with the same paving used in its circular driveway.

The new headquarters reflects the Art Deco heritage of many buildings in downtown Cincinnati. The sloped pyramidal roof, for example, echoes that of Carew Tower, the city's tallest building, the Times-Star Building and Union Terminal. Although P&G's Central Building already had a plaza, KPF was given freedom to virtually tear it up and start over to link the two main structures in the headquarters complex, Mr. Crafts says. "John Smale [now chairman-CEO] in particular wanted a unified complex, and if it meant tearing up the plaza to do it, we would expend those kinds of funds," he says.

When the building was ready for occupancy in

The Gwynne Building was the home for Procter & Gamble from 1914 to 1956, when the headquarters moved to what is now called the Central Building.

February 1985, it contained 836,000 square feet and office space for 4,600 people. "This building creates a bridge between the past and today, and [it establishes] Procter & Gamble's image as a conservative, dependable company that is proud of its history," says Mr. Kohn. "With a company like Procter & Gamble, it's appropriate to create a building that links the past and the present."

Not everyone agrees. John Meunier, director of the University of Cincinnati School of Architecture & Interior Design, believes P&G missed an opportunity to make a statement about how corporations relate to their communities in a more collaborative way. Mr. Meunier, who is taking a post in September as dean of the College of Architecture & Environmental Design at Arizona State University, Tempe, has been a vocal critic of P&G's headquarters complex as a member of the city planning board. "It's a wonderful example of this very peculiar attitude that I think America has toward corporations. Quite clearly, the corporation has replaced the church and the state as the unchallengeable authority. We have no trouble poking fun at our presidents. We have no trouble pillorying our religious leaders, but the corporation remains an almost holy sanctuary, which none dare attack," he says. "The sense of oligarchy is so strong. The sense of hierarchy, autonomy and a decision-making process from the top down is so clearly there," he says.

Contrast this with the social attitude in Europe, where corporations are secondary to the state and the unions, says Mr. Meunier, who originally is from the U.K. "Here in America you have a sense that the corporations rule." The building also fails, in Mr. Meunier's estimation, to reflect changes in our culture since the 1930s-era after which it is modeled. It ignores the esthetic tensions of modern art, music, literature, film and architecture, he says. Mr. Meunier says the building reminds him more of a classical French play with its unities of time, place and action rather than a

work that celebrates the changing consciousness of late-20th century art, where the classical unities often are disrupted and fragmented.

"In the case of P&G, it's all laid out for you. What you see is obvious at first sight. There are no surprises. The whole thing evokes the nostalgic and fictional stability of the past," he adds.

Mr. Meunier also criticizes what he feels is an overblown sense of self-importance in the headquarters complex. "I'm sometimes struck with the thought that what we're looking at is awfully like the United Nations, complete with flags of countries out front—a sort of secretariat of a huge international organization. There is a seriousness about this which one would sort of like to prick the balloon of," he says. "I find the seriousness of this amusing when you think about what they're selling, which is disposable diapers, detergent and soap. The image certainly fits their sense of themselves as a very serious and major organization."

Mr. Meunier says the building was done at the peak of the post-modernist period in architecture, which he considers a reactionary phase in which the more utopian ideals of modernism have lost their conviction, and a sense that a more conservative attitude towards building in cities was appropriate. This is so that buildings make sense to a wider public than those built during the modernist period. "It's a building in a funny way that is appropriate to is time and place in that both the time and the place are conservative, as is the organization itself," Mr. Meunier says. "Also, it's an organization that values its independence and autonomy, and to a certain extent its privacy. Though it's a very public building, it also has a peculiarly private presence in a very public context."

As an example, Mr. Meunier compares P&G's old plaza, which was virtually inaccessible to the public, with its new public park and plaza. "When they built the new park in front of this building they made noises about its being much more accessible to the building. In fact, it has been designed in such a way that it remains a very private place. Even when the chains are down, you still feel in a way that you are trespassing. "It is not a park that has been designed in a way to make the community feel that they have any rights there. They are definitely the guests of P&G and are very much there on P&G's sufferance, so to speak. Everybody is aware that there are guards around with pocket radios who will chase you out if you start to do something that P&G doesn't approve of," he says.

This attitude is perhaps a reflection of the traditional values held by the people of Cincinnati—respect for privacy, hard work and a sense of control over the environment, Mr. Meunier says. "I think P&G has always created an ethos around if of being a very extreme example of something that is valued in Cincinnati generally. It is a city that values reserve and the right of the individual to remain private. The case here is that the corporation as an individual has the right to retain control over its environment," he says. "And yet in another way, the image fits very well," Mr. Meunier adds. "One of the things that makes Cincinnati a stable economic environment is the stability of companies like Procter & Gamble. General Motors can abandon its Tomorrow assembly plant [as happened recently], but everyone knows that Procter & Gamble would be very unlikely to [leave Cincinnati]. They take their civic responsibilities here very seriously."

Did P&G miss an opportunity to take a look into the future through the construction of its new headquarters?

"Whether P&G could ever have done that I don't know," says Mr. Meunier. "Certainly, there are relatively few instances where a major corporation has an opportunity to build a major building that will have an important impact on a major city. There aren't many lessons to be drawn from this particular case," he concludes.

Mr. Kohn takes the criticism in stride. "He is

certainly entitled to his opinion," Mr. Kohn says. Many in the architectural profession appear to side with Mr. Kohn. KPF was chosen this year as winner of two American Institute of Architecture Design Awards, the highest honor given by the profession, for the P&G headquarters complex, and for a commercial building at 333 Wacker Drive in Chicago. Both also figured prominently in a poll by *Progressive Architecture* asking architects to rate the top buildings constructed in the world over the past five years.

"I don't think it is appropriate to totally ignore the context in which a building exists," Mr. Kohn argues. "The challenge was to relate to [the Central Building] while creating an updated image in a building with more personality and character that could contribute to the architectural heritage of the city. To find a way to make it special and yet relate to the past was the challenge presented to us," he says. In the case of the garden, too often open spaces are ignored in major cities, especially in downtown areas, Mr. Kohn adds. "Procter & Gamble has chosen at great expense to create a garden that provides light and air for all. It's an amenity for P&G employees, for the city of Cincinnati, and it's a statement that says this is the center, the world headquarters," he says.

"With regard to appropriate behavior in the park, I don't see anything wrong with certain rules and restrictions on how to behave in a space. I don't think you need to throw wild parties and throw papers around to demonstrate that it's a public area. It is Procter & Gamble's property after all."

Mr. Kohn also takes issue with criticism about an inflated sense of importance in the headquarters complex. "As a corporate headquarters, you know the people who are going to live there, and you are designing for the lifestyle of a company. You are representing the company's feelings and its attitude toward itself. Procter & Gamble was our most challenging project to date because it was a major corporate headquarters in the downtown of a major city."

A close look at the new headquarters complex also reveals that it is very modern inside, despite exterior resonances with Cincinnati's past. The most telling feature is the use of open-floor plans, a system of modular offices that places upper-level executives around two atriums in the centers of the floors. Floor plans have a fixed circulation pattern around the perimeters, says Patricia Conway, senior partner at Kohn Pedersen Fox Conway, a KPF affiliate. A drawback of open-plan construction is that it doesn't provide as much privacy or status as private offices, but it offers more flexibility to reorganize floors with changing needs, she says.

True to form, P&G researched every aspect of open-plan construction before finalizing details, Ms. Conway says. Executives visited a variety of companies using such systems. "They wanted assurances that the open-plan concept would not degenerate into chaos, that you would not need a guide dog to get through the floors," she says.

P&G's decision not to build a splashy high-rise office tower fits closely with the Cincinnati 2000 Plan, adopted in July 1982. That plan designates areas where commercial and residential development should take place. Such planning is critical in Cincinnati, where an accident of geography created what may be the smallest downtown area of any major city. The city is hemmed in to the north and east by hills and to the south by the Ohio River. The U.S. government completed the job by looping the edges of downtown with an interstate system that skirts the base of Cincinnati's hills. The result is a downtown that cannot sprawl. Almost any destination in the downtown area is within 15 minutes on foot.

One aspect of the Cincinnati 2000 Plan is that buildings rise to a peak at the center of downtown. The focal point is Fountain Square, and the tallest buildings are located within a block or two of Fifth Street, the main east-west thoroughfare.

The dominant structures in this area include the 50-story Carew Tower, completed in 1930, and the 34-story Central Trust Center, completed in 1913. This area also includes several buildings in the 30-story range.

P&G also saved the city a great deal of money by privately acquiring all property for the project, says Nell Surber, director of Cincinnati's Department of Economic Development.

The company has a distinction of having the only major construction project in the downtown area that was built without assistance or tax abatement from the city, she says. "They never asked us for a penny." How much the P&G project could have cost the city is illustrated in a project by J.M.B. Federated, a developer 80% owned by J.M.B. Realty, Chicago. Upfront costs for the $250 million office and hotel tower near Fountain Square could exceed $30 million for site acquisition, relocation of businesses, demolition and repaving of streets and sidewalks, Ms. Surber says.

Although P&G is tight-lipped about how much it spent on its new headquarters, local developers estimate the price tag exceeded $100 million. A second-level walkway that P&G built between the Central Building and the headquarters probably cost $700,000 by itself, Ms. Surber says.

Perhaps the most beneficial aspect of P&G's headquarters in terms of downtown development is that it provides a beautiful anchor on the east side of downtown, Ms. Surber says. "Although the architects designed a building that seemed logical to them, they could not have designed it better for our purposes if we had asked them to," she says. "The complex provides an entryway to the city from the east, and the park looks like [the formal gardens of] Versailles. You can see it from almost any tall building in the city."

The P&G headquarters is a model for future downtown development, she adds. "It demonstrates that the area is vital, economically healthy, and a secure place for future development."

CHAPTER FIVE

Heeding the (Toll Free) Call

In her 37 years at the company, Dorothy Puccini has seen and heard almost everything. Her staff receives training in dealing with consumers and what can happen when a product is used incorrectly.

SINCE 1974, WHEN PROCTER & GAMBLE CO. put its first toll-free number on a box of Duncan Hines fudge brownie mix, millions of consumers have called the company with questions, complaints and compliments for P&G products. "It's like having a mother handy," says Dorothy Puccini, P&G's manager of consumer services in Cincinnati.

Thirty-seven years ago, when Ms. Puccini joined the department she now heads, "we were primarily letter-writers," she recalls. Then in 1970, someone suggested calling up the consumers who wrote to P&G, in order to do a little follow-up. "From this it was a logical next step—but a big one—to get consumers to *call us*," says the consumer contact veteran.

By 1981, all P&G products carried an 800 number, "and the effect on our consumer contact volume has been enormous," says Ms. Puccini.

While the company averaged 160,000 letters a year before the 800-number, it now receives 200,000 letters and 800,000 phone calls fielded by 100 agents. The phones are manned mostly by part-timers, weekdays from 9:30 a.m. to 7:30 p.m. (ET). Before becoming phone agents, employees must complete three-to-five weeks of training in their specialized category, such as paper products or detergents.

In training, they learn not only how to deal with consumers on the phone, but also the history and marketing strategy of every product in their niche. They're also taught what can happen when the product is used incorrectly.

The consumer services staff's preparation and expertise in consumer relations recently have been put to the test in rather dramatic fashion. What had begun as a Southern-based story earlier, came to a head in the early 1980s. Procter & Gamble found itself in the midst of controversy that linked its corporate logo with Satanism. The rumors were generating 5,000 queries a day from New York, New Jersey and Pennsylvania by 1985. The curious called P&G's toll-free number, where extra help had been hired to set them straight. From 1981 to 1985, P&G answered 100,000 calls and letters that generally went like this: "A friend of a friend of mine saw the head of your company on 'Phil Donahue' admitting that you worship Satan. Your logo shows Satan as a ram, surrounded by the diabolical numbers 666." Ridiculous as these charges may sound, they cost the company untold aggravations and distractions—and sales.

Of far more urgency was the report issued in June 1980 by the Atlanta-based U.S. Center for Disease Control that linked the sometimes-fatal disease toxic shock syndrome to the use of tampons. Further findings indicated a disproportionate number of women who had contracted TSS had been using P&G's superabsorbent Rely brand. The company acted quickly to withdraw the product and later suspend its production.

P&G was inundated by calls from concerned, frightened consumers seeking answers and assurances. According to "Crisis Management: Planning for the Inevitable" by Steven Fink, the company has no data on the number of calls that were actually related to Rely. However, because this was the same 800 number found on the back of all P&G products, the company initially was insensitive to female callers who felt uncomfortable talking to male operators, Mr. Fink writes. After a number of complaints, however, all Rely calls were routed to female operators. No medical information was given out; callers were counseled to speak with their own doctors. According to P&G, callers were alerted to the symptoms, given details of Rely's contents and encouraged to return the product for refund. (Seven years later, the matter is still in litigation.)

These incidents illustrate the importance of this department as a vital link in the bond of trust the company has built with its public. Of course, most situations the agents field lack the urgency of the Rely and Satanism affairs.

At Christmastime, for example, the department's baking goods specialists expect a batch of calls from consumers who misplaced their favorite Crisco recipes. In April, those agents specializing in household cleaning products are kept busy with calls from spring cleaners. And in June, according to Ms. Puccini, the baking mix experts field questions from mothers who are baking their daughters a wedding cake using Duncan Hines products.

The gist of every call is noted and compiled into monthly reports for brand managers in each division. Moreover, P&G management—including Chairman-CEO John Smale and President John Pepper—occasionally listens to tapes of calls that have been recorded with the consumer's consent.

While the company does not depend on incoming calls for consumer research, it was 800-number users who convinced the company to include instructions for baking Duncan Hines brownies at high altitudes. They also alerted P&G to the fact that Downy liquid fabric softener had a tendency to freeze easily during cold spells.

When a consumer recently complained of "unfudgy" Duncan Hines fudge brownies, the sympathetic phone agent queried her first about methodology: "Did you use an 8-by-8-in. pan?" She did. "Did you bake for 24 to 27 minutes?" She did. "And you added the oil, egg and water?" Again, yes. The agent expressed surprise and regret, and promised to send the caller a coupon for one free package of the mix, "so you can give it another chance."

In this way the 800 number serves a twofold purpose: "It helps consumers with questions and problems," concludes Ms. Puccini, "And we make sure that what consumers are saying gets to the right person."

CHAPTER SIX

No Dust in the Attic
P&G's Active Archives

Active archives become even more so under an archivist who stresses a system of collecting, documenting and storing materials for the future.

THE CORPORATE ARCHIVES, THAT GREAT grab bag of Procter & Gamble Co.'s cast-offs, assorted baubles and historical artifacts has come to life under Corporate Archivist Ed Rider. The archives is poised to relocate from a basement into specially outfitted quarters on the sixth floor of the Sycamore Building, which is symbolic of the value P&G places on its history. Begun in the 1950s, the archives formerly was staffed by part timers but now is run by Mr. Rider, a professional who was lured away in 1980 from the Cincinnati Historical Society.

Mr. Rider's archives certainly isn't gathering dust. Much of it remains on active duty as brand managers and their assistants struggle with timely questions. An example: Why did the push-button Crest toothpaste dispenser only become popular today, although it first was introduced 30 years ago? "Why didn't it catch on then and why is it coming back now?" asks Mr. Rider. Another example is Crisco shortening, a revolutionary product that engendered a massive education program when it was introduced in 1911. "Maybe we should do that again," Mr. Rider says.

"The value of an archives is to provide our marketing people with the same understanding of the history of our products that the consumer has," Mr. Rider says. "This is important when you consider that most brand managers are in their 20s and 30s," he adds, "and yet we have consumers who conceivably have been using our products since they were introduced." Historical records are relevant because they indicate how brands and images have been shaped. Continuity is vital, he says.

"It is important to see what we've been telling consumers. Obviously, you can't copy things exactly as they were then because today's consumer is different. But you have to have some appreciation of that history. People are sensitive to that," he says.

Mr. Rider frequently gets letters from women in their 80s and 90s who still remember how the introduction of certain P&G products affected their lives. "You have to have some appreciation for that consumer," he says.

For example, how many consumers under the age of 40 are even aware that there was a real Duncan Hines? Mr. Hines, who died in 1959, was a traveling printing company salesman who became America's foremost where-to-eat authority. Restaurants nationwide once clamored for listings in Mr. Hines' travel guides, but first they had to pass personal inspection. Only then were they allowed to display the coveted "Recommended by Duncan Hines" sign, which appears on brand packaging today.

P&G's corporate archives is assembling materials Mr. Rider believes will help brand managers and executives understand brand history and make informed decisions in the future. "Historical resources are becoming more and more important, particularly as Procter & Gamble grows and diversifies," Mr. Rider says. "It's especially important for new employees to understand not only the products but the image that these products have held historically in the mind of the consumer."

This attitude fits well with the image Mr. Rider is attempting to cultivate for his own department. "It's OK to think of the archives as a corporate attic, but it's really a corporate historic resource center," he says. One example of the role an archives can play is as a resource in resolving disputes over trademarks and logos. Dated samples of packaging can provide documented evidence on when a company introduced certain packaging or made key claims.

The archives also is a vital resource when it comes to legal proceedings such as cases of product liability claims. "We would need to know which label the consumer had at the time to determine if there was product misuse. By the time we get to the legal case, it could have changed three times," Mr. Rider says.

In this regard, a corporate archives takes a different viewpoint from the local historical society, he adds, saying, "We have to be more aware of the company's needs and of confidentiality. The corporation is to make a profit and to look ahead into the future."

For obvious reasons, it also is advantageous for important company materials, documents and artifacts to end up centralized in one department, rather than being distributed around the general offices. "It makes more sense to know where something is, rather than try to find out who's got it squirreled away somewhere," Mr. Rider says.

But keeping track of advertising and product samples for more than 150 brands marketed worldwide through the years is an enormous task. And it is one that has been performed inconsistently in the past, he says.

"Prior to the early 1970s, we just had thousands of negatives of TV commercials with no information on what they were or where they came from. We didn't even know if they had ever even aired," he says. The archives reluctantly disposed of most of the materials, he says. To flesh out P&G's collection of TV commercials, Mr. Rider now is asking for copies of historic reels from the 17 agencies P&G has used in the past. And to simplify collection of current TV commercials, he is asking each brand manager to select a single TV spot that represents the current year's commercials. Master tapes of the selected spots are then cataloged and stored in a climate-controlled warehouse in Cincinnati. For print advertising, P&G has made arrangements for each agency to send proofs to Cincinnati of every piece done in the past year, he says.

Another duty of the archives department is to develop a system of safeguarding product samples and records of companies acquired by P&G. When Crush International was acquired in 1980, for example, Mr. Rider found several original Norman Rockwell paintings created for the Crush brand from the 1920s. "When you're packing up a location, naturally the historical records take second place to the actual business. But it's important for me to get in there and see that important finds are saved," Mr. Rider says.

Other examples are Richardson-Vicks, Wilton, Conn., acquired in 1985, and Norwich-Eaton Pharmaceutical Group, Norwich, N.Y., acquired in 1982. Norwich-Eaton already had an archives, which remains at the divisional headquarters, he says. But at Richardson-Vicks, the founding families donated many early documents to the University of North Carolina at Chapel Hill, he says.

The division soon will be consolidating its headquarters and research facilities, and Mr. Rider intends to be ready with an archives system. "Whenever a company moves, that's when everybody starts cleaning out their drawers. I want to make people aware that there is an archives in Cincinnati."

Collecting and cataloging materials is not the extent of Mr. Rider's duties, however. The corporate archives also performs a variety of other services at P&G. An example is management of company relics, such as a magnificent antique English silver coffee and tea service once owned by J.A. Folger & Co., which was acquired in 1963.

Another responsibility is responding to consumer inquiries. Some are seeking to sell artifacts, while others are simply inquiring about P&G's history and its brands. But this generates some interesting letters. A recent letter and baby photo from a 62-year-old Missouri woman asks whether she was an Ivory Soap baby [portrayed in an ad] in 1925. Mr. Rider shakes his head as he examines the photograph. "I doubt it," he says. "At that time we used illustrations. She could have been a model for the painter, though."

Another responsibility is planning presentations for trade shows. Mr. Rider recently created a huge display for the lobby of the new headquarters that celebrates P&G's 150th anniversary.

Collecting artifacts is an interesting aspect of Mr. Rider's job. He sometimes buys items from people cleaning out their attics and basements. Recent finds include a case of the discontinued brand of Polo Soap, circa 1915, and an ad for Ivory soap from 1900. "I don't spend my weekends in dusty attics or at flea markets, but it doesn't seem to matter. When people find things they tend to call me anyway," he says.

And that is how Mr. Rider managed to acquire four 1905 stand-up window displays advertising Lenox Soap. The hinged, wooden displays, which are in mint condition and still in their original boxes, had been shipped by train in the early 1900s to Montana. Apparently, they never reached their destination and were found a few years ago in the rafters of a train shed that was being torn down. "It's one of the most significant finds since I've been here," he says.

CHAPTER SEVEN

Memorable Images

*From Ivory babies to Ozzie & Harriet,
P&G has long been a part of
the public consciousness.*

Circa 1925

January 1928

November 1941

June 11, 1958

May 1956

January 1950

November 1934

August 18, 1928 *Drawing by Gluyas Williams, 1928, 1956, the New Yorker magazine.*

June 14, 1959

1924

Salesmen in the 1930s often carried display cases containing
samples of P&G products.

November 1934

September 1953

June 1936

May 1946

II

THE PEOPLE

CHAPTER EIGHT

Leaders of Distinction

Seven men have served as P&G's chief executive. Each has built upon the principles of its founders. And each has made a difference.

WILLIAM ALEXANDER PROCTER, SON OF founder William Procter, became Procter & Gamble's first president in 1890. He was a philanthropist, making large, often anonymous, donations to various institutions. During his tenure construction on Ivorydale started, marking P&G's first period of growth.

William Cooper Procter, P&G's general manager since 1890, became president after his father, William Alexander, died in 1907. He pioneered many labor practices at P&G, most notably Saturday afternoons off with pay and an employee profit-sharing plan. Under his leadership, the company began opening new plants outside the Cincinnati area and entering the overseas market.

Col. Procter (as he was popularly known from his days as a commander in the Ohio National Guard's infantry) was elected board chairman in 1930. When he died on May 2, 1934, the *Cincinnati Post*, recalling the many progressive programs he had initiated over the years, wrote, "Col. Procter was animated by the most human instincts. He was a great philanthropist and a great industrialist . . ."

William Alexander Procter

Richard R. Deupree became president in 1930 and board chairman in 1948. He served as honorary board chairman from 1959 to 1974.

Mr. Deupree began his P&G career as a clerk in 1905; by 1924 he had become a member of the board. He played a leading role in making the guaranteed annual employment plan practical by developing a revolutionary direct-selling marketing plan that ensured steady, year-round production. His edict concerning long-winded memos—"Boil it down to something I can grasp"—resonates today in P&G's practice of containing memos to one page. Mr. Deupree died in 1974.

Niel H. McElroy joined P&G in 1925 as an ad department mail clerk. He became promotion director in 1929, advertising and promotion director in 1940, VP-advertising in 1943 and VP-general manager in 1946. He became company president in 1948. The only job he held outside P&G was U.S. Secretary of Defense under President Dwight D. Eisenhower from 1957 to 1959, after which he returned to P&G as board chairman. He retired in 1971.

Mr. McElroy is credited with crystalizing the company's brand-management system. Also, he was ad manager during the years that P&G became heavily involved in daytime radio. Mr. McElroy died in 1974.

William Cooper Procter

Richard R. Deupree

Howard J. Morgens, like Neil McElroy before him, came up through the P&G ranks by way of the advertising department where he had been brand manager, advertising department manager and VP-advertising. He was made exec VP in 1954.

After graduating from the Harvard Graduate School of Business Administration in 1933 he joined P&G, starting as a salesman. Mr. Morgens was transferred the next year to the brand promotion section of the advertising department; in 1946, he was named manager; in 1948, he became VP-advertising. He became exec VP in charge of U.S. operations in 1954.

Mr. Morgens became company president when Mr. McElroy left for Washington in 1957. He became chairman and chief executive in 1971. (According to a company source, the title chief executive was first designated in 1971—"the outside world knows it as chief executive officer." This new management structure was seen as a move to pave the way for Neil McElroy's retirement that year.) Mr. Morgens became chairman of the executive committee in 1974 and chairman emeritus in 1977.

Edward G. Harness was president from 1971 to 1974, when he was promoted to chairman-CEO, a position he held until 1981.

Neil H. McElroy

Howard J. Morgens

Before becoming P&G's president he rose through various merchandising, sales and brand management positions. In 1960, Mr. Harness was named advertising manager of the U.S. soap and detergent division. He went on to head the toilet goods division and then the paper products division. He was named VP-group executive in 1966 and exec VP over all consumer products divisions in 1970. He died in 1984.

John G. Smale, who joined P&G in 1952, became P&G's president in 1974 and acquired the additional title of chief executive in 1981. In April 1986 he was named chairman-CEO.

John Smale is a member of the trustee board of Kenyon College and the Cincinnati Institute of Fine Arts and is chairman of Cincinnati's infrastructure commission.

Under his tenure P&G has become the largest manufacturer of otc drug products by acquiring Norwich-Eaton Pharmaceuticals, part of G.D. Searle, and most important, Richardson-Vicks. The R-V acquisition is the largest and most important acquisition in P&G's history, dramatically increasing its position in the health and personal care field and laying the foundation for future growth worldwide.

Edward G. Harness

John G. Smale

Making the Grade
How P&G Recruits Winners

The company scours the countryside for recent graduates and military veterans to fit its goal-oriented system. When the newness wears off, staffers' futures hinge on speed, accuracy and creativity or they are diplomatically shown the door.

I T'S THE BEST GRADUATE EDUCATION YOU'LL ever get."

"They'll teach you action under fire."

"It's one experience you'll never forget."

These accolades from former Procter & Gamble employees sound like slogans from military recruiting posters. In fact, each of these people, who have successful careers in advertising, public relations and brand management at other companies, once were recruited by P&G, a process they both loathed and loved.

Each year, P&G hires nearly 1,000 people from 200 graduate and undergraduate programs around the world to fill all of its available posi-

tions. The company employs some 75,000 people in Cincinnati and 55 installations in the U.S. and abroad. The recruiting process begins not on college campuses, but deep inside P&G's Tower building in Cincinnati, where the company's personnel recruiting staff identifies positions expected to open in the coming months. The company (which would not comment on its recruiting practices) works at defining the different personality traits and professional qualifications necessary for each job.

"P&G [assesses] the types of people they need and exactly how many they need," says Richard A. Stewart, director of university placement services at Purdue University, West Lafayette, Ind. "Then we indicate P&G's needs to our students, and they begin signing up for interviews. We also run student data through our computer," Mr. Stewart says. "If P&G says they want a chemical engineering major with a B-plus average who wants a job in process engineering, we can get them a list of names and resumes within two minutes."

P&G's recruiters pore over resume books sent by university placement staffs, looking for qualified student candidates. P&G does a fine job, they really take it seriously," Mr. Stewart says. "They put the time and effort into getting who they want. They say that 60% of their new hires are pre-identified" from resume books and university recommendations.

P&G also runs several programs during the school year to help identify good student prospects. "They [P&G recruiters] come in early in the year and have receptions and presentations," says Joyce Watts, assistant dean and director of career development and placement at Northwestern University's Kellogg Graduate School of Management, Evanston, Ill. One year P&G took over a pizza parlor near Northwestern for a night and entertained 200 student prospects. Similar events are held in New York, Cincinnati and on university campuses around the country.

P&G also offers mock-interview situations in front of the students, Ms. Watts says. "Not everyone would do that. They put the time and effort up front so that people know them, and they know their people. They have a profile of what skills and characteristics are necessary to cut it in Cincinnati," Ms. Watts says. "While they are personnel people, they really are grounded in P&G and know what it takes to be successful there," she adds. "They're trying to create a win/win situation for the students and the company. They're consistent, they don't lead anyone on and they don't make exceptions. They know their policy."

P&G also keeps in constant contact with university placement people, while many recruiters from other companies simply fly in and fly out, Ms. Watts says. "It keeps them on top of trends in the graduating class, the new teachers, new clubs and salary ranges" offered by competing consumer product companies.

The company often targets first-year M.B.A. students with a special weeklong Summer Camp held at corporate headquarters in Cincinnati. It's attended by one recruit from each of the graduate business schools it favors. P&G offers seminars and group projects designed to familiarize the student with P&G. These sessions also help in judging whether these students are recruitment material.

On campus, P&G interviews students it has targeted from the resume books and those students with the fortitude to sign up without a prior nod from P&G. At most schools, the company interviews a minimum of 50% by invitation and 50% on an open-list basis. Some schools, including New York's Columbia University, allow P&G to run a 90% to 100% closed schedule because P&G recruits so heavily from the school, says Fredric Way, associate dean and director of placement, Columbia Graduate School of Business.

Fear of rejection caused one former P&G recruit, now a brand manager at a leading cosmetics company, to avoid signing up for a P&G interview. "I was being recruited by the top investment houses on Wall Street and several consumer products companies. But I wasn't going to have Procter & Gamble tell me no," he says. When P&G called him, however, he jumped at the chance for an interview and was offered a job.

Other students make it their goal to get a job at P&G. When Richard Edler, now exec VP-general manager of McCann-Erickson, Los Angeles, was pursuing his M.B.A. in the late '60s at the University of Iowa, he made up his mind to get a position at Procter & Gamble. To realize that goal, he did his master's thesis on consumer attitudes about laundry detergents, focusing on P&G's brands. Impressed with his knowledge and enterprise, the company hired Mr. Edler in 1969 as a brand assistant in the packaged soap and detergents division, where he stayed for seven years.

Just what does P&G want in a new employee? "They want the best and brightest and the most articulate students. Everyone wants the best, but P&G wants the *creme de la creme*, and they get it," Mr. Stewart says. The company says it looks for employees with a "strong motivation to achieve, an outstanding record of leadership, strong oral and written communication skills, a high level of intelligence and creative flair," according to a P&G college recruiting brochure.

P&G's new brand-manager hires typically come from 25 different states and several foreign countries and attended 30 graduate schools and 50 different undergraduate institutions. Most are fresh out of school, others have had some work experience before attending school and some come from the military, the company states in the recruiting material. P&G uses two interview occasions, including a visit to Cincinnati and a written Scholastic Aptitude Test-type math and English exam, to make its decisions.

"They asked four questions designed to get the applicant to talk about himself. They want to gauge your scope of accomplishments, persuasiveness, leadership and overall initiative," recalls Myron Lyzkanycz, now VP-account director at J. Walter Thompson USA, Chicago. After completing graduate work at the University of Wisconsin in Madison, Mr. Lyzkanycz worked as a district field representative for the P&G Distributing Co., as its sales and distribution division is known.

"P&G wants to know what benefit you will give to them rather than what your best attributes are. You may have worked for a company, but P&G wants to know what you have accomplished," he says. "They're looking for people

who want to jump in and get their feet wet on a brand right away. They want people who are impatient for responsibility because it's easier to rein you in than to light a fire under your butt," says one former P&G staffer, now a brand manager at a major cosmetics company.

P&G also looks at students with a B-plus or higher grade point average. Despite appearances, P&G isn't necessarily looking for superior academics, says Gary DiCamillo, VP-marketing at Black & Decker Corp., Hunt Valley, Md. An M.B.A. from Harvard University Business School, Mr. DiCamillo spent five years at P&G as a brand manager on Charmin bathroom tissue and Luvs disposable diapers. "They're looking for people who are well-rounded leaders with the accent on 'What did you get done?'" he says.

Interviews begin with students being questioned on one or two specific things from their resume, ranging from experiences on summer jobs to club memberships. "They want to see how you attack things and how you get things done," Mr. DiCamillo says. "Elected leadership is high on their scale because it's important to work through people to get things done," he says.

P&G hires only recent college graduates—never employees from other companies—for two reasons. First, it wants to promote from within, which helps motivate those who already work there. Second, it wants to indoctrinate people from the start on how P&G works, Mr. DiCamillo says.

P&G also likes student athletes because they've shown a dedication to excellence over a long period of time, another former brand manager says. He adds it's for this same reason that P&G is attracted to people who've served in the military.

P&G recruiters don't waste time asking questions that could be answered by a glance at a resume, said Lee Rushlow, partner with Group 3hree Corp., a Pompano Beach, Fla.-based advertising agency and a P&G salesman in the late

1960s. "They were more European in their approach. Instead of asking specific questions that were a matter of record on my resume and application, they were very interested in getting to know me as a person." What P&G isn't looking for is the analyst-type who just crunches numbers, says Randy Powell, assistant dean for company relations, Indiana University graduate management school, Bloomington. "The gregarious type is more likely to get the nod from them. They also tend to pick people who are very all-American looking."

Goal direction also is a necessity, he says. An undergraduate would have to walk on water to get hired, he says. But if undergraduate students are convinced they belong in brand management and can convince the company of that, they have a good chance of being hired, Mr. Powell says. Once recruits get to Cincinnati, there's a 70%-to-80% chance they'll get offers, Mr. Powell says. At that point, P&G is as much selling itself and Cincinnati to the recruit as the student is selling himself to the company.

Once the hiring decision is made, P&G puts on a full-court press, Mr. DiCamillo says. "It's certainly more satisfying to go to a company that really wants you. P&G cares enough about you to send nine people to follow up or to fly you and your spouse [to Cincinnati] to house hunt."

P&G also is very sympathetic to dual-career couples. Ms. Watts recalls one couples' difficulty in deciding to accept the P&G offer. P&G sent a counselor to Chicago to talk to them. They later flew the couple to Cincinnati to help them find housing. "The wife wants a Ph.D., and P&G got her in contact with the University of Cincinnati.

P&G is sensitive in a way that makes it easy for everyone to have their needs met," Ms. Watts says. They treat people well with good benefits, especially for female executives who want training and family, without worrying about losing ground in their career, she adds.

One woman recounts being called once a week for four months as she weighed the decision. "When I hesitated, they began calling me every week, sending me boxes of products. I appreciated their concern—it was very personal. It's something you don't expect from a giant company," she says.

P&G's recruitment process is so intense because it wants to make the hire before a competitor gets the chance, another former P&G staffer says.

One thing Wim Slootweg, senior VP-managing director of Ogilvy & Mather, Chicago, appreciated about being hired at P&G was that they treated him in a very businesslike manner. "They laid out everything very clearly, from job duties to compensation and to whom I would be reporting. They were very fair," he says.

Given P&G's reputation for career development and brand-management excellence, most recruits don't even hesitate to accept a job offer. "I hesitated for about 10 seconds," says Robert L. Lauer, a former public relations executive at P&G, now VP-corporate affairs at Chicago's Sara Lee Corp. "I would have gone if [the salary offer] had been less," he adds. "The starting salary was not all that generous, but the benefits were extremely good; they were pioneers in profit sharing. But with the chance to go to work for P&G, I would have paid them."

CHAPTER TEN

It's "One Year ... and Up or Out"

At a meritocracy with strict regimentation, the key is creativity without failures.

PROCTER & GAMBLE CO. TAKES GREAT CARE in the professional development of new personnel. But if an employee doesn't live up to expectations, his career with the Cincinnati consumer products giant will be quickly over. Brand management recruits spend their first six-to-nine months learning P&G's system of using a one-page memorandum to communicate ideas and plans. It is a system that is both praised and ridiculed.

"Thinking is important," says a former P&G staffer, now a brand manager at a major cosmetics company. "They work very hard at teaching you how to think. A lot of people ridicule the memo system, but for a black manager [as he is], it was great," he says. "Procter is a meritocracy. They judged you on the quality of your work and your ideas and on little or nothing else. On a memo, they didn't know your race or sex or anything about you."

P&G managers have to digest a lot of information to make decisions quickly. The memo system inculcates the P&G method very quickly, says Michael Clowes, New York-based editor of *Pensions & Investment Age*, a Crain Communications publication. "It's like basic training and a haircut in the Army." Mr. Clowes was recruited by P&G from Columbia Graduate School of Business in 1971 to be a brand assistant on bar soap.

Once an employee gets beyond Memo Writing 101, he is expected to be creative, especially in product promotions and selling techniques, says Mr. Clowes. "You get ahead by not making any mistakes and by showing sparks of creativity."

P&G offers great on-the-job training ranging from management games to plant tours. It also holds seminars on subjects like the creative side of advertising and what makes a TV commercial work, he says. "It's a well-organized system of people teaching people. Everybody looked at what you did and criticized in constructive ways," says Wim Slootweg, senior VP-managing director of Ogilvy & Mather's Chicago office, who worked in brand management for P&G International in Belgium and Canada.

All P&G employees establish SMAC (specific, measurable, achievable and compatible) goals every three months, so it's easy to see who will stay and who will go, says Myron Lyzkanycz, a former P&G sales representative, now an account director at J. Walter Thompson USA, Chicago. "You never get lost in the shuffle because one person is responsible for your achieving your goals. There is accountability at all levels," he says. P&G "honestly, truly believes that their greatest asset is people." In fact, district managers are judged both on sales and on planned-vs.-unplanned turnover. The rule of thumb, though, is "one year, up or out. You have to prove yourself in terms of being promotable or you're out the door," Mr. Lyzkanycz says.

One woman ready to start at P&G this fall says she was surprised to find that upper managers are graded on how well they develop their employees. "It's nice to know that upper management has some commitment to my development," she says.

Mr. Slootweg says he didn't really want to leave P&G, but the advertising world promised fun and variety. What bothered him the most about P&G was the regimentation and the structure. He recalls being "sent home to change into a suit," after showing up for work in a blazer—perfectly acceptable business attire in Europe.

With such stringent controls, it's hard to believe P&G rarely fires employees. Instead, they are subtly forced to resign. "It's so competitive, you must perform. If you don't, you realize it and quit. They're pretty outspoken about performance. They give you a second chance, then you're out," Mr. Slootweg says. Still, many more employees just wake up one day and decide to leave. "I left because we weren't doing the kind of marketing I wanted to do," one former brand manager says. "I wanted more seat-of-the-pants-type stuff, not 'research it to the nth degree.' P&G isn't consciously trying to blunt the entrepreneurial spirit, but it becomes blunted because Procter has too many safety nets in place. . . . They don't put people in situations where people make risky decisions," he says.

"I knew within six weeks that I didn't like it," says Mr. Clowes, who worked at the company 11 months. He had been a foreign correspondent before entering Columbia University. "It was hard to switch from being a Lone Ranger at a newspaper in New York to a militaristic organizational structure. When I decided to leave, I told my supervisor that I was unhappy. He told me not to rush it, that I didn't want to complicate it by making another bad decision," he says. "They gave me full pay during that time and paid to fly me to other job interviews. In some ways it was very hard to leave a company that would show that much concern for its employees.

"They were so considerate because they felt that after the interviewing process and the exposure to the company, they must have misrepresented P&G to us [him and his wife]," Mr. Clowes says. "P&G felt they must have misled us, so they felt they bore part of the responsibility to help us relocate and find happiness."

Some people later admit regretting having left P&G. "I left for all the wrong reasons. If I had it to do over again, I wouldn't have quit," says Kenneth Silvers, senior VP-group director at Hicks & Greist, New York. He spent two years as a brand assistant on Crest toothpaste after getting his M.B.A. from the University of Illinois. He left P&G to become a product manager elsewhere because he wouldn't be a product manager at P&G for another four years. But, reality set in when he realized that "product manager in one place isn't the same responsibilities as at Procter.

"I thought then that Procter was over-regimented. There was 'a P&G way' and that's how you did things. I later found out that other places had no 'way,' " Mr. Silvers says. "Procter has a method that's working for them," he explains. "They don't waste time on how to do something and how to say something, because that was standardized. [Instead] you'd concentrate on developing an idea because they [had already] greased the skids for you."

A Blue Chip Education

The ranks of many Fortune 500 companies are filled with executives who learned the ropes at P&G.

LOOK IN THE EXECUTIVE RANKS OF MANY OF the *Fortune* 500 companies, and the odds are there'll be former Procter & Gamble Co. managers filling many of the highest-ranking positions. To name just a few: Ronald Ahrens, president of Bristol-Myers; Joel Smilow, president-CEO, Playtex Inc.; Robert Beeby, president-CEO of PepsiCo's International division, and William E. Phillips, chairman-CEO of Ogilvy Group.

Although no one has counted the number of former P&G-ers who've gone on to bigger and better career opportunities, there is at least one ex-

ecutive recruiter who tries to keep track of the recent alumni. John T. Thomas, a P&G alumnus and partner in the Chicago office of Ward Howell International, painstakingly compiles the unofficial annual Procter & Gamble Marketing Alumni Directory, relying on fellow alumni to help keep track of P&G grads. P&G people "like to stay in touch with each other," says Mr. Thomas, "and every year ex-P&G-ers contribute new names to the directory. It's like a never-ending chain letter."

This year's edition is the fifth compiled by Mr. Thomas. Almost 1,000 entries are cross-

Robert Beeby, PepsiCo International Division, Somers, N.Y.

referenced by year of hiring, P&G division and, most important, current location. The idea for an alumni directory grew out of the infrequently held gatherings of former P&G-ers. The first reunion, organized by alumni Vada and Ted Stanley, was held Nov. 17, 1980, at the Stanley home in Westport Conn. The party brought together all those who worked on the ninth floor at P&G's Sixth & Sycamore St. headquarters during the 1950s. (The Stanleys met and married when they were working in brand groups in the soap product promotion/advertising division.) More than 140 former P&G-ers, spouses included, gathered to reminisce and exchange new business cards.

They came because former P&G-ers have a lot in common. "Our time in Cincinnati was like playing for the [New York] Yankees," says Mr. Stanley, now chairman of MBI Inc., Norwalk, Conn. "We lived, breathed and worked the soap

business out there in Cincinnati. We'd go to parties and talk business; we were neighbors, car-pool members and Saturday touch-football team members. It was an unforgettable, intense experience."

Inspired by the enthusiasm for the Stanleys' soiree, Mr. Thomas began planning for a national P&G alumni reception. He got some names from the Stanleys' list and others from West Coast-based P&G-ers, who had held a party of their own. "Then, being an ex-Procter guy and promotion minded, I decided to have a big spring party and make it self-liquidating because my former company, Wilkens & Thomas, couldn't afford it," Mr. Thomas says. In late April 1983, more than 330 P&G alumni and guests gathered at Chicago's Field Museum of Natural History for an evening that included a satirical skit by the Second City theater group. All attendees received the first edition of the annual directory.

The directory certainly makes it easy for executive recruiters and competitors to find P&G grads, Mr. Thomas says. "P&G, after all these years, still is considered a gold mine for marketing talent."

Herewith are some reminiscences of several well-known P&G alums:

Robert Beeby, president-CEO PepsiCo International division, Somers, N.Y.

Robert Beeby joined P&G in 1959, "straight out of Northwestern University graduate school." After completing the obligatory field sales training and a year as brand manager for a test-market soap product, he was named Tide brand manager. During his three-year tenure, Tide had sales of $150 million, he says.

"We had a $16 million ad budget, and that's a lot of marketing power for those times. When I was on the brand, our task was to reverse a volume decline, which we did by airing the first-ever 30-second TV campaign to be used in the soap business. We did a lot of trade ad coupons and in-trade ad refunds. At the time, it was a novelty to offer the trade advertising refunds," he recalls. "Tide maintained its leadership position by carefully monitoring the competition. Whenever we saw a high level of spending that was out of proportion to a competitor's market share, we would step in with a heavy counter-spending attack.

"Tide was special. It was *big time* marketing in the sense that there was a lot of media open to us that wasn't available to other brands, even other P&G brands," he says. Despite the rewards of working on P&G's most famous detergent, Mr. Beeby left P&G to join Glendinning Cos., a Westport, Conn.-based consulting company founded in 1960 by former P&G-er Ralph Glendinning. (It has been a mecca for a number of P&G alumni.)

"I left because I was frustrated with the P&G system and my inability to control my destiny. You waited, did what you were supposed to and you were not called to move up until it was your turn," he says. "I didn't want to wait anymore."

After five years with Glendinning, Mr. Beeby joined PepsiCo in 1972 as an executive assistant to the president. He worked his way up the PepsiCo hierarchy, serving two-year stints at the company's Frito-Lay snack foods division and Wilson Sporting Goods Co., then owned by PepsiCo. In 1983, he was named president-CEO of PepsiCo's International division.

Like many former P&G-ers, Mr. Beeby doesn't regret the time he spent in Cincinnati. "There's such a tremendous shared experience among alumni. If my son said he's going to work for P&G, I'd be proud. The company hasn't lost its luster."

James Ferguson, chairman of the executive committee, General Foods Corp., White Plains, N.Y.

World War II veteran; graduate of exclusive Hamilton College; Harvard M.B.A. . . . James Ferguson's credentials were tailor-made for P&G, which he joined in 1951. Beginning his career there in brand management on what was then the

James Ferguson, General Foods Corp., White Plains, N.Y.

toilet-goods division, he worked on the Gleem, Lilt and Shasta shampoo brands. He then worked in the paper-products division on Charmin, the introduction of White Cloud, and Puffs facial tissue before leaving as an associate brand manager in 1962.

"I went to P&G intending to stay three years—and stayed 11," Mr. Ferguson says. He finally left because he "couldn't see spending his whole career in Cincinnati" and wanted to return to the East Coast. Mr. Ferguson tips his hat to P&G—as so many other alums do—as "a first-class place to learn the package-goods business."

He learned his lessons well. Mr. Ferguson's career at General Foods has been a study in corporate upward mobility. Beginning in 1963 as an assistant to the marketing manager of the frozen

James McManus, Marketing Corp. of America, Westport, Conn.

about being the market leader in so many consumer-product categories, he says, and adds it may not be as easy today for P&G to maintain its strangleholds. "The fact that they're in the market [with a competing product] doesn't mean other companies roll over and play dead." He certainly should know: GF is one of P&G's arch-rivals for leadership in the coffee business. "But with the momentum P&G has, it would be hard for them to screw up badly. When you have the people they do, imbued with their philosophy, you may get a B, but it's hard to get an F."

James McManus, founder/president-CEO, Marketing Corp. of America, Westport, Conn.

As a college student, James McManus never doubted that some day he would work for P&G. While in graduate school, "I wrote a letter to them [P&G], telling them I had decided I wanted to be in marketing and advertising. Since they were and still are the champion consumer-package goods marketer, that's who I wanted to work for." His letter worked. Within weeks after receiving his M.B.A. from Northwestern University in 1956, he went to work in what was then called the toilet-goods division.

"I came in as a staff assistant on Oxydol, went out on sales training four months later, then worked on Cheer, Ivory, Dash and Top Job. Every year or two, I'd get promoted to another brand, another position. It was a chance to show what I could do. And if you didn't like one supervisor, the next year you'd be working for another. Your performance didn't hinge on just one manager's opinion.

"P&G in the years I was there was going through a tremendous expansion period," Mr. McManus says. "Soap was the heart of the business, but seven years later, they were into food, personal care, and paper goods. Soap went from 12 to 24 brands. Gleem and Crest [toothpastes] were coming out. It was a booming place, and at

foods division, he has served as a corporate VP (1968); group VP managing the food service, beverage, dessert and cereal divisions (1970); exec VP in charge of the Maxwell House and three other divisions (1972). He became CEO in 1973; chairman and president in 1974; and vice chairman of Philip Morris Cos. a year later. This year he became chairman of the executive committee of GF's board.

Mr. Ferguson recalls the marketing principles that guided P&G: Create products that are superior, distinctive, and "exploit them in a full-blown way. These [P&G's] principles—superior products and building a strong consumer franchise—are very valid today."

Does he detect any slight chinks in P&G's armor? "The company has a touch of arrogance"

William E. Phillips, Ogilvy Group, New York.

the heart of it all was advertising." What impressed Mr. McManus most about P&G was its dedication to its employees. At P&G, people were given ample opportunity to find their niche. "When I started at P&G, there were 22 people in my 'class.' Five years later, only two were left in the advertising side of the business. There was that kind of high turnover rate, but that was part of P&G's plan to weed out people. They demanded high performances out of everyone. It was an up-or-out policy. If you weren't promoted, you left," he says.

Mr. McManus left in 1964 for a consultant's berth at Glendinning Cos. Seven years later he decided to strike out on his own. Working with a stake of $100,000, Mr. McManus built Marketing Corp. of America into what is now a $300

million conglomerate, with interests in restaurants, real estate and commuter airlines. Mr. McManus says he relies on skills learned at P&G to run his own business, particularly the attention paid to detail and business strategy. "P&G has a commitment to excellence. There's an assumption of energy and integrity on the part of every employee and it's all directed at the same goal," he says. "That's how you achieve leadership."

William E. Phillips, chairman-CEO, Ogilvy Group, New York.

Although he now heads an ad agency that lists P&G competitor Lever Bros. as a top client, William Phillips was actively courted by P&G while he was finishing his M.B.A. at Northwestern University. P&G apparently liked the fact that Mr. Phillips obtained his M.B.A. while supporting himself as an appliance salesman for Polk Bros., a Chicago retailer.

"I was part of the new foods division. P&G had just bought the Nebraska Consolidated Milling Co., a regional mill that had a regional brand, Duncan Hines," he says. "As brand manager, I supervised the first brand that came out, Duncan Hines Deluxe Cake Mixes," he says.

More than the "thrill" of marketing for P&G, "what was more amazing is that all of us were recruited out of college, from similar backgrounds, and thrown together in a strange town. . . . There was a lot of company socializing, from car pools to Saturday touch-football games. The company dominated your life. It was an efficient way to sell soap, and a great learning experience, but I decided I didn't want to live that way forever. I wanted more diversity and fewer restrictions," he says.

After four years with P&G, in 1959 he joined Ogilvy & Mather, rising to become president of the U.S. agency in 1975, chief executive of the parent company in 1981, and chairman a year later. He has supervised a number of major client accounts, including General Foods Corp., P&G's chief competitor in the coffee business.

"P&G is a capable competitor in many fields, and it's been fun competing against them in everything from detergents and soaps to diapers and coffee," he says.

Perhaps the most important thing Mr. Phillips carried away from Cincinnati was P&G's commitment to the community in which it makes its headquarters. "P&G was special because it taught its people to be community minded, and that's something I've carried over to Ogilvy," he says.

James P. Schadt, president-CEO, Cadbury Schweppes North America, Stamford, Conn.

Like many of his fellow P&G alumni, James Schadt in 1960 began his marketing career at P&G following his graduation from Northwestern University. But unlike many new P&G-ers, Mr. Schadt didn't have an M.B.A. "That was unusual. There weren't many non-M.B.A.'s at P&G," he says. He joined the paper division and became a brand manager of Puffs facial tissues just a year after P&G bought the Charmin Paper Mills. P&G had developed a way to make paper "thicker, softer and less costly" and was gearing up to introduce a slew of new products. "Tissue-making had been around for 100 years and here comes this new company that can make softer tissue at a lower price. With that, we were introducing Puffs, a new Charmin, White Cloud and Bounty. Puffs even beat out [Kimberly-Clark Corp.'s] Kleenex in midwestern test markets," he recalls.

"P&G then was a pure environment; achievement and hard work were valued. Virtually everyone I worked with worked every day until 4:30, then came back after dinner and worked until they turned out the lights at 10:30. This happened every day, except Friday, and even included a full day on Saturday. And we didn't complain. It was fun, there was so much growth, and

James P. Schadt, Cadbury Schweppes, Stamford, Conn.

people were getting promoted quickly," he says.

In 1965, Mr. Schadt left P&G for Glendinning Cos. "So many of us went to Glendinning in the early days, built that company up, and then left." Mr. Schadt moved on to general management of Beech-Nut Baby Foods, and handled the divestiture of Beech-Nut for Squibb Corp. in 1973, which brought him to the attention of PepsiCo. At PepsiCo he reported to the president of the parent company. He acquired and managed several international snack-food companies for PepsiCo before becoming president of the then-new PepsiCo Wine & Spirits business.

After several years with Consolidated Foods Corp. (now Sara Lee Corp.), in 1981 he joined Cadbury Schweppes, responsible for the London-based company's North American beverage operations. Mr. Schadt says he's been able to use his P&G training and experience in his marketing career. "A P&G marketer makes sure every part of his product, from graphics to packaging, is the best it can be, while other companies don't pay as much attention. Like in toilet paper. P&G made it a little softer and thicker, and advertised that. And it became No. 1. Who would have thought you could advertise toilet paper as an image product? But P&G did," he says. "P&G in my mind still is the finest company I've ever been involved with or know about in consumer-products marketing."

Hercules A. Segalas, senior VP, Drexel Burnham Lambert, New York.

Hercules Segalas is known on Wall Street for his tough-yet-fair evaluations of his former employer. Yet when he was finishing his undergraduate work in civil engineering in 1955 at Yale University, working for P&G was not part of his plans. "I never even signed up to talk to P&G. One day I got a phone call from the P&G recruiter, who'd gotten my name from a professor, and suggested that I come down to Cincinnati for an interview. I was flattered enough that I went down for the interview never thinking I'd end up working for a soap company, but they made it fun," he says.

Mr. Segalas worked in P&G's paper division, helping run the first experimental paper plant in Cheboygan, Mich., which led to P&G's purchase of the Charmin Paper Mills. "Very early in my career, P&G assembled a task force, about eight people, and shipped us to Cheboygan, where there was an old defunct paper mill that had been run into the ground during [World War II], and left in a frozen state with ten feet of frozen pulp in vats sitting out. We spent quite a bit of time up there making all kinds of calculations, and it eventually led to P&G's decision to get into the paper business," he says.

In 1963, P&G sent Mr. Segalas, who's fluent in

Hercules A. Segalas, Drexel Burnham Lambert, New York.

five languages, to Brussels, to supervise the construction of several buildings in Brussels and Frankfurt, West Germany. The "freedom" of living in Europe eventually led to his decision in 1965 to leave P&G. "I left because I had developed a life style in Europe better than the one I had in Cincinnati. I also wanted to go into marketing, and I wanted to move back to the East Coast, all of which led me to IFF [International Flavors & Fragrances]," he says.

Mr. Segalas joined IFF as assistant to the president of IFF-U.S., and later served as president of IFF-Latin America. In 1968, he joined the newly opened brokerage house of William D. Witter Inc., where he covered a broad range of consumer-package goods companies, with particular attention paid to the household-products in-

Theodore Stanley, MBI Inc., Norwalk, Conn.

dustry. "I felt I had a point of difference in my coverage of the industry. Coming from a business background, I found it was easier to understand Wall Street than to learn industry," he says.

Prior to Witter's merger with Drexel Burnham in 1976, Mr. Segalas was exec VP and board member of Witter and chairman of its Investment Policy Board. At Drexel Burnham, Mr. Segalas also is a member of the board. While continuing coverage of the household-products industry, he increasingly has been active in the company's mergers and acquisitions unit. His 10 years with P&G have paid off in his coverage of the company. "Like on sucrose polyester [olestra], I would call a P&G alum, introduce myself, and talk about my project. I'd never met [the alum] but either they'd heard of me or we could talk

about mutual friends. From an investment-banking standpoint, it's a major benefit. I get calls from former Procter guys who want to do business. They feel comfortable coming to me because we've gone through the same system," he says.

"P&G people miss two things when they leave the company: The technological backup and the financial support. A number of my [fellow alumni] have told me that when they left P&G, they felt naked. Because at P&G they take it for granted that they have all this . . . support. But when they joined other companies they found they don't have the support groups," says Mr. Segalas. "That's the biggest difference."

Theodore Stanley, founder-chairman, MBI Inc., Norwalk, Conn.

"I'm not very famous, but I've done very well," says Theodore Stanley, who, after leaving P&G in 1961 for Glendinning Cos., went on to found MBI Inc., which has become one of the largest U.S. direct-marketing companies. He and Vada, his wife and fellow P&G alumna, helped create the tightly knit P&G alumni network by throwing one of the first reunions.

Mr. Stanley was with P&G from 1953 to 1961, with two years out for required Air Force service. He worked on Dash in "the very early days before it hit the market" and was involved with the national expansion of Zest soap. He also was one of the early brand managers on Cascade automatic dishwashing detergent "back when the automatic dishwasher was first coming in and P&G got into the business."

In the 1950s, P&G was an exciting place for a young brand man. "I came in seven years after World War II, but P&G still was riding high on the tremendous advances they had made with Tide. Those were the dynamic days, the glory days of P&G," he says. However, even P&G's glory days weren't enough to hold him in Cincinnati. Mr. Stanley in 1961 joined Glendinning

Cos. "I wanted to get away from the big company; I didn't feel it was the best place to spend my life. Back then, people didn't tend to leave P&G, but Ralph Glendinning changed all that. We were among the first of what became a real mass exodus during the early '60s," he says. "The large number of people leaving has made it difficult for Procter to compete, but then again, they have talent stacked up like cordwood there."

Despite the exodus, P&G remains the best marketer and a "perfect model" for MBI. "The main thing I've tried to copy is this bearing in on getting good products and doing things right, which is a never-ending task. I run my company on the same principles as P&G, which is getting the best products and the best people in your organization." P&G stays on top in the household products industry because "it's not that they're doing something right, but they're doing more right than other people," he explains. "That's one of the keys to P&G. You're not just marketing, you're marketing for P&G. It's an elitist and somewhat arrogant attitude, but in P&G's case, it's justified."

John T. Thomas, partner, Ward Howell International, Chicago.

John Thomas initially held manufacturing line responsibilities as glycerine department manager when he joined P&G in 1958, fresh from getting his M.B.A. from the University of Michigan, Ann Arbor. He was the Ivory bar soap department manager until mid-1961, when he asked to be transferred from manufacturing to marketing. "My plant manager made it very clear that if I went through the interviews downtown, then my career in manufacturing [at P&G] was finished. There was a large brick wall between the functions," Mr. Thomas says. Despite the warning, he went ahead with the interviews and aptitude test, required of all incoming brand managers. He passed "with flying colors," went out on sales training and came back as a brand manager, work-

John T. Thomas, Ward Howell International, Chicago, Ill.

ing on Comet cleanser, Ivory liquid detergent and Top Job, which he took to test market in late 1963.

"If you wanted to go into business in a big company, P&G was the place to be in the 1950s, '60s and '70s. They had the reputation as the best-managed company in America." P&G thrived on the competition that came about as a result of putting so many talented people together in one place. "You were competing with some pretty good people. P&G wants the Ivory dishwashing detergent people to compete head-on with the Joy people. And they get some real battles going over who can lay claim to what."

Mr. Thomas joined the crew at Glendinning Cos. in 1964, staying 10 years before joining Ero Industries, Chicago, as exec VP-chief operating officer. He later moved to Lamalie Associates, Chicago, as VP for the national executive search company. The experience of conducting executive searches with *Fortune* 500 companies led him in 1981 to E. N. Wilkens Co., Chicago, which in 1985 was renamed Wilkens & Thomas. This August Mr. Thomas was named a partner of Ward Howell International.

Mr. Thomas says P&G's training and management style are so unique that many of his clients don't want to hire P&G-ers straight out of the Ivory Tower. "They say they want someone that's gotten more into the real world, that has at least one other company's experience under their belt. That's because P&G's support functions can't be truly duplicated outside the company and ex-P&G-ers have to adjust to life without P&G's support," he says.

P&G has had to adjust to a different marketing climate and the new competition for the top business graduates. "Today, the top 10% of business school grads want to go to Wall Street where they can make three times [P&G's] starting salary. P&G now has to pay the price to hire M.B.A.s," he says. "But in other ways, P&G hasn't changed. The brand manager still thinks the universe revolved around him or her."

Family Albums

Not only do people make lifelong careers at Procter & Gamble, so do entire families, from one generation to the next.

The Junker family, headed by Conrad and Sophia (seated), has seen four generations work at P&G. Standing (from left) are children George, John, Peter, Albert and Estelle.

The Junkers

When the Junkers have family outings, it might be easy to mistake the gathering for a P&G company picnic. Through four generations, the family has an incredible 250 years of combined employment.

It started with great-grandfather Conrad Junker, who worked about 30 years starting in the 1890s at Ivorydale. Of his five children, two sons followed him to Ivorydale: John, a mechanic and millwright for 33 years, and Peter, who worked in plant security for 40 years. The third generation included three P&G employees: Bill, who retired in July after 40 years in P&G's toilet goods division warehouse; George, with 40 years in industrial engineering; and Dale, who retired in 1984 after 42 years in accounting for the industrial chemicals division. Dale Junker, 63, says he met his wife, the late Dorothy Junker, at the pencil sharpener when both worked at P&G. The fourth generation is represented by Dale's son Michael,

37, and daughter Melanie, 26, and by Bill's two sons, Jeryl, 20, and Joby, 18, who are part-time line operators at Ivorydale.

"What attracted me in the first place was the family relationship," says Dale Junker. "I don't know that my father ever said, 'You've got to work for P&G,' but he impressed upon us things about his relationship with the company. And I remember that even when I was a little boy during the Depression, my dad was working when other kids' fathers weren't. I didn't recognize what stability was at that time, but in retrospect I had a sense about it."

Dale's father, John, was a mechanic who started at P&G in 1920. During the Depression, John Junker worked in a labor pool, which performed whatever tasks were necessary regardless of the worker's skills, he says. Laborers were guaranteed 48 weeks of employment per year and frequently found themselves performing make-work tasks such as putting in sewers. When the Depression ended, P&G eliminated pool gangs, and John Junker became a mechanic, a job he held until his death in 1947.

Dale Junker was the oldest of four brothers. His father's influence led to his seeking a job at P&G. "I didn't think there was any choice," he says. Mr. Junker's first job was in the foods division,

tracking rail tank cars filled with margarine. But his responsibilities gradually grew into a career in accounting, despite the fact he had no college background. Once he became trained in industrial accounting, Mr. Junker could easily have changed jobs, but he remained loyal to P&G.

"There were opportunities, particularly at General Electric, that were paying very well. But I don't think I ever questioned my continued employment at P&G. Maybe the company did, but I didn't. I enjoyed my relationships with people and the company." He never really thought of his work as a career until his retirement, he says. "At my retirement party, my boss went through all the details of my job description, and I didn't realize until then that I have had a career at P&G. It's funny that I had to retire to find that out.

The children of Dale Junker (from left) represent the fourth generation: daughter Melanie, a food sales rep and son Michael, in Citrus Hill's sales merchandising unit.

Three generations of the family get together: (from left) Conrad, John and Dale, who spent 42 years in accounting. An uncle, Al Haeufle, did not work for P&G.

"I always felt retirement was kind of a gradua-tion ceremony—you get a warm feeling for the person. I still get together with [former co-workers] for a poker party every couple of months."

Dale's daughter Melanie did not consider it her destiny to work for P&G. "If anything, I pushed away. I was a rebel," she says. Ms. Junker worked two years in Cincinnati for the Purex division of Omaha-based Armour Food Co., as a food sales representative. She joined P&G in a similar capac-ity in 1985. "After two years in consumer prod-ucts, I came around to thinking that maybe it would be better to work for a company that could further my career. My counterparts from P&G seemed to be top notch and the elite, which is something I really wanted. It helped that I had this dedication to P&G through my upbringing," she says.

Michael Junker is perhaps the best example of how P&G develops the human potential of em-ployees. After dropping out of teachers' college, he worked at a construction site until the winter layoff. He then got a call from P&G for a job as night janitor, which he viewed as an opportunity. "Richard Deupree [the first non-member of the founding families to reach the office of president] started as an office boy," he says. "Mr. Deupree once said something like, 'I never looked toward the future, I always looked at the task at hand.' If you look at the task at hand and do it well, you will be rewarded," Mr. Junker says. The philoso-phy seems to have worked in his case. Mr. Junker was night janitor for only a year and was pro-moted to the mail room, where he worked two years. He was promoted again to a clerical posi-tion in art and package design department, then to an entry-level management position in the same department. From there he was promoted into brand advertising on the Citrus Hill orange juice brand. He now works in Citrus Hill's beverage sales merchandising department. "Looking back,

I guess the opportunity was always there," he says. "This company is built on evolution from within."

His sister adds, "The company is continually challenging you. However, there is never a situa-tion that is placed in front of you and someone says, 'Do it or else!' For as large a company as P&G is, it's extremely people-oriented."

One of the buzz phrases now circulating at P&G is "Ownership in the business," Melanie Junker adds. "All of us have a form of ownership. As we grow within the company, our ownership grows in terms of benefits and in the way you go about your daily job. You reach the point that you are doing something because you are part of P&G, whether it's a small task such as paperwork, or a more important [matter], such as how you treat your customers," she says.

With ownership, each employee is an entrepre-neur, responsible for setting his or her job direc-tions, she adds. "[Management] encourages us to tell the company what's right for the business."

As an example of this concept, P&G's internal newsletter, "Moonbeams," tells of a P&G em-ployee who was shopping in a local discount store that featured a huge display of Tide. Because of the way the display was stacked, people were hav-ing difficulty pulling down boxes. The employee corrected the problem by remaining in the store for several hours, helping people as they came along.

Michael Junker says this take-charge attitude is part of the corporate culture of P&G. When a job needs to be done, it is everyone's responsibility to see that it gets done, he says. I'm amazed that the company works so well given the diversity of peo-ple who work here. But if there is a common thread, I think it is the character, integrity and commitment we all share in offering an excellent product at a competitive price. That's what we're here for. It's a pervasive attitude."

Reuben Lambert, who spent 43 years as an analytical chemist, is flanked by his granddaughter, Linda Ulrey, a 15-year employee, and son Stan, a 38-year veteran.

The Lamberts

With more than 100 years of combined employment spanning three generations, the Lambert family has a unique perspective on some of P&G's first efforts in analyzing and testing the effectiveness of P&G's products.

Beginning with the late Reuben Lambert, who retired in 1968 after 43 years as an analytical chemist, and son Stan, who retired in 1986 after 38 years, the family has been deeply involved in product research. The family now has one active employee in Stan's daughter, Linda Ulrey, with 15 years experience, and one former employee in son David.

For a brief period in 1968, three generations—Reuben, Stan and Linda—worked in P&G's package soap and detergent division. Ms. Ulrey has since taken a position as a manager in the public relations department, and David, who worked five years in P&G's process development department, where laundry and dishwashing products are formulated, now works in Phoenix for Santa Clara, Calif.-based Intel Corp.

David Lambert is listed on one patent as a co-developer of a formulation of Dawn dishwashing liquid for his work on cleaning and sudsing agents. "He still has the patent proudly displayed at his home," says Stan Lambert, who is listed on dozens of P&G patents for products and packaging.

Ms. Ulrey's career began in 1967 with summer jobs as a laundry technician in the product development division. "When you tell your friends that you're working at Procter & Gamble, they think you've got it made," she says. In reality, it was hard work. Once she got her hand caught up to the elbow in the wringer of a laboratory's conventional washing machine. Although she was uninjured, it was embarrassing calling for help, she says. As a result of the incident, the washing machine company later modified the automatic release mechanism of the wringer's design.

Ms. Ulrey is a good example of how P&G promotes motivated employees. After becoming a full-time employee in 1972, she moved up from a laundry operator to technician, and from there took on special tasks in the division, such as organizing an affirmative-action program for women. Later she became engaged in issues pertaining to government regulations and how they affect soap and detergent products. "Eventually, they needed someone in public relations and, voila, here I am," she says.

Stan Lambert's most vivid impression over the years is that the P&G family fosters a strong sense of integrity about work and about products. He recalls participating in a $2 million recall of Joy dishwashing liquid because a batch didn't suds well. "Those are the kinds of things that make you believe in what you are doing," Mr. Lambert says. "It's a feeling that you owe something to your customer." But this is an attitude also handed down from his father prior to his decision to join P&G. "My father was a devoted P&G employee. The company was the ultimate thing in his outlook. Obviously, some of that rubs off on you as a child," Mr. Lambert says.

After his Army discharge and four years of college, where he worked in a cooperative program with Chicago-based Container Corp., Mr. Lambert was hesitant about applying at P&G because of its reputation for hiring only top students. With his father's encouragement, he took P&G's employment tests. Mr. Lambert was hired in product research in 1949, a position he held for 20 years before moving into technical packaging. The atmosphere at P&G was a big change from Container Corp. "Everyone [at Container] hoarded every bit of information, waiting for the proper moment when it could help their careers. That was the general attitude there." By contrast, P&G managers took a keen interest. Early on, Mr. Lambert was asked to report to a superior, who sat him down for a long talk. "Given my background, I wondered if he was setting me up. But, in fact, he had gone completely out of his way to help me. That was the general attitude, and a way of life at P&G," Mr. Lambert says.

Employment at P&G also had a big impact on his personal life. Recently married, he had wanted to buy a house and a car, but had no income or credit, until he started with P&G. "All I had to do was say that I worked for Procter & Gamble and the world opened up. Everybody was willing to do anything and everything. [On the other hand,] you were expected to be a leader in the community and in the church. You automatically assumed this role because you were a P&G person," he says.

Church and civic groups cleverly would recruit employees of large local companies, such as General Electric, P&G, and Cincinnati Milacron, placing a representative of each in charge of fundraising groups, Mr. Lambert says. "It was a competitive thing, and I was upholding the honor of P&G. We couldn't allow a GE person to outdo P&G. I was much too sophisticated to fall for that ploy, but of course I did anyway."

The sense of pride in being a part of P&G held whether on or off the job, he adds. "I felt responsibility not only to myself but to my father. It's a feeling that whatever you are involved with also reflects on your family. But very quickly you get this feeling that you're also a part of the company. That was deeply embedded in all of us, partly because my family is involved with P&G and partly because of a general attitude there," Mr. Lambert says.

When Mr. Lambert started, P&G had just begun a long period of rapid growth. "My dad had just given up on knowing the names of everyone in the technical division. He was frustrated that he could no longer keep up with everyone," Mr. Lambert says. Despite growth, however, individuals still held their professional individuality. "There is a belief and an attitude that exists in this kind of a setup that you have a responsibility to be true to your discipline and still be a valuable contributing member of the company," he says. "You did things based on what was right. For example, you would never use an edible flavor or odor with detergents or laundry products. The reason was that we feared it would encourage children to ingest the product," he says.

Mr. Lambert recalls one instance where Dreft laundry detergent registered an ingredient with the department of agriculture that would inhibit bacterial growth and greatly reduce the risk of diaper rash. Clinical studies supported the claim. "The next [time] we ran another series of tests, lo and behold, we didn't show any advantage. We agonized over that, and finally we went to the department of agriculture to bare our breasts of this horrible lack of sufficient data. Their response was, 'Oh well, that's the way these things go.' " P&G withdrew the claim pending further evidence, he says.

"These were the kinds of things from which you developed a feeling that there is something beyond making a buck, that you do have a responsibility."

The Hafers

The Hafer family counts itself among the elite at P&G with more than 275 years of combined employment. The family history offers insights into the ever improving working conditions at P&G.

The Hafer association began in the late 1800s, when William F. Hafer began his 34 years in the utilities and water treatment area at Ivorydale, where its heat, water and power is produced. It is the same area where a grandson works today. His wife, Rosina, also worked in the soap-packing line at Ivorydale for eight years before their marriage.

The second generation of Hafers at P&G included five children with long terms of employment at Ivorydale. They included: William, an engineer in charge of electricity at the plant, 48 years; Howard, a machinist, 46 years; Walt, a machinist, 49 years; Hilda, a Crisco line worker, 25 years; and Alvin, a laboratory analyst, 42 years.

The third generation is represented by Walt Hafer's son, Walt Jr., 39, a technician who started in 1969 in fuel procurement. He now works in the instrumentation and electrical area at Ivorydale, where his grandfather worked. (The plant is completely changed from his grandfather's day, following several modernizations.) Walt Hafer Jr.'s wife, Donna, 38, also worked at P&G for 13 years before they were married, and returned to work in June 1987 at P&G's Sharon Woods Technical Center.

Walt Hafer Sr., 74, who retired in 1978, recalls his start in 1929, at the height of the Great Depression. He was 16 and home for the summer, a vacation he intended to make permanent. His father had other ideas, issuing an ultimatum: " 'Go to school, or you're going to work!' " he says. Walt Hafer Sr. chose the latter, taking a job with Globe Soap Co., St. Bernard, Ohio, which was later acquired by P&G. Working conditions were rugged during his five years at St. Bernard because huge grinding machines spewed soap and deter-

William F. Hafer, holding a grandchild, started in the late 1800s in the utilities and water treatment area at Ivorydale. He worked at P&G for 34 years.

gent dust in the plant. "There was so much dust you could cut it with a knife. I was nervous about this because I liked sports, and I'd always read that dust is bad on your lungs," he says. When P&G later acquired the plant, its first action was installing dust collectors, he recalls.

The conditions drove him to seek employment at Ivorydale, just down the road. And his sports prowess helped secure his position. "I loved baseball and basketball. It was right down my alley," he says. "At the time, each area at Ivorydale had competitive sports teams. A good way to get a transfer into the plant was to be good at a sport." The elder Hafer became a machinist and played on several championship softball teams. Ivorydale today has a wall of old photographs in the administration building of company sporting events.

"I loved my job at Ivorydale," he says. "If you have to work for a living, you can't beat it." Despite this, P&G had a reputation then as a hard-driving employer, he says. "I don't mean to be degrading but P&G had a reputation for being cheap throughout the [Ohio River] valley. You had to work your fanny off, and you weren't getting paid for it. But it has changed an awful lot since then. It has become one of the best places to work in terms of money, incentives, and their stock program is one of the best anywhere," he says.

The elder Mr. Hafer believes a change in P&G's reputation occurred as a result of innovations in employee relations. Ivorydale workers were among the first in the U.S. to organize in-house unions, which tended to work out problems with management before they reached crisis proportions. P&G also was an innovator in employee ownership through stock programs. These are among the reasons why Ivorydale has never had a strike, he says."We never did go to an outside union. We had our own representation made up of people who work here. We were always able to sit down in a meeting and talk it over with [management], and come to an understanding."

Steel and chemical workers' unions attempted to organize P&G in the Cincinnati area, but with no success. Employees recognized that, as stockholders, they would be hurt by a strike more than anyone. "The outside unions couldn't better our situation. If they could have given us something

better, maybe we would have listened," Mr. Hafer says. International and national unions do represent P&G at other plant locations worldwide, however.

"The unions say we were riding their coattails, but I don't believe that," says Mr. Hafer, who was an in-house union representative for 15 years. "We were bettering ourselves. I think we had something good."

Among the changes that improved conditions was increased emphasis on worker safety. "Number one, P&G believes in safety," Mr. Hafer says. New employees were guided through a safety booklet and expected to follow the rules strictly. "All of these rules were learned the hard way over the years by somebody losing an arm or fingers or getting burnt," Mr. Hafer Sr. says. "If you didn't work safely, you would be called down to the office, and if you argued, you were out. That's it."

One safety rule forbid employees from wearing long sleeves or gloves when operating a lathe. A second rule required protective eyewear, he says. P&G also was an innovator in encouraging a safety attitude, he adds. The company periodically threw cake and ice cream parties in the cafeteria for plans with good safety records and recognized safety achievements with special flags and plaques.

As P&G improved, the demand for jobs there grew, Mr. Hafer Jr. says. Several years ago, when P&G advertised employment opportunities at Ivorydale, 5,000 people applied. Some camped out overnight at the hiring office.

One reason why people clamor for jobs with P&G is the opportunity for training and advancement. Walt Hafer Jr. recently began a three-year training program in the instrumentation and electrical department.

Prior to his promotion, Mr. Hafer worked in the department that ordered fuel at Ivorydale. "We're into a high level of commitment at Ivorydale, and part of that means that P&G will train people from within for technical jobs. There is plenty of room for advancement, and there are many opportunities to go from one area to another," he says. "That is one of the good parts about working for P&G. You can control your own career. If you show enough initiative and you want to get ahead, they offer you opportunities," he says.

P&G tested Mr. Hafer Jr. thoroughly in math, mechanical aptitude, logic and basic comprehension before accepting him into the program, he says. He also interviewed with plant electricians and instruments people. Despite opportunities at P&G, Mr. Hafer Jr. says he found it difficult to imagine his future employment in the power plant when he first started in 1969. "A utilities plant is a hot, dirty, noisy place. When I first walked into that place, I thought there was no way in the world that I was going to work there. There must be something better," he says. "The way it worked out there wasn't anything better, even in the Ivorydale area," he adds.

The reason is the position offers freedom to be your own boss, he says. "Aside from the fact that you're responsible to someone, you run your assignment area the way you want. The flexibility and freedom P&G offers is tremendous." Flexibility includes such perks as allowing utilities employees to control their own schedules.

"The lifestyle has been very good to me. As far as pay and incentives go, P&G is very generous. I agree that if you have to work for a living, this is a tremendous place to work."

III

THE PRODUCTS

CHAPTER THIRTEEN

One Brand, One Manager

Neil McElroy's memo in 1931 in effect created a system that has been copied by nearly every major American package-goods company. The driving force remains: one person must devote single-minded attention to all aspects of marketing a brand with the help of a support team.

On May 13, 1931, yet another memo wound its way up the decision channels at Procter & Gamble Co. In a company where memos were, and are, an art form, this one stood out. Perhaps no other memo in the company's long history has had its impact—on P&G and on consumer marketing in general.

The memo was written by Neil McElroy. His subject was brand management. Mr. McElroy, a Cincinnati native who had joined P&G fresh out of Harvard in 1925, was at the time working on Camay soap advertising. (He went on to become P&G's president and, later, Secretary of Defense in the Eisenhower administration.)

He was vexed by the slow sales of Camay, which had been introduced in 1926 as the company's second bar soap, after the venerable Ivory. To boost sales, the company in 1929 had moved the Camay business from ad agency Blackman Co. (later to become Compton Advertising), which had handled both soaps. That was a significant step, marking the first time P&G—and perhaps any U.S. company—was allowing two viable brands to compete. Previous intracompany brand competition at P&G always sought to replace an older, fading brand with a newer one.

The new agency was Pedlar & Ryan, New York. Mr. McElroy was appointed to work with the agency on Camay advertising, becoming, in effect, Procter's first brand manager. Camay's fortunes improved, but before Mr. McElroy could fully exploit the possibilities of the new set-up he was sent on assignment to London. While there, he honed his thinking on brand competition by observing how it was practiced at Unilever. After returning to Cincinnati to work on Camay, Mr. McElroy became convinced the idea of having one person working solely on the brand's advertising was a good idea as far as it went. It just didn't go far enough.

The brand-manager position was still largely experimental. It lacked the official blessing of the company and sufficient resources to do the job. Without both, the brand manager was still just one man trying to move a brand against entrenched loyalties to the flagship Ivory, which had no trouble getting the company's attention or funding.

In his now-famous memo—which ran to three pages, flouting another tradition begun by Richard Deupree, the one-page memo—Mr. McElroy argued there simply weren't enough people caring about Camay the way they should. He argued that the brand manager should devote single-minded attention to *all* aspects of marketing a brand and should have a team to help him. There should be a brand assistant to take over some of the office work and become groomed for brand responsibility himself. There also would be "check-up people," who would spend most of their time in the field monitoring sales operations.

Previously, P&G's approach was largely functional, with marketing, sales and other managers dividing their time among various products.

In time, Mr. McElroy argued, many marketing functions shouldered by the sales force, which, after all, had to sell several brands, would be assumed by the brand-management team.

The memo was okayed by VP-Advertising Ralph Rogan, who had heard Mr. McElroy's entreaties on many occasions. But this obviously was a decision that would require top management commitment, not just of money, but to what some P&G veterans saw as a house-against-itself philosophy that amounted to pure heresay. The memo ultimately reached the desk of Mr. Deupree, P&G's president. He was the right man in the right place, a restless innovator known for his insistence that customary practices be subjected to continuous scrutiny. Mr. McElroy's idea made sense to him. He okayed the memo, and the brand-management system was born in 1931.

It since has been copied in some form by nearly every major package-goods company in the country as well as many other marketers of consumer products and services, ranging from banks to the U.S. Postal Service. The reason: It works.

According to P&G, the company competed in 38 consumer product categories last year in the U.S. It had the No. 1 brand in 19 of them, and the first, second or third brand in all but five. Of the total U.S. industry sales of the categories in which it competes, P&G commands about a 25% share, the company estimates. A key reason is that the brand-management system has kept P&G brands healthy in defiance of product life-cycle theory. Comet is 31 years old; Joy, 38; Tide, 41; Zest, 35; Crest, 32; Prell, 41; Camay, 61; and Ivory, the brand that started it all, 108 years old. None of these, and many other P&G brands that span generations, are candidates for the graveyard any time soon.

"The brand-management system is still the best way there is to manage market-driven companies," says Gary Stibel, a former P&G brand manager who is founder and a partner of the New England Consulting Group, Westport, Conn. "And P&G's brand-management system remains one of the best, if not *the* best, in the world."

The system also has proven to be the route to the top at P&G. Every chief executive since Mr. Deupree has had brand-management experience, and all four of its present senior executives—Chairman-CEO John Smale, President John Pepper and Vice Chairmen Thomas Laco and Edwin Artzt—were brand managers at one time. "Everybody who comes in here thinks he or she is the new John Smale or John Pepper," says Patrick Hayes, a former assistant brand manager and now P&G's associate director-public relations.

The pyramid gets ever narrower toward the top, of course, so a lot of brand managers fall by the wayside in time. Many of them land on their feet. Some get good jobs elsewhere within the company. Some go to other companies: P&G brand alumni constitute a virtual Who's Who of U.S. consumer-product marketing executives.

And for the many who choose a consulting career, P&G brand experience is tantamount to the keys to the kingdom. At New England Consulting Group, for example, about half the partners are former P&G brand managers. "Brand experience at P&G is a very marketable skill, and I've got three houses to prove it," says Gordon Wade, a former P&G brand manager who has his own consulting company, the Cincinnati Consulting Group.

The underlying tenet of brand management remains what it was in 1931. Every P&G brand merits the single-minded attention of managers bent on thrashing all competitors—including their own company's.

Mr. Laco, a former Cascade and Comet brand manager, says, "It's basic. A brand is a business. Somebody, especially when you've got lots of brands, has to be responsible for each business in toto as his sole responsibility." Brand management "was inevitable," Mr. Laco says. "Not just at P&G, but everywhere. If we hadn't come up with it, somebody else would have."

There are about 100 brand managers at P&G. With a few exceptions, each handles one brand, or the basic brand plus its extensions (Always sanitary pads and Always Plus, for example). Some are in charge of brands that haven't yet made it to market. Managers of established brands oversee businesses that average $100 million a year in sales. The "typical" P&G brand manager is in his (or her—about a third of P&G's brand managers are female) late 20s or early 30s. He has been a brand manager for about three years and with the company for six to seven years.

He started as a brand assistant, probably plunging right into a sales-promotion project. (There is no formal training program at P&G). In about 15 months, on average, he became a sales trainee, spending a couple of months in the field working on shelf facings, displays and store managers. He then became an assistant brand manager, probably on a different brand. Then, typically about three and a half years after starting with the company, he became a brand manager.

At many companies, the brand manager comes from sales or ad agencies. At P&G, chances are he was recruited directly from college. It was the brand manager for whom he would work who carried the most weight in deciding to hire him.

Contrary to popular belief, P&G isn't overloaded with Harvard M.B.A.s or other Ivy Leaguers as brand managers, the company says. That's not because P&G altruistically wants to spread its hiring around, but because it hasn't found a relationship between place of education and performance. "We've researched that," Mr. Laco says. "There's no correlation."

Each brand manager heads a brand group, typically of three to four people, though some brands have more, depending on such things as sales volume and competition. The Always group, for example, has seven members. The brand manager reports to an associate advertising manager, who oversees three or four brand groups. The associate advertising manager reports to an advertising manager, who in turn reports to the general manager of one of eight consumer divisions. It is at the division level that profits are measured at P&G; the brand group isn't a profit center.

It is sometimes claimed that P&G brand managers aren't even told how much profit their brands are producing. That's not so, P&G says. Typically, not only the brand manager but everyone in his group sees regular reports detailing the brand's financial results, a company spokesman says.

The company won't say what brand managers earn; Mr. Laco will say only that it's "a lot." P&G followers say it's $40,000 to $60,000 a year. In return for his pay, the brand manager must build the business. If his brand is No. 1, he must keep it there and build its lead. If it isn't, he has to get it closer. He is expected to know more about his brand that anyone in the company.

The brand manager develops a marketing plan—formally known as "a basis for marketing"—determines what advertising, promotion and packaging measures will be necessary to implement it and requests the company to fund it. Whether he gets the money he wants depends on how strong a case he presents. Final funding approval typically is made by the division VP.

Devising and executing the plan require him to tap the services of a variety of line and staff organizations including sales, finance, manufacturing, market research and promotion services. The brand manager has no formal authority over any of these groups; he must use the power of his ideas—often conveyed in memo form—to establish a kind of intellectual authority. It helps immeasurably that top management stands staunchly behind the brand-management concept, and that everyone in the company knows it.

Yet the lack of formal authority, coupled with what appears to be formidable responsibility, is sometimes the source of friction with other managers as well as of great frustration, former brand managers say. Within the marketing function itself, it isn't always clear what decisions a brand manager can make on his own. Brand managers themselves differ on how much autonomy they believe they have. Larry Zigerelli, Crest toothpaste brand manager, says he considers himself "the president of the Crest company" and top management, his bankers. The implication is that he has wide latitude.

Ron Doornink, brand manager for Pampers, sees his job more as one of recommending and facilitating. "Our main role is to recommend to the company the right course of action and provide a rationale for that. And the company chooses to agree or disagree. It's not like we're little dictators on our own brands—we're not," he says.

Stories abound of seemingly minor decisions that are made at very high levels at P&G. One, for example, is that Mr. Smale himself decided what

color cap (gold) would go on Folgers instant decaffeinated coffee. (P&G says it can't confirm, but
doubts that it happened.) The company says the
notion that its brand managers have little authority is bunk. "I know from the time I was a brand
manager that our typical brand manager has more
autonomy that significantly higher executives at
other companies," Mr. Laco says. He asserts that
the P&G brand manager, in fact, has more freedom than the typical company owner who
"spends most of his time raising money."

If a P&G brand manager has a good idea, "we
have the money to invest," Mr. Laco says. "What
we've achieved, in effect, is an entrepreneurial position within the company." There are no rigid
rules governing a brand manager's role, Mr. Laco
says. "It depends on the brand manager."

A number of studies of brand management
have taken issue with the brand manager-as-
entrepreneur idea. One survey of brand managers
at U.S. companies, reported in the Harvard Business Review in 1975, found that their decision-
making was limited to the number and timing of
promotions. "In all other decision areas," the
study found, the managers are "at best . . . participants in the decision process, and in a number of
areas they play even lesser roles."

At P&G, Mr. Laco acknowledges, any decision
"that will obviously affect the general manager's
profit forecast—where the brand's interests inter-
cede on the interests of the division in a significant
way" will be one on which "the general manager
is going to have a real impact." That applies not
just to spending outlays but to "significant"
changes in product, packaging, advertising and
other marketing elements, Mr. Laco says.

"But the test," asserts Mr. Laco, who can become worked up about the issue, "is what the hell
is happening in the marketplace. If you look at the
number of initiatives coming out of Procter &
Gamble—the new brands, the improved brands,
the line extensions, the changes in advertising, the

innovation in media—those are all initiatives that
are importantly developed, decided, controlled
and directed by brand managers."

Advertising agencies know about brand-
manager clout. Agencies sometimes complain of
brand managers' inexperience and reverence for
research, but they know the brand manager represents a lot of ad dollars—and that advertising that
doesn't satisfy him simply will not run. They also
know the brand manager is their entree to a client
that pays more than lip service to the notion of
agencies as marketing partners. In crucial budget
meetings, for example, the brand manager and
agency account exec appear before the division
manager and other executives as a team to present
their case.

Brand managers have considerable discretion in
approving advertising in a continuing campaign.
Any change deemed substantive, such as a new copy
strategy, will have to be passed up for approval,
however. Interestingly, under the Procter & Gamble
structure, the VP-advertising usually isn't involved
in approving ads. Rather, that's the province of the
brand manager and his line superiors.

Brand managers spend a lot of their time monitoring the competition, through A.C. Nielsen Co.
reports, tips from the field, trade publications and
the like. It is through such sources that they also
must learn what competing P&G brands are doing. It is bad form, to say the least, for the Tide
manager to wander into the Cheer manager's office and ask him about Cheer's market share. The
Cheer manager won't tell him that anyhow, or
anything else that might give his rival an edge.

In "In Search of Excellence," consultants
Thomas Peters and Robert Waterman Jr. recount
telling an ex-P&G quality control manager that
the company's brand managers seemingly "would
almost rather cannibalize a fellow brand manager's product than beat the competition." The
former P&G staffer agreed.

In evaluating brand managers, the company

says it places as much importance on the development of subordinates as on business results. This is especially vital at P&G because of the company's longstanding tradition of filling all management positions from within. "We really watch brand managers to see that they are bringing along their people," Mr. Laco says. Subordinates are "strongly encouraged" to talk to the brand manager's boss about their development or lack of it, he says. Superiors are particularly watchful for indications that the brand manager can't get along with those who work for or with him. "The ability to deal effectively with people is, I think, the most important characteristic" of a successful brand manager, Mr. Laco says.

Impatient, table-pounding, Patton-esque personalities seldom rise very high at Procter & Gamble," agrees Mr. Wade. P&G sometimes send abrasive managers to what is known in the company as "charm school," normally outside P&G at classes offered by organizations specializing in "people skills." P&G declines to identify the specific outside resources it uses.

Brand managers receive twice-yearly performance reviews from their bosses, who share their evaluations with their own superiors. Brand managers must review their subordinates twice a year. (Employees above the brand-manager level are reviewed annually.) In recent years, partly to weed out nonproductive employees and reduce costs, P&G has refined the employee-review process. Each year, managers must group their subordinates by ability and state what they will do to further the careers of the good ones and to make the marginal ones productive. The next year they must report their progress.

P&G's brand-management approach periodically comes under attack for alleged deficiencies. Inroads by competitors in recent years have caused a new wave of skepticism and a spate of business press articles about "P&G's Rusty Marketing Machine" and competition-induced "cul-

tural change." In the early 1980s, for example, Crest and Pampers both suffered market-share losses. Crest was slow to respond to the introduction of gel toothpastes and pump dispensers by Colgate-Palmolive Co. and others. When P&G did come out with a pump-dispensed toothpaste, it was plagued by production problems.

Pampers, meanwhile, gave ground to Kimberly-Clark Corp.'s Huggies. Kimberly-Clark out-Proctered Procter, analysts like to say, by developing a significantly improved product that consumers were willing to pay more for.

P&G since has recovered ground in both categories. But the testing and repeated management scrutiny of ideas mandated by the system can be a weakness as well as a strength, company followers say.

The brand manager labors under the presumption "that everything has been done correctly in the past," says Mr. Wade. Indeed, the brand manager's own bosses likely participated in many of the decisions that the brand manager has to challenge to protect the brand, Mr. Wade notes. Thus, "the brand man is required to marshal an enormous amount of fact and analysis to make a major change," he says. "I have seen Procter move with the speed of light [in withdrawing Rely tampons from the market, for example], but that is still the exception rather than the rule," says Mr. Stibel.

P&G's strategic mindset also can blind it to tactical threats or opportunities, Mr. Stibel says. The company's concentration on getting Tartar Control Crest to market, for example, may have left it vulnerable to Colgate's tactical moves to sell toothpaste in pumps or as a gel, he says.

P&G counters that its brand-management system is continually reshaping itself. One of the most notable recent twists is the formal institution of the business-teams concept, which encourages far more participation of other departments, divisions and staff people in decisions affecting a brand. Business teams began in 1979, primarily as part of a manufacturing productivity drive. Now they are widely used in brand marketing. The business-team approach was explained by Mr. Smale in a 1985 interview in *Harvard Business Review*. Before business teams, he said, a brand manager proposing a change in production of his brand, for example, would send a memo to manufacturing. Manufacturing would respond by saying whether the change was possible or not.

But as a part of a business team, the manufacturing manager would be asked for his thoughts before the proposal is finalized. He might say, for example, that by altering the proposed procedure he could reduce production cost by 50 cents a case. "Under the old system, it was much more difficult for manufacturing to get that point of view inserted," Mr. Smale said in the interview. This, he said, is "a major change" for P&G.

There are now more than 50 business teams at P&G, the company says. One of their big advantages is that decisions are made more quickly than they were under the previous memo procedure.

P&G says a business team took Liquid Tide, introduced in 1985, from test to national distribution in just nine months, which the company said is one-half to one-third the time it would have taken previously. Liquid Tide is the most successful new laundry detergent brand in 15 years, the company adds. Among other recent successes P&G also attributes to business teams is the decision to sell Pringle's potato chips in single containers rather than the double-canister package that consumers perceived to be uneconomical. Before the change, "there was a question of whether the brand was going to survive," Mr. Laco says. Now, he says, Pringle's "is a rousing success, challenging our capacity."

Mr. Laco rejects the idea that business teams represent an erosion of the brand group's power. In the Pringle's case it was the brand group's "analysis, their redesign, their thrust" that turned the brand around, he says. "This is a brand manager's success."

P&G's productivity drive under Mr. Smale also has pushed the brand manager more heavily into non-marketing functions. "They spend [more] time in our plants," Mr. Laco says. "They spend time worrying about capital appropriations that are much more complex than the machinery that I had to worry about. Costs and efficiency . . . are all very important elements of competition now," Mr. Laco continues. "So the brand manager's job is much more like a general manager's assignment than it was when I was a youngster. We had the luxury of concentrating on a narrower band of issues that affected marketing pretty much alone."

Another significant development is the emergence of new-brand groups. Sometimes called "futures groups" internally, these are "groups of people whose charge is to look at the next generation" of existing brands, says one P&G follower. "Thus you have the existence of a Tide brand group but also of a Tide futures brand group."

Changes in the marketplace will continue to test P&G's brand-management system, company followers say. Most serious at present, they say, are trends that strike directly at P&G's traditional emphasis on strategic thinking with a national focus. These include an erosion in the coverage and power of national media, particularly network TV so beloved by P&G.

In addition, retailing is consolidating into fewer, more powerful hands; according to Campbell Soup Co., by 1990, just 9% of grocery outlets will be doing 50% of industry volume. Furthermore, the Universal Product Code and computers are arming retailers with precise knowledge of the profits of each product they stock; no longer must they feel compelled to stock and generously display a product simply because it is P&G's. The trade is now in a position to exert some muscle of its own, just as P&G over the years has used national ad dollars to muscle retailers into line, often with cavalier haughtiness.

The use of coupons and other retail promotions also has soared. That may be causing a serious erosion of the kind of brand loyalty P&G and other package-goods companies have so assiduously cultivated over the years. "There is a new brand in town and it's called Deal or Discount," Graham Phillips, Ogilvy & Mather's chairman-U.S. and president-North America, said in a recent speech to U.S. marketing executives. "We have done a great job of teaching the consumer to buy on price." By design, selling on price has never been a P&G forte.

In addition, some marketers, including Campbell Soup Co. and General Foods Corp., increasingly are tailoring their products and tactics to regional tastes and conditions. This typically involves allocating more marketing funds to regional sales operations and reducing brand managers' control from headquarters.

Officially at least, P&G disdains regionalism. It flatly denies reports, including one in ADVERTISING AGE (AA, April 20, 1987), that it is moving in that direction. A regional approach clearly would run counter to the ingrained P&G culture. Mr. Stibel, the former P&G-er, remembers internal P&G marketing literature repeatedly telling brand managers that "it's not a good idea until it's national." He says that thinking still permeates the company.

P&G naturally takes issue with the idea that it won't be able to cope with change. "P&G has al-ways been changing," Mr. Laco says. "It would be poor business for us to take a share loss and not react to it in some intelligent way."

Thus, to competitors seeing fresh chinks in P&G's armor, the company's response is what it always has been: The ultimate test is what happens in the marketplace.

In addition, some marketers, including Campbell Soup Co. and General Foods Corp., increasingly are tailoring their products and tactics to regional tastes and conditions. This typically involves allocating more marketing funds to regional sales operations and reducing brand managers' control from headquarters.

Officially at least, P&G disdains regionalism. It flatly denies reports, including one in ADVERTISING AGE (AA, April 20, 1987), that it is moving in that direction. A regional approach clearly would run counter to the ingrained P&G culture. Mr. Stibel, the former P&G-er, remembers internal P&G marketing literature repeatedly telling brand managers that "it's not a good idea until it's national." He says that thinking still permeates the company.

P&G naturally takes issue with the idea that it won't be able to cope with change. "P&G has always been changing," Mr. Laco says. "It would be poor business for us to take a share loss and not react to it in some intelligent way."

Thus, to competitors seeing fresh chinks in P&G's armor, the company's response is what it always has been: The ultimate test is what happens in the marketplace.

CHAPTER FOURTEEN

Brand Builders

Who are the Procter & Gamble brand managers? What do they do? How do they feel about their jobs? To explore such questions, Advertising Age *talked to three current brand managers chosen by the company to be interviewed.*

Ron Doornink

Ron Doornink, 32, is brand manager for Pampers disposable diapers. He joined P&G in 1982 after working at an ad agency and a consumer drug company. He is single and an avid competitor in triathlons, having participated in six of the grueling swim-bike-run events last year.

Pampers is P&G's largest business, with estimated sales of $1.148 billion last year. It has a 41% share of the $2.8 billion category, analysts say. P&G spent $25.6 million on Pampers advertising last year according to LNA. The Pampers agency is D'Arcy Masius Benton & Bowles, New York.

I was born and raised in the Netherlands and I came over to the United States about nine years ago. I'm still a citizen of Holland and am a permanent resident of the U.S. I came to the U.S. really to go to school. I wanted to get my M.B.A. at Columbia, which I did. I didn't really have a plan after that. I got a job offer from P&G to go back to Holland, but I wanted to really work in the U.S. But I didn't have a working visa, and that prevented me from joining P&G in Cincinnati.

Some companies—very few—were willing to go along with that risk. One of them was Compton Advertising in New York. So I worked a year and half as an account executive on P&G business with Compton. Then I worked a year in product management at Block Drug in Jersey City. After my visa problem had been resolved, I again started negotiations with P&G. After having worked with another company and having seen several others, I knew I wanted to work for P&G because of its quality.

I started as a brand assistant on a new paper towel brand called Merit, which no longer exists. We were involved in opening a test market and basically taking a product that had a name and packaging, but no marketing plan at the time. We sold our plan to the company. Its execution involved running the introductory sales meetings, executing a promotion program and so on. We learned some very important things about the mid-priced segment in the paper-towel category. We found we did not have a successful marketing plan. Our marketing mix simply was not delivering the kind of consumer interest in the product that we hoped, and we decided to withdraw from that segment. I was no longer in the business when that happened, but it's disappointing as a brand person to see a project not succeed.

I had moved on to sales training in the Detroit sales district, and then to the facial-tissue business as assistant brand manager. I did that for about a year. Then I became an assistant brand manager on Pampers. In a little less than a year I became brand manager.

My challenge with Pampers is to keep the business growing at a rapid rate. I enjoy the challenge, and I would like to think that we're meeting our objectives for Pampers. It's very early to tell. I've been in this business eight or nine months now. Generally, it takes a bit longer before you can really measure the impact of a new manager on the business. But I'm excited about what we are doing and feel good about it. Generally speaking, most of my time is spent on the development and execution of marketing plans and strategies. I'm also training a number of people in the business. I can spend as much as 10% of my time looking at research. It varies with what the issues are, whether we have a new product initiative, whether the competition has a new product initiative or whether we are getting research back from tests that were fielded a while ago.

I like to set six-month objectives for my brand group, and I sell that to the company as our plan. Then I work back from that into monthly project lists, and from that back into weekly project lists. That is a way for me to control the productivity, if you will, of the brand. Planning is critical in brand management; therefore, we try to use planning tools like project lists. I work from to-do lists and I make sure my people do, too. The challenge is to deliver marketing plans and strategies—that's where you win, competitively speaking—and not get preoccupied in plan execution.

Historically, the diaper category has been a product-driven one. It's a fairly young category relative to other categories, which explains the product's importance. As our product begins more closely to meet consumer needs it will be more difficult—and more costly—to win from a product standpoint. So the role of marketing in the diaper category has become very important. I think a specific part of my charge was to help develop superior marketing programs. We field promotions almost on a monthly basis. You could look in your Sunday newspaper and find coupons or joint promotions with the General Motors car key. All those things are being worked on and executed by the Pampers brand group. I can do very little of this on my own. It's important to recognize that a brand manager is very much an advocate of plans, a recommender of plans, with some latitude within his budget to do certain things himself.

You develop principles, objectives, strategies. From that flows, for example, a promotion pro-

gram. It's a once-a-year kind of project, with some checks along the way. Essentially, you've presold the program. All you do after that is make sure it is executed with excellence. You can vary a lot of the details, but it's not as if I might decide what kind of coupon runs next month. It is a very systematic approach, based largely on strategic and tactical thinking.

I do have a lot of flexibility to react to the marketplace. I can change promotions today. All I need to do is figure out a good rationale for doing it. I wouldn't hesitate a moment to change anything in my marketing plan if it were the right thing to do. I can't change an ad campaign, but I can initiate the change and provide the rationale for it.

There are established levels from where approval has to come, depending on the decision. Sometimes it's the amount of expense involved that determines whether a change is made. But that's not the only consideration. Sometimes if you change a campaign it really doesn't affect your expenditures, but it does affect the way in which you expose yourself to the outside world. I have a significant amount of influence on how much we spend on advertising Pampers each year. You can work to increase spending aggressively if you feel you can justify it.

I feel I have enough authority, but if you mean being able to lay down rules and laws, this is not the place where you would have it. You wouldn't have it in any company that practices brand management. Brand management is, by definition, a job of collaboration, motivation, inspiration. If you're adept at that part of it—at influencing the system and making recommendations with very solid rationales—it's like autonomy. You have to be good at it, and you have to enjoy it.

Long term, I'd like to go into general management, probably at P&G. This is an excellent company and I've enjoyed it so far. I don't think much about how long I'll be in my present assignment.

The company feels strongly about continuity in assignments like this. I think time is not really the key factor. I think it's feeling you're learning, that you're developing as a marketing individual. And that if you aspire to general management, you continue to learn in that area as well. As long as that's the case, I'm happy. And that's been the case the five years I've been here.

I do have a couple of frustrations. I think the way you win in brand management is to invest most of your time in developing smart marketing plans and strategies. Yet, there is this ever-present challenge and pressure to execute the plans you sell. That takes time, and there always are day-to-day problems.

Then there is what I call internally generated pressure. I think this is fairly typical of brand managers here; you want to do a lot of things quickly, you want to do it all. And that's simply, logically, not feasible. I'd definitely come here if I had to do it all over again. It's a very stimulating place to be. It's a place where we all try to be the best marketers we can be.

Beth Kaplan

Beth Kaplan, 29, is brand manager for Always sanitary napkins. The Omaha native was a summer intern at P&G in 1980, after receiving a bachelor's in finance from the Wharton School of Finance at the University of Pennsylvania. In 1981, after graduate work at Wharton, she joined P&G full time. She is engaged to a Cincinnati real-estate broker. She has "a passion for ballet" and serves as a director and head of marketing for the Cincinnati ballet company.

Always had estimated sales last year of $149.8 million and an 18% share of the $832 million category, analysts estimate. P&G spent $22.6 million last year on Always advertising according to LNA. D'Arcy Masius Benton & Bowles, New York, is the brand's agency.

With a summer at Procter under my belt, there are a lot of different places I could have gone. The bottom line was the people here. I identified with them. They had the same ethics I had. They had an energy level and tenacity for the business that I was really turned on by. There's never any sense of grayness about what's right and wrong here. There's a very strong sense of ethics imbued in you from day one: Do what's right for the consumer first and foremost—business needs can be secondary if they're in conflict with the consumer's needs.

My very first day on the job as an intern I was given a promotion to develop for the Bounty brand. I was given the shipment objective for the quarter and I had to figure how to meet that objective. My promotion included some consumer premiums and some trade promotions. [The assignmment] also called for working very closely with our sales organization. I remember initially being overwhelmed by the magnitude of it all. In fact, that's really the way we manage our folks. You want to make sure people get the opportunity to succeed right off the bat. You want to give

them something under their belt that gives them a taste of how to work in the organization and an understanding of how we do business. So you get something very concrete to do, right away.

When I came to work full time in 1981, I worked on Pampers as a brand assistant. Everyone starts at the same level in this organization. I had some promotion responsibility, and I also had a more far-reaching project responsibility. That involved developing a larger count-size for the brand. Diapers were conventionally sold in packages of 30, and this was a mega-package of diapers. I was a brand assistant for a little under a year. Then I went on sales training. I went back to Philadelphia for about three months. During sales training you work very closely with the unit and district managers to learn how the plans you developed back at the office actually were executed in the field. I learned that you needed to be very tuned in with the needs of the trade, that very little was going to happen unless you were meeting the trade's needs. Overall, we've become a lot more sensitive to that kind of thing. I was in the stores a lot. We set the shelves. We met with the store manager, trying to sell him on why he should feature our brand that week.

I spent time putting together what are called key account presentations. That's when you go in on a major new brand initiative and you work with the buyer to establish distribution, merchandising and shelf space. I came back to Cincinnati and was an assistant brand manager on the Charmin business about a year. So I became a brand manager in a little under three years, and have been one for about three years.

Before Always, I was brand manager for a while on the mid-priced Banner toilet tissue brand. It was a smaller business, a relatively new brand. I was supposed to get it healthy—get its share up and start making some money. We did it. I was on Banner a little less than a year. Then I was asked to move to the Always brand.

Always had been in the market a little less than a year. It was very exciting to be able to carve out the brand's national strategy. Basically, we had come out of a period of sort of hand-to-hand combat with the introduction. The brand was on the shelf and now it was up to me to figure out how we were going to make it successful over a long term—to meet the share goals and the profit goals. And make this an attractive business for the company to be in. We are on track meeting all our objectives. We're very pleased with the brand's success.

We really had to get into the consumer's head and figure out what motivated her, not only on the surface, but also underneath. We had to figure out the best way to meet her needs so we can truly win in the category. And that really becomes the thrust of our marketing effort. We do qualitative and quantitative research, we spend time asking the consumer about all kinds of subjects—advertising, products, her thoughts about being a woman. It runs the complete gamut.

We have a business team on this brand. They come from all the key functional areas closest to the business: product development; engineering; manufacturing; purchasing; sales. I was in charge of establishing the team, of which I'm the leader. We meet weekly. I spend a lot of time with my brand group, working on marketing plans and execution. And a lot of time training, supporting them. I'm their key contact and first-line manager, and their development and training is very critical. When those people walk in the door, I'm responsible for their success or failure. One of my biggest highs is watching somebody really grow. People I had trained as brand assistants now are brand managers.

I spend a lot of time with our advertising agency working on copy strategy, developing advertising, evaluating its effectiveness. And I spend a great deal of time with my business team.

I have all of these functional responsibilities, in terms of marketing plan development and execution. I also have a similar level of responsibility in overall business development strategies: What's our next product? What's the next target audience we should be looking at?

I also do a lot of traveling. I just got back from the plant last week. I was with the manufacturing manager, and we were out there working the lines, talking to the people, understanding what their issues were in the manufacturing. I also spend a lot of time in the field working with the sales organization, so I go all over the country.

This afternoon I have a meeting with my business team to decide what our priorities should be for the next two years. I can make all the decisions in terms of our marketing plan elements, what promotions we're going to run, what the right advertising campaign would be. I may seek counsel from my boss or other people in the organization. But, by and large, I call it. I can make decisions, along with the business team, in terms of what are the key projects that we should be working on—new sizes, new formulas or whatever—over the next year.

It's safe to say I know more about the category than anyone in my management hierarchy does, especially when you've been on the business for a number of years. So it would be rather foolhardy of them to try to make the decisions for me. And we've made a lot of decisions that I'm pleased with. Always has been very successful. To some extent, we really have revolutionized the way the category advertises.

We have a campaign we lovingly call "Quotes." It is a campaign of women talking about how they feel about our product. If I were to define it, it would be as a stylized testimonial. It's very high energy, very colorful, highly styled, with wonderful music. We're trying to communicate that Always understands women and their needs, be they physical or emotional, better than any other brand.

We introduced Always Plus about a year ago, and it's been very successful. The business team made a joint decision that introducing Always Plus was the right thing to do for the brand. My business team developed that product. That's what turns people on. That's how you keep good talent in this organization—by giving them big chunks of business and letting them run with it.

Someday I'd like very much to become a general manager and run a bigger chunk of business. But to be honest with you, I don't get wrapped up in that. There are enough role methods in the organization of people who do well and are rewarded with more responsibility. So my focus is on the things today that can really make a difference.

I guess if there are any frustrations, it's really around the kind of person I am. I'm not really different from my peers here. We're all successful, dedicated, energetic people who like to see things work. So if I've got any frustrations, it's when things don't work out the way I want from a business standpoint. Because of the way the organization is here, I've become at one with my business. It's sort of hard to separate Beth Kaplan from the Always brand, to be honest with you.

Larry Zigerelli

Larry Zigerelli, 28, who hails from Monaca, Pa., is brand manager for Crest toothpaste. He joined P&G in September 1980, a few months after graduating from Yale University with a bachelor's degree in administrative science. A guard on the varsity basketball team while at Yale, he continues to participate in sports, especially basketball and softball for P&G corporate and intradivision teams. He recently married a P&G market researcher.

Crest has annual sales of $368.5 million and a 39% share of the $945 million U.S. toothpaste market, analysts estimate. P&G spent about $31.7 million on Crest advertising last year, according to Leading National Advertisers. D'Arcy Masius Benton & Bowles, New York, is the brand's agency.

I'm from the P&G class of '80. About half of them are still here, I'd say. I didn't know anything about P&G before I interviewed with them. I didn't really have a business background. In fact, I wasn't even sure I was going to go to work. I thought perhaps I was going on to graduate school. But the woman in career advisory was a big basketball fan. She called me one day and said she'd help me with a resume and fix me up with some top companies. So I talked to Morgan Guaranty for finance and IBM for sales. And I talked to P&G for both sales and marketing.

From the initial campus interview, I still wasn't sure what the P&G advertising job was all about. But I was interested enough that I did come out to Cincinnati for a full day. Basically, it was a day of exposing me to every aspect of what I was going to be doing, spending time with a brand assistant, talking to brand people, interviewing with people I was going to be working with, as opposed to the personnel department. They really encouraged me to make sure I fully understood the whole job. It meant a lot to me. I had no background in business and really didn't know what I was getting into. I think the one thing that really stood out to me in the interview process was the incredible

amount of honesty and integrity everyone has and their compassion for the company.

One of the people who hired me advised me not to make any conclusion as to whether I liked the place for six months, because I really wouldn't understand what the job was all about. So after six months I did a gut check. I decided I really like this; I'm going to give it a shot. Then six months later I did it again, and basically I saw that I really enjoyed it and pretty much decided then I wanted to stay and move on here.

I started as a brand assistant in what was then called our toilet goods division. I was developing marketing plans for a product that was going to have a test market. I can't really talk about the product. I did that about a year. Then I was in sales training for about two months in New Orleans, and then I worked as an assistant brand manager on one of our deodorant brands for about a year. Then I worked for a few months on Chloraseptic and Pepto-Bismol, brands we got when we purchased Norwich Pharmaceuticals. I was promoted to brand manager in little less than three years with the company. I've worked on a couple different brands as a brand manager. I've worked in the Scope mouthwash business, and a little bit on Pepto-Bismol. I've been on Crest for over a year.

Basically, my day runs anywhere from 10 to 11 hours, 8:30 a.m. to 7 p.m. I spend a lot of time with all the marketing areas, and I deal a lot with the advertising agency. I spend time developing creative promotion plans and looking at long-range plans. I also work with our professional services group on programs with dentists and professional associations. We do a lot of qualitative focus-group interviewing and quantitative research through our market research department to get to know the consumer. When I'm doing field checks in stores and I see people buying products, I stop and ask them what they think and why.

On average, I travel once a week, mostly to the

advertising agency in New York, and sometimes out in the field to work with the sales people or check on a test market. Tomorrow I have a meeting with product development. I also have to go over some documents, a couple of proposals that were forwarded to me from my assistants. Tomorrow afternoon, I have a key meeting with our sales force about what's going on out in the field right now. We deal with the salespeople, the voice for the field, here in the general office.

I spend a lot of time with my subordinates because 50% of how I'm evaluated is how well my people are trained. I get involved in recruiting. When I recruit people, I assess how well they measure up in five areas: leadership; how motivated they are; do they seem to have worked well with people in the organizations they've been in; what's their thinking like creatively; and do they communicate well? Were they editor of a magazine? Were they on the debating team? Are they good oral communicators? Pretty much size them up the way they're going to be evaluated here.

I don't think I should talk too much about my work on Crest. I just don't want to say anything that the brand manager of Colgate may get turned on by. It's been no secret, if you look at the Nielsen shares that Crest is . . . uh, we're doing okay. I did work on a new advertising campaign that's out there now, testimonials, real people. We are doing a lot in the promotion area.

The thing that I've always really enjoyed at P&G, which I was a little concerned about before I started, was what kind of impact I can really make if I have a good idea? I've seen time and again on every job that if you develop good plans, management buys them and you can implement them, even on a brand the size of Crest. How long it takes them to respond depends on what I'm asking, but it's always within days. We propose everything related to the brand's budget: total spending; how it's broken out by individual marketing element; long-range spending. The case

rate—spending tied to the volume of the brand—is kind of the framework we start with. Then it depends on the competitive situation. You may get to spend more if you feel it's appropriate.

The job is basically running the Crest company, and viewing management more as the bankers. They're generous bankers, too, and they're creative bankers. Often you'll go to them with an idea and they'll say, "Great, but have you ever thought of doing it this way," putting some topspin on it, because they've all done my job at some point. I can't remember the last time I was disappointed in my budget request, that I thought, boy, we really missed the mark here, we're not going to make our volume. The proposals that brand managers tend to make are reasonable enough. Even if you don't get exactly what you ask for, it is a negligible difference.

Where decisions are approved here depends on how big the decision is. I think you learn, after having worked here for a while, who the person is you need to have the final agreement from. A promotion that's going to go into the field, I know I don't have to propose to John Pepper [P&G president]. But I know who the person is. Sometimes, instead of a formal written recommendation, I lay out the recommendation in what we call a talk piece. Then I go into a meeting, pass it out and say, here's the objective and here's rationale point No. 1. Then I'd expand on what's on the paper. It helps expedite things.

The thing I really like about P&G, and marketing per se, is the pace. The only thing constant about marketing is change. Reassessing priorities and getting the most important things done is what I do, but I wish I had more hours. But I'm the kind of person who thrives on more to do than I have enough hours in the day. I see it as fun, as kind of a game. You're basically trying to outsmart the competition. It's analogous to my sports background. You always try to work harder to become the championship team.

P&G's Research Powerhouse

At least twice as aggressive as the next best company, P&G — with more than 800 Ph.D.s and $479 million budget — stands alone in research and development for its products.

O THER CONSUMER-PRODUCTS COMPANIES pride themselves on their research and development. But none more so than Procter & Gamble Co. Product research always has been the driving force behind P&G's 150 years of progress. Even before Messrs. Procter and Gamble signed their famous partnership agreement, James Gamble regularly consulted a chemist in Philadelphia for the latest information on soap and candlemaking.

Starting with James Gamble's individual efforts, P&G's R&D staff has grown to more than 6,000 researchers and made possible its blockbuster breakthroughs in detergents, paper products and healthcare. Many of the researchers have an average of 5.2 years of graduate school and/or a doctorate degree in the life sciences or physical sciences, according to Geoff Place, P&G VP-research & development. There are more than 800 Ph.D.s currently working in P&G's six main research, development and engineering facilities worldwide. (Many of the company's subsidiaries outside the U.S. also have the product-development laboratories and engineering facilities.) At P&G, Ph.D.s are not limited to the laboratory. Many Ph.D. scientists can be found at the associate director, director and VP levels throughout the company's research organization.

"P&G is the most aggressive company when it comes to basic research," says Hercules Segalas, a senior VP-director at Drexel Burnham Lambert, New York, and a former P&G manufacturing staffer. "P&G is at least twice as aggressive as Unilever, and it is the only company with basic research comparable to Proctor's."

Mr. Segalas says P&G's commitment to research "started at the beginning. P&G is first and foremost a technology-driven company. They have determined that it always costs too much to become just another 'me-too' company." Most package-goods companies pay lip service to research. Their idea of research is 'reciping,' coming up with a new shape, color, flavor, or viscosity," he adds.

In fiscal 1986, P&G spent $479 million—3% of its $15.4 billion in sales—on research for new and existing products. Professionalism and strong financial commitment underlie P&G's tradition of developing and marketing products both new and demonstrably different from those of the competition.

"It's clear that the original founders were very interested in understanding what they were doing," says Mr. Place. "That interest has carried through to a very strong desire on the part of the company to understand consumer needs; the market; and product technology."

According to company records, the first P&G research laboratory was set up in the corner of a machine shop in the 1850s. The first official chemist, an Englishman named Gibson, was hired in 1875 to "help with the production of soap, to understand the production better, and make it more efficient, resulting in higher quality products," says Mr. Place. Mr. Gibson (his first name doesn't show up in any corporate record) worked in a makeshift research laboratory with founder James Gamble's sons, James Norris and David. The three men had one goal: to find a formula for a hard, white soap comparable in quality to the castile soaps highly prized by homemakers for their rich, foaming lather. However, the castile soaps, based on expensive, imported olive oil, were priced beyond the average consumer's reach.

The company's search for the "right" white-soap formula was aided by the purchase of another company's soap recipe. James N. Gamble recorded in his diary in the late 1870s: "We bought the formula for a very moderate sum and proceeded to make soap according to the prescription, but after some experience, we changed it considerably." Finally, in 1878, James N. Gamble was able to report that he and his research associates had developed a white soap that was "satisfactory in every way." In 1879, the White Soap became Ivory.

127

P&G from the start has been able to transfer its understanding of one technology to development of another product. For instance, in learning how to make Ivory and other soaps and detergents, P&G's researchers became experts on human skin. This led in time to the development of hand and body lotions like Wondra.

Years of crushing and processing various seeds, especially cottonseed, for oils and shortenings sparked P&G's interest in papermaking. Its purchase of the Charmin Paper Mills in Green Bay, Wis., in 1956 opened the door further to understanding the papermaking process. After inheriting some technologies—and improving on others—P&G entered the disposable diapers category with Pampers in 1961.

"There's a tendency to think of cutting-edge science and technology as belonging to sophisticated industries like electronics, aircraft or defense," says Mr. Place. "What makes P&G unique is it brings a comparable quality of science to bear on everyday-type problems. We've deliberately targeted our R&D against the everyday, every-person needs," he says. Competitors have a difficult time trying to stay one step ahead of the company. P&G is notoriously tight-lipped in public, believing any statement is an indication to the competition of future marketing or research strategy.

But in 1976, P&G's then-chairman, Edward G. Harness, dropped a small hint: "A reasonable description of our potential future markets for U.S. consumer business would be those kinds of products normally sold through food, drug and variety stores. Viewed this way, there is a consumer goods market in the U.S. [then] totaling $125 billion at wholesale, and our share of that existing business is in the range of 3%." In other words, Mr. Harness was indicating that any kind of household item that consumers want, that can be mass-produced and sold at low cost, is the kind of product P&G will market.

During the annual shareholder's meeting last October, John Smale, P&G's current chairman-ceo, reiterated the company's position on product research. He called the continuing flow of new and improved products the "lifeblood" of the company's growth. "The success of our brands depends first and foremost on our skills in fashioning products which offer consumers meaningful advantages compared to competitive products . . . it is our goal to be the world leader in the relevant science and technology for every category in which we compete," he said.

Although Mr. Smale did not say what products are in P&G's pipeline, an indication of P&G's new-products interests can be found in the more than 500 patents filed annually with patent offices in the U.S., Canada and Europe. Leo J. Shapiro, head of the Chicago-based research company bearing his name, for more than 10 years has been regularly and systematically following P&G's patent filings.

"P&G likes to start with a natural-occurring substance, like the coffee bean, and modify it to become more stable, effective and controllable," he says.

Mr. Segalas is one of the few Wall Street analysts closely following P&G's patent filings. "In the last five years, P&G increasingly has filed patents in the healthcare industry, particularly for ethical and proprietary usages. A lot of their work has to do with bone chemistry, immunology and the cardiovascular system," he says.

Mr. Segalas says P&G's "thickest" patent file is in laundry products. Then follow healthcare products, personal care and food, "especially those that fall in the 'good-for-you' "category, he says. One promising new venture is what Mr. Segalas calls "medical foods." After 20 years of R&D, in May P&G filed for Food & Drug Administration approval of one such "medical food," olestra (sucrose polyester or SPE). Olestra is a calorie-and-cholesterol-free fat substitute. The man-made compound has both food and drug potential. In foods, P&G wants to use it to replace at least 35% of the fat in its Crisco and Puritan home-cooking oils; 75% of the fat in salty snacks like Pringle's potato chips, and in cooking oils it sells to restaurants.

In future FDA filings, Mr. Segalas is sure P&G will ask to use olestra in a prescription-only cholesterol-reducing drug for control of heart disease. "All the drugs that are out there that reduce cholesterol actually aggravate gall stones. [Olestra] helps dissolve those stones," says Mr. Segalas.

The push into healthcare is not surprising, considering the company's traditional emphasis on hygiene, the analyst adds. More health-related developments, particularly in skincare and haircare, can be expected in the next seven years.

"A quarter of our R&D efforts are directed against our traditional soap and detergent busi-nesses. The new areas, like healthcare, are now as significant, [accounting for more than 20%] at this point," says Mr. Place. He says P&G's ongoing research is necessary because "consumers' needs are very different today than they were 150 years ago."

While Mr. Place says he is confident P&G will stay one step ahead of consumers' needs, he admits the new-products pace has become faster. "We're now in a worldwide market, with competition from Japan, Germany and Great Britain, not just American companies. That wasn't true 25 years ago when travel was more difficult" he says. "Now, there's always somebody, somewhere thinking they can do it better, produce a better product, and do it more cheaply. From a research and development point-of-view, there's no peace."

CHAPTER SIXTEEN

Rely Tampons
The Decision Was Easy

Years of research and planning created the Rely brand. Its successful introduction was well worth the effort. Then, after a terrible series of consequences, within days P&G took action to withdraw the product from the market.

To the marketing world, it seemed a shocking, stunning blow. After a terrible series of consequences, the late Edward G. Harness, then chairman-CEO of Procter & Gamble Co., made the decision: withdraw the company's highly successful new Rely tampons from sale nationwide. He would later call it one of the easiest decisions he ever made.

What led to the September 1980 decision that represents in many circles the height of corporate social responsibility occurred, as far as P&G is concerned, over a period of about three months—quickly, considering that the pulling of the product undid a reported 20 years of work by the company. One of P&G's most successful marketing efforts had ceased, and within days the company was conducting an unprecedented product retrieval and public information campaign—using advertising. P&G was, in effect, de-marketing Rely, a product it had spent much of the 1970s introducing to the market.

A promising beginning

It had started out so well. As was typical of the times, competitors in the feminine-hygiene market had spent months—maybe even years—preparing for P&G's first rumored, then anticipated, then fully expected, entry into their consumer-product field.

During the fall of 1973, the industry's grapevine was spreading the word that the nation's most feared marketer—to competing companies—was putting together its launch of a tampon product. Rumors about that possibility had started circulating at least as early as 1968, and it was with anxiety that such companies as Tampax, Inc. (now Tambrands), International Playtex (now Playtex Inc.) and Kimberly-Clark Corp. looked to 1974. By December, it was definite; Procter & Gamble's new tampon, named Rely, would begin test marketing in Fort Wayne, Ind., when the new year began.

What would the country's preeminent package-goods company do? What product difference would it bring to the tampon category, long dominated by products made up of basically the same thing (cotton) with only minor added-benefit variations, e.g., rounded plastic applicator or a deodorized version? What technological improvement had P&G's noted research laboratories produced? Additionally, and importantly: What would the nation's No. 1 advertiser bring to the tampon marketplace, at the time representing only about $130 million in sales and requiring brand ad budgets of only about $4 million annually?

Only recently had broad-scale advertising been used in the category. Tampon ads mostly were in magazines targeted to young women and teen-age girls. The ads primarily were end-benefit oriented, portraying young women active—in sports, for example—during their menstrual period. In fact, TV commercials for feminine-hygiene products had only been allowed by the broadcasting industry since 1972. Only Playtex, in the tampon segment, had used the medium.

What would P&G do in getting across to the consumer its expected product difference? Com-petitors found out in February 1974, when ads created by Benton & Bowles (now D'Arcy Masius Benton & Bowles) began running in the 11-county market area surrounding the northeastern Indiana city. Spread magazine ads used visual comparisons with "the leading tampon," but targeted users of sanitary napkins, too. "The most absorbent tampon ever made," the print ad read. "New Rely is incredibly absorbent because it's made of hundreds of tiny sponges—super absorbers that work a lot better than other tampons' compressed cotton and rayon ever could. . . . These sponges are made of soft foam and a revolutionary new man-made fiber and they're encased in a silky soft covering—twice as absorbent as the leading tampon. . . . gently and quickly expands into a unique cup shape that gives you wall-to-wall internal protection. . . This means Rely not only works better than other tampons, but it also works better than napkins."

P&G demonstrated this to the area's retailers. "They came in here with a new-concept pitch," one grocery distributor told ADVERTISING AGE at the time. P&G salesmen, calling on distributors and retailers, brought in samples of Tampax, Playtex and Rely and performed demonstrations, dipping the three tampons into water to show absorbency. After removing the product, "Rely held the liquid and it could not be squeezed out," the distributor recalled.

Not only did P&G use TV commercials to support Rely, but it concentrated its TV time in the evening hours, to reach the increasing number of working women. The low-keyed spots featured a woman explaining that there was a "revolutionary" new product on the market, and referring viewers to magazine ads for details. Despite the fact that feminine-hygiene products—primarily sanitary napkins—were being advertised on TV at that time, the company closely watched reaction to its commercials in the Midwestern community. Local-station executives reported that Benton &

Bowles continually checked for viewer complaints. The spots reportedly were well received.

Competitive reaction to Rely was immediate. Playtex began moving boxes of its tampon brand into the market pre-priced at 99¢ (normal retail price then was about $1.93). Cents-off couponing also was used. Of course, P&G was the biggest user of couponing and sampling, with free boxes of Rely being given to customers in the beginning stages of the market test.

One of the purposes of an actual product-marketing trial in a test city or cities is to gauge competitor reaction, and over the next several years both Playtex and Kimberly-Clark (marketer of Kotex) made changes in their products. By mid-1974 Playtex had introduced nationally a new rounded-tip applicator similar to Rely's. Kotex also had come up with an applicator entry. Although it had been first introduced in 1972, the Kotex line extension still was in limited distribution by 1974, because of production problems. But more significant changes would take time—R&D time—and it was several years before the competitors hit the market touting tampons with improved absorbency.

Meanwhile, P&G moved Rely into another market—Rochester, N.Y.—for further testing in January 1975. And it was there the product first encountered negative publicity, when a local group or groups attacked Rely's formulation, which included polyurethane as an absorbent material. News media reported that polyurethane may pose a health hazard, although that was not substantiated. Because of consumer concerns, however, P&G did change from its polyurethane foam to a cellulose-sponge material, in November 1975. (Rely's formulation was changed again in late 1976, to one containing polyester foam and cellulose.)

The development in Rochester obviously slowed the company's progress in rolling out Rely (and, as far as is known, had no connection with Rely's future problem). One industry analyst said reformulations cost the company a year and a half in its race to national market.

The big test

By 1977, the major tampon brands had played their hands in the area of product improvement. Kimberly-Clark, Playtex and Tampax had gone back into their labs and come out with more absorbent tampons. Kotex's heavy-duty tube tampon claimed to be "twice as absorbent as the best-selling super" in 1977 ads, which added that "you'll probably never wear another napkin." Ads for Playtex's new Playtex 2 product claimed: "The tampon that absorbs more than a napkin in actual use . . . with new Maxi-Sorb fiber." New Super Plus Tampax was "50% more absorbent than the super tampon you may have been using . . . last month could be the last month you needed both a tampon and a pad." Also, by mid-1977, Johnson & Johnson, which marketed the No. 1-selling napkin, Stayfree, was in test market with its own "o.b." brand of tampons. (The product was developed in Germany; o.b. means "*ohne Binde*," without sanitary napkin.)

P&G decided to do battle with the "improved" competitors in one of its favorite large-market test sites—Kansas City, Mo. A real battle ensued. "Consumers in Kansas City are receiving more samples and seeing more advertisements for tampons than anyone else in the world," one top Kimberly-Clark executive was quoted as saying in *The Wall Street Journal*. P&G's advertising at the time was focusing on Rely's "unique cup shape" and sponge configuration, while continuing to stress absorbency—"Rely even absorbs the worry" was an ad tagline.

Significantly, the feminine-hygiene market was changing rapidly, and by 1978, the tampon market was estimated to be $300 million in annual sales nationally; the segment nearly matched the size of the napkin segment. When Rely first entered Fort Wayne, the national tampon market was just a little more than half the size of the napkin market. (At that time, an Indiana drugstore wholesaler had told an ADVERTISING AGE reporter, "I wouldn't be at all surprised to see a reversal, with tampons over napkins.")

Tampax, which steadfastly had refused to advertise on TV, finally did so during fall 1977. The brand once had dominated the category with an 80% share, and was by this time holding 44%. And Rely was still in test stages. Although segment growth was contributing to its diminished share, new products and an aggressive Playtex were hurting the once-dominant brand.

The process of expanding Rely began soon after the advertising and marketing fine-tuning in Kansas City. Oregon and Washington got Rely, then other areas of the West coast and upper Midwest in the first wave of the national expansion (in August 1978). By February 1980, the national rollout was complete. How had Rely done during the tests? It had attained a high 40% share of market in Fort Wayne. In Rochester, its share was an estimated 28%. In 1979, during the phased rollout, most industry sources said Rely was "averaging" about a 20% share in the areas where it was already sold.

Rely, a natural outgrowth of P&G's paper-products research and development, which had virtually created the huge disposable diaper business, was on its way to market—and possibly market leadership.

Disaster strikes

In 1977, James Todd, a physician in Denver, diagnosed his third curious case involving staphylococcus aureus and an unusual "shock" reaction to the staph infection. That year an eight-year-old boy died from what the doctor suspected was a new disease. He later labeled it toxic shock syndrome. Within three years, TSS was known throughout the country as a sometimes-fatal disease, receiving enormous media coverage.

In May 1980, the federal Centers for Disease Control in Atlanta issued a report noting the incidence of 55 cases of TSS and their association with menstruating women. Although the CDC knew of the Denver physician's discovery and had studied his reports (making no connection with menstruation), it based its report on cases from the upper Midwest (Wisconsin, Minnesota, Illinois). Doctors there had reported a majority of their cases involved young, menstruating women. Newspaper headlines like "New disease striking young women" made the connection stick. Follow-up CDC surveys—and news reports—went further and made a statistical link not only with menstruation but tampon use. On June 13, 1980, CDC asked P&G and other manufacturers for information on tampon usage, and on June 19 it talked to the company and alluded to a connection between TSS and tampon use. Backing up the latter statement was a CDC telephone survey of 52 women who had contracted TSS and an equal number of those who had not. Meetings were held with tampon manufacturers later that month, with CDC requesting brand and brand share data.

During July and August, P&G did its own investigation of the disease (outsiders had no access to CDC data at that time) and could find no evidence of special risk associated with its product. Mr. Harness later reported that even after receiving bacteria samples from CDC, P&G lab tests found no evidence that Rely's super-absorbent materials encouraged the growth of the particular strain of staph aureus. (At the time, non-scientific information given to the news media was the theory that superabsorbent tampons were removed from the body less often, which might have meant a greater bacterial-incubation time.)

In mid-September, however, P&G was informed of CDC's latest findings making a statistical link between TSS and Rely. The news media prominently carried the name Rely in their reports. That link came from telephone interviews of 50 additional TSS victims, asking about tampon brand usage. In addition to the high probability factor—Rely was the most heavily advertised brand of tampon in the country during 1980 and, as a new product on the market, getting a great deal of trial usage—CDC interviewers specifically asked about Rely in the phone surveys; it was the only brand mentioned, a fact that mystified P&G.

Although CDC itself and other scientific groups said the evidence did not show Rely was causing TSS, there was a "statistically significant difference" that made Rely stand out, a CDC epidemiologist is quoted as saying in a later article reviewing the TSS situation, published in the January/February 1985 issue of *Science '85* magazine. The article said CDC's outside, supporting documentation in September 1980 was preliminary case figures from Minnesota, which showed that "35% of women were using Rely at the onset of toxic shock syndrome." (That article went on to quote the Denver doctor who first reported TSS cases as saying those figures told him "65% of victims . . . were not using Rely.")

Nevertheless, on Sept. 22, 1980, P&G announced it was suspending the sale of Rely tampons. As Mr. Harness explained at the company's annual meeting in October, P&G's scientific advisers "could not assure [P&G] that the results of the latest study, though fragmentary and inconclusive, could be safely ignored." On Sept. 26, P&G voluntarily signed an agreement with the federal Food & Drug Administration that called for extensive advertising informing consumers of

the symptoms and risk of TSS and asking consumers to return boxes of Rely tampons for full refund.

The four-week ad campaign began on Oct. 5, running in the same media the company had been using to promote Rely and receiving a greater "reach"—percentage of women receiving at least one message—than had its earlier ad schedule. (Through September, Rely had received about $12.3 million in national advertising support in the six media measured by the Leading National Advertisers monitoring service.)

Fortune later summed up Rely's market success and significance to that point: "It was P&G's first entry into a U.S. market for sanitary products (called catamenials) that is . . . around $1 billion in size and not given to fads. . . . Market research showed that Rely . . . was significantly preferred by women over other tampons and sales seem to validate that finding. By September . . . Rely was getting about 25% of the tampon market, a remarkable share for a product so new. Rely may have been on its way . . . to 'driving Tampax right out of business.' "

At the October shareholders meeting, Mr. Harness said the company was taking a $75 million after-tax writeoff on Rely. "The financial cost to the company of Rely's voluntary suspension will be high," he told shareholders, "but we believe we have done what is right and that our action is consistent with the long-held Procter & Gamble view that the company and the company alone is responsible for the safety of our products. To sacrifice this principle could over the years ahead be a far greater cost than the monetary losses we face on the Rely brand."

Aftermath

THE EXACT CAUSE (OR CAUSES) OF TSS STILL is not known. Although the number of reported cases has declined (from a 1980 high of 890) over the years, CDC stated that 1986's 110 reported cases represents a "gross underestimate" of the disease. Dr. Benjamin Schwartz, of the Atlanta-based CDC, told AD AGE the government unit does not detect the majority of TSS cases, noting that there were probably five to 10 times the number reported last year. (Of those reported cases, he said, 56% were menstruation related and 44% were unrelated to menstruation.) He believes TSS cases, including unreported ones, have been "relatively stable" over the last several years.

However, the prevalent attitude is that the use of absorbent tampons increased the risk of TSS for women, and the prevalent theory about why it is that the newer absorbent materials may have contributed to greater amounts of the toxin associated with TSS being produced in the body.

In 1985, both Tambrands and Playtex withdrew from the market versions of their tampon brands containing polyacrylate, another absorbent material. This second (after Rely) product-retrieval program also included advertising.

A number of lawsuits were filed against P&G and the other tampon manufacturers; the exact number is difficult to determine. As for Rely-related lawsuits, P&G disclosed only that there have been three trial verdicts involving the company—none of them found the product defective; there were no punitive damages awarded; and in only one case was compensatory damages awarded, in the amount of $300,000.

All of the companies have contributed funds to support continued research on the disease. P&G reports it has contributed $4 million in financial assistance to 24 outside university-based research groups as of summer 1987.

CHAPTER SEVENTEEN

Back to the Basics
P&G's Turnaround Tactics

*When products falter in the marketplace,
P&G recognizes that it has lost touch
with its fundamental priority: meeting the
consumers' needs.*

In 1981, a *Fortune* article called the 1980 market withdrawal of Rely tampons "agonizingly disappointing" to Procter & Gamble. But P&G today remembers that period of time differently. "Obviously you don't have that happen without some sense of loss," P&G President John E. Pepper says in referring to the Rely incident. "But people weren't moping around thinking about wasted effort or a lost brand. It really was a feeling of, we did the right thing," he says. "There was never any looking back, not ever."

Mr. Pepper, who at the time of Rely's problems was group VP responsible for the company's key packaged soap & detergent and bar soap & household cleaning products divisions, recalls that "that was the only consideration. It wasn't a question . . . of what the liability would be . . . or what about the years of effort. . . . Nor was that really the subject for a lot of discussion. Every company has certain things that occurred in its history that give life to its beliefs, that make them real and substantive," he continues. "The Rely decision, in this company's history, is—if not unique—one of the very select group of events" that illustrate the "value . . . of maintaining integrity in all we do, in doing what's right for the consumer."

In November 1986, as the company was preparing to enter its sesquicentennial year, Cincinnati employees were gathered at Cincinnati Coliseum and Mr. Pepper introduced to them a formally adopted Statement of Purpose. Its language is strikingly similar to those comments. The second paragraph of the basic three-paragraph statement begins and ends: "We will achieve that purpose through an organization and a working environment which . . . maintains the company's historic principles of integrity and doing the right thing."

The newly decreed Statement of Purpose addresses the company's philosophy on managing its brands. It "is not new in one sense," Mr. Pepper told ADVERTISING AGE later. "It's really a reflection of our history, of what we've believed in for as long as this company's been around. . . . The first paragraph: 'We'll provide products of superior quality and value that best fill the needs of the world's consumers.' When we're doing that, when we're really providing superior quality and superior value, then we don't have [what could be termed] problem brands. If we have a problem brand, it's because we are somehow failing to do that."

The company has had its share of problem brands in recent years, notably Pringle's potato chips and, somewhat surprisingly, Pampers disposable diapers. (Rely should not be included, because throughout most of its existence it was just the opposite. Rely "fulfilled all those things that we expect a brand to do to succeed. It was a better product; it was well advertised; it was a good value," notes Mr. Pepper.)

"It's kind of a fact of life when you have roughly 100 national brands," says the executive, who was exec VP in charge of all U.S. consumer products before being named company president in 1986. "And when you have a problem brand," he says, defining that as either a new or established brand "that's not achieving the degree of share and profit progress we'd like," then "what's usually at the roof of it is you are not doing right—or as right as you need to be—by the consumer. You are not offering a competitive advantage to the consumer . . . [Or] you are not communicating [a benefit] well enough . . . or you have a pricing—a value—issue."

In most cases, he believes, "The key to improving [it] gets right back to the fundamentals: knowing the consumer better, what they want; delivering that better than the competition, in our product; communicating that . . . in our advertising . . . [and] having a competitive price. If those sound like generalities," he adds, "I guess they are. But it really reduces itself to that."

In discussing brand struggles (eliminating those

products in test marketing, which are, in effect, still in development, albeit the final—and public—stage of their development), Mr. Pepper admits: "The situation on Pampers is a classic."

Textbook case

Pampers, of course, also is a classic in a more positive sense. Introduced into test market in 1961, Pampers disposable diapers was the first successful such product. Not immediately, of course; there first were problems with pricing, and then with building the production capacity for a growing demand. But by mid-1970, almost 20 years after a P&G engineer had gotten the idea for it while baby-sitting with his first grandchild, Pampers was available nationally in the U.S.

It had virtually created the disposable-diaper market, which today is a $5 billion worldwide business. It solidified the company's leadership position in the even larger paper-products field. It provided a marketing textbook success story of unparalleled proportions. By the late 1970s, the story of the creation of Pampers was being used to help educate the public—particularly young people—on our economic system. A P&G-produced booklet still being circulated today is titled, "Consumer Choice, the Driving Force of a Market Economy" (AA, April 4, 1977).

But, as Mr. Pepper notes, in the mid-1980s, years after it had become a "classic" example of a successful consumer-product brand, Pampers was in trouble in the marketplace. "We were in bad shape share-wise two and a half or three years ago. The reason was that we had lost adequate touch with the consumer, in knowing what they needed. We didn't have product superiority," he says. A competing product, Kimberly-Clark Corp.'s Huggies, an elastic-leg disposable diaper, was doing extremely well in the market at the time; in fact it had taken a slight market-share

lead, a true accomplishment considering that Pampers had held that lead for close to two decades. So P&G publicly declared its intention to go all out to turn around its disposable diaper business—which by now included a second brand, Luvs—with a budgeted $500 million commitment to researching and upgrading its diaper lines.

"By learning that [it had lost touch with what consumers wanted], by getting more technology and better benefits into Pampers, we moved back out ahead of Huggies," Mr. Pepper declares. "We gained 10 share points, and to stay there we're going to have to keep doing what the consumer wants, better than our competition."

Under Mr. Pepper's criterion for what constitutes a "problem" brand, the company at any given time may be struggling on a brand with virtually no knowledge of that struggle outside its headquarters (and the offices of the brand's ad agency and key competitors). Pampers' recent trouble is an example; the brand was still widely considered the far-and-away leader of the diaper category during the early days of Huggies' market-share gains. On the other hand, at times a brand's problems will be very visible—the talk of the marketing community, in fact.

In the late 1970s, while Rely tampons were rolling up an enviable sales record on the way to national distribution, that was the case with the company's still relatively new Pringle's brand.

A "newfangled" phenomenon

Pringle's potato chips went into test marketing in Evansville, Ind., in the fall of 1968. The brand created an immediate uproar in the industry, which viewed the entry as revolutionary. Not only were P&G's "newfangled" chips of uniform size and shape and stacked upright in a "tennis-ball container," they had a long shelf life. Regular potato chips are bagged (and broken); within a fairly short time they become stale and are removed from grocery shelves. For this reason, the potato-chip industry is, with a few exceptions, made up of local or regional companies that make and deliver the chips fresh to retail stores.

Pringle's, delivered via the same grocery warehouse distribution channels as Duncan Hines baking mixes or Tide detergent, were a really threat to the "chippers." And, initially, Pringle's uniqueness carried the day, despite massive counter efforts by competitors. Those efforts including copying P&G's product and product-packaging idea; publicly attacking its preparation methods; and, in the end, cooperating with one another region-by-region by sharing marketing strategies to combat the interloper. Frito-Lay, the king of the potato-chip hill with a national fleet of delivery trucks, tried—through a specially created subsidiary—warehouse distributions of its own "stackable" chip (AA, Aug. 12, 1974).

The efforts to make P&G put the words "imitation potato chips" on Pringle's, made from dehydrated potatoes, came to naught when the Food & Drug Administration sided with P&G, although it did require prominent display of the words "made from dried potatoes" on Pringle's packages after 1977 (AA, Dec. 1, 1975). Despite that setback, the regional potato-chip companies did employ a successful marketing strategy against Pringle's, playing up their chips as "natural"—the real thing vs. the "fabricated" chip. Potato-chip companies that already had faced Pringle's in market battle sent copies of their marketing plans to other chippers in cities yet to see the P&G product, which was rolling out market by market.

Pringle's was in national distribution by mid-1975, and within no time, it seems, much of the controversy and marketplace excitement was over. Although the new brand was taking a reported 10% or 15% share of the market, that was nowhere near the 25% share many in the industry were expecting when the incursion started. The regular chippers had held their own against the P&G powerhouse. By 1978, Pringle's was being labeled a failure—a "bomb," in marketplace parlance. By all outside reports, Pringle's sales had peaked three years earlier at about $110 million, far below the $200 million the company was said to have envisioned, and sales were trending down. The brand's share of market was put at 8% that year (AA, June 5, 1978).

If controversy remained, it was internal. And it did. Although P&G was not talking, Pringle's survival was at issue. "Pringle's indeed was a problem brand," acknowledges Mr. Pepper now. "We lost volume on it for many years." But, in 1979, "we commissioned a special team [to work] on Pringle's," and as a result the brand's "now a real bright spot for us."

Industry sources estimate current Pringle's sales at slightly more than $130 million, a sizable increase from the eight-digit figures attributed to the product during the late 1970s. P&G does not release brand sales figures, nor does it comment on outside estimates. What came out of the special business team put together to turn Pringle's around? "The key," Mr. Pepper continues, was "to go back and understand what the consumer wanted. . . . We learned we needed to do better on taste."

Flavor "fever" rises

To the consumer, Mr. Pepper states, "Flavor was No. 1, No. 2 and No. 3 in priority . . . and we needed a variety of flavors, not just one. The can [cylindrical container] was important, but it had become more important to us than to the consumer." And, he says, "our pricing needed to be more competitive." An improved Pringle's potato chip hit the market in early 1981, supported by a new advertising campaign touting: "We've got the fever for the flavor of a Pringle's."

Wells, Rich, Greene, New York, had succeeded Tatham-Laird & Kudner, Chicago, on the account, and the new campaign turned out to be a long-running one. The company recently introduced Pringle's seventh flavor, Light Bar-B-Q (AA, June 15, 1987).

Another action recommended by the business team was to sell—and price—Pringle's cans individually, dropping the shrink-wrapped double-canister packs. This negated a perception of higher price vs. regular chips. "The solution really did grow out of understanding the consumer better," Mr. Pepper states. "Again, all this 'knowledge of the consumer' sounds so basic, but it really was going back to the basics" that saved Pringle's.

On business teams—a relatively new management technique at the company—Mr. Pepper went further, "A big component of this [Pringle's story], as in any part of our business, is: How are people working together? And whenever we're in a high-challenge situation—a new brand we're launching or a problem brand—the premium is greater than ever on having a really tight-knit group of people across all [the various company] functions. . . . Our people are what really makes the difference. And . . . as somebody who's lived through what we've been through on Pampers over the last three years, it's been the character of the people and the teamwork, the commitment behind it, that has made that [turnaround] possible. The same thing on Pringle's."

The company president notes, with no trace of intentional understatement: "As long as we think we can bring something to the market . . . we tend to be very patient. We try to take a long-term view."

Pringle's certainly attests to that. Still, what took so long? "From my perspective, what took the time was defining what we needed to do. . . . To define what the core of the problem was— taste, price—and then to define what we needed to do. Once you can define what you need to do,

then, with the people we have in this company, 'Katie bar the door.' "

More recently, Mr. Pepper states, "Pert [shampoo] would qualify as a problem brand." The brand, introduced nationally in 1980, was "not delivering a benefit . . . that was good enough, distinctive enough," he says. But "we came up with a very important piece of new technology about two years ago which, for the first time, combines the benefits of a shampoo and conditioner in one.

"We had been on a strategy on Pert we were feeling good about . . . 'wash and go.' It was directed at young people, athletic, who don't have a lot of time to do three or four different steps on their hair," he says. "But it was on our regular shampoo, so we saw this new shampoo and conditioner made to order—this was a formula for Pert." So P&G put the new formula into Pert, now called Pert Plus, and test marketed it in Seattle. "It [became] the third-largest shampoo brand there," Mr. Pepper says, "tripling the business, going from a 2 [share] to a 6½ share." It is, he believes, another "outstanding example of how you never should give up on a brand. If you can find a new consumer benefit, a new technology to deliver, and if the brand has a positive image in a broad sense, it can be made into an important equity.

"There were many times when we wondered whether we ought to persist on Pert. And we said yes, we ought to keep looking for a benefit, a product formula. . . . And it appears from what we've seen in test that that's what's going to happen here on Pert Plus." (Pert Plus was introduced nationally earlier this year.)

"The drama of this to me," he continues, is that when a brand is "quote—in difficulty: What are the dynamics of turning it around? There isn't an inevitable decline. A brand that's in trouble is not inevitably doomed to continue on a downward spiral. Even in what can be seen as the toughest of situations, ones that would lead many people to walk away and say we will work on something else—if you're able, if you have people who are able to understand the consumer, understand [what] your product is doing or not doing . . . whether it's an established brand or a new one, it can be turned around."

Mr. Pepper had one additional example to prove his point. Looking at a box of Dash laundry detergent, a newly reformulated and repackaged brand, he continues: "That brand has declined every year for 20 years. That's not a scientific count, but it's about right; it's gone down every year for 20 years." But the new "lemon fresh" Dash, introduced nationally shortly after Pert Plus rolled out and positioned for fighting both dirt and odors in clothes "tripled the business in six months" in test, he reports. "So I think it's exciting what you can do on a brand, if you get back and really understand the consumer," Mr. Pepper concludes. "It works, it really works."

CHAPTER EIGHTEEN

Ivory:
A Classic's Redesign

Ivory soap's current packaging seems fresh and contemporary after more than two decades, which is remarkable considering many consumer products live and die within that time span.

Since 1965 Ivory soap has had one package design and logotype, the longest run of any package or logo the brand has ever had without change. It also became the basis for all Ivory product packaging.

PRODUCTS THAT ACHIEVE ALMOST LEGEND-ary status are not easily changed. When Procter & Gamble Co. redesigned Ivory soap's packaging in 1963, it made sure the new look wouldn't sink its famous floating soap in the marketplace.

"Ivory soap is thought of as the pillar of the company," says Don Baker, who retired as P&G's manager of art & package design last year. "I remember when the [artwork for the new wrapper] was finished, either [P&G's then-President] Howard Morgens, or one of his assistants, drove all the way out to Glendale, an exclusive suburb of Cincinnati, to show a little 80-year-old lady the design—just to make sure she was happy with it." She happened to be Mary E. Johnston, William Cooper Procter's niece, who was P&G's largest single stockholder, Mr. Baker says. Ms. Johnston "thought it was beautiful."

This particular packaging redesign was not the first by any means in the product's history. The first curlicued and checkerboard-patterned wrapper of the late 1800s, according to a brochure published by P&G in 1979 to celebrate Ivory's 100th anniversary, "looked well on the shelves of kitchens . . . a partner to the scrubbing board, the pot-bellied stove and kettle. . . ." It also concealed dust that gathered on packages in general stores. In 1923 the first major change was made in deference to modern times: Most of the curlicues were dropped. Over the years, competition and modernized grocery stores wrought other small changes in the wrapper. In 1940, a major technological breakthrough—the continuous hydrolyzer process in soapmaking—called for another change: A bright blue color was added to the package. The antique design, by and large, was still intact until, three years later, little blue wavelets were added top and bottom and the logo was updated. Slight alterations were made through the 1950s. Then came the 1960s.

"P&G always updated packaging on an evolu-

tionary basis," Mr. Baker says, making changes if a product "was tired, if a competitive move was needed, or if there was a product improvement. Starting around 1961, P&G felt Ivory's packaging was tired and needed updating." Some of P&G's packaging ideas have been revolutionary as well, including: the first plastic consumer-product bottle (Ivory liquid); the first hollow plastic handle (Downy liquid fabric softener); fluorescent inks that didn't dry on the printing press or fade on the package (Tide); reverse-printing poly film for wrapping paper products (Charmin bathroom tissue).

The Ivory redesign project fell to Walter Dorwin Teague Associates, one of two New York-based industrial-design companies P&G was using for the bulk of its design projects. (The other was Deskey Associates.) Tom Richardson, now head of the Riverside, Conn.-based package-design company that bears his name, recalls that particular "evolution" very well. He should. He came up with the design motif—the stylized waves and sans-serif type treatment—that has remained unchanged for more than 20 years. And he wasn't even working on the Ivory project at the time. "I was a senior supervisor in graphics and packaging working on new P&G products: Scope, Head & Shoulders shampoo and [the recently acquired] Charmin bathroom tissue. I knew P&G had asked us to come up with a fresh, contemporary look for Ivory. There was a trend in P&G in the early '60s toward a lighter, more sensitive touch" in packaging. Teague, which got the P&G business in the late '50s, hired Mr. Richardson from Yardley because "of my background in toiletries products package design.

"I was asked by another new senior designer for a suggestion, because an Ivory presentation was being readied for approval in Cincinnati by the late Charles Gerhardt," then head of P&G's art and package design department. "I made one design sketch." And P&G chose his design. "After that, I continued as the Ivory design director at

Teague until I left to join BBDO. I guess it was a matter of luck and timing," he says.

Harold J. Vanderhyde, the retired former head of Teague's technical packaging group, recalls, "Charlie Gerhardt got his staff thinking of packaging as something that could be a sales tool; he had management's backing—and they took the wraps off the budget" on an as-needed basis. "We worked on projects following a set of written objectives—that was Gerhardt's doing. The objectives were reviewed by management and the art section before we got any project. Presentations were weighed against them. They were a challenging, inspiring client. And they were thorough," he says.

P&G was thorough from start to finish. Ivory's redesign was chosen in 1963; the new package didn't enter the national market until 1965. "Never before had a package been so thoroughly tested," Mr. Baker says. For six months P&G did pre-test market consumer research using panels and door-to-door surveys, getting a handle on consumer attitudes toward the old Ivory package. The new-design Ivory was test marketed in the South for two years. Finally convinced that the new package wouldn't turn off consumers, P&G in 1965 sent Ivory's new waves into national waters. "We tried to update it again in the late '60s," Mr. Baker says, "but P&G has never beaten that design. It just hasn't dated at all."

IV

MARKETING AND ADVERTISING

CHAPTER NINETEEN

The Man Who Built P&G's Market Research

❦

The doggedness of "Doc" Smelser provided a foundation based on knowing the consumer better than the competition.

ONE MAN'S EXTRAORDINARY CURIOSITY and singlemindedness is credited with the founding of a market research department at Procter & Gamble Co. D. Paul Smelser, a newly minted Ph.D. in economics from Johns Hopkins University, the story goes, joined P&G to work in an economic-research department set up in 1923 to study commodity markets. But Mr. Smelser turned out to be more interested in consumer purchasing and product-usage behavior than in fluctuations in commodity prices.

According to "Eyes on Tomorrow," P&G's official corporate history, "In conferences . . . Smelser would ask questions like, 'What percentage of Ivory soap is used for face and hands and what percentage for dishwashing?'" Corporate

officers—William Cooper Procter, then president, and Richard R. Deupree, who would become president in 1930—admitted they didn't know. Mr. Smelser—throughout his long career at P&G, he would be known simply as "Doc"—kept pecking away. Finally, an exasperated Mr. Deupree told Mr. Smelser to "go out and find the answers to those damn questions yourself."

Thus, a formal market research department was created in 1925, and "Doc" Smelser, the first manager, was empowered to take off on a fact-finding career that didn't end until his retirement in 1959. Considered a conservative man with "strong feelings and beliefs" by those who knew him, Mr. Smelser shaped an organization unique to U.S. industry at the time.

The company then, and, to a large degree, still

D. Paul ("Doc") Smelser

today came to be characterized by: a heavily quantitative orientation; a strong advertising-media orientation; a commitment to spending the time and money necessary to develop new, better data-collection techniques; complete objectivity achieved by independence from operating divisions; self-sufficiency; and secrecy. After all, Mr. Smelser and his co-workers knew better than anyone the marketing leverage inherent in a better understanding of the consumer than that of the competitors.

As one former P&G advertising manager is quoted in "Eyes," "People were forever wondering how Procter & Gamble managed to make so many brilliant moves. Much of that brilliance rose out of the market studies made by Smelser's group." Not to say that this data came quickly or easily. Oldtimers in MRD remember sitting together in a bullpen, and noting that Doc would

leave his desk every morning at 10 a.m. for an hour and then again at 3 p.m. for another hour. Later they discovered he was walking around the advertising/marketing department, making himself accessible, proselytizing this newfangled thing called market research. Apparently Doc, a small man and a natty dresser, did an outstanding job. One advertising agency veteran long associated with P&G was asked, "What would you say distinguished P&G from other advertisers?" His answer: "There are several things. First, they never forget the consumer is making the buying decision; they are fanatics on this and they'll research consumers' reactions on virtually anything. . . ."

The investigators

By 1934, Doc Smelser had 34 people on his MRD staff. His operation emphasized the fundamentals of marketing research. And this focused on quality field work. In the late 1920s, MRD started to build its own field force of interviewers (called investigators), almost all of whom were young female college graduates. They would be brought to Cincinnati for four months of training and then sent out in groups, traveling the U.S. by train or bus to conduct door-to-door interviews on MRD projects. (Men recruited for brand-research work in MRD went through the same training in those days, often spending up to two years as field investigators.)

Patron saint of the investigators was Maggie Downing, MRD's first field director. Doc Smelser assigned her the duties of recruitment and training. "We recruited college women," recalls Richard G. Shepherd, who later served as manager of MRD's field operation, "because they had the maturity to travel alone." Intelligence counted, too. The interviewing techniques being developed by the Smelser/Downing team called for investigators to memorize all instructions, questions and answers in an interview. No clipboards, pens or

147

questionnaires were in sight. These things, it was felt, might inhibit a natural, conversational tone that would lead to an open disclosure of feelings and attitudes. After the interviews, investigators would run to their cars to write down the respondents' answers.

Doc Smelser was very selective about his investigators and interviewed each one before she was hired. He wanted prim and proper young women who wouldn't intimidate housewives, and he frowned on extraordinarily good-looking women who might be considered threatening. In the beginning, MRD investigators were required to wear high heels, a hat and gloves while interviewing; sweaters were frowned on. Men had to wear a dark suit and white shirt, as was the rule at P&G in those days.

Eventually, Mr. Shepherd estimates, more than 3,000 young women passed through MRD's training program. Today, some are still with P&G in other capacities; some work for outside research companies; and more than 100 of these women, it is estimated, are married to men now working for the company.

In the mid-1960s, with the cost of door-to-door interviewing becoming prohibitive, and with the advent of the telephone WATS line, a long-distance package, MRD started to fold its field investigator force and train the young women for telephone interviewing.

DAR research

P&G's MRD embraced new research techniques, a prime example of which is the on-air copy-testing methodology DAR (Day After Recall). DAR measures a TV commercial's memoriability in a natural on-air viewing situation. The technique apparently began with some academic studies related to the training of Navy pilots in the 1940s. These studies came to the attention of the late George Gallup Sr., who became intrigued

with measuring TV commercial effectiveness in an environment of 60-second spots running on single-sponsor shows. The Gallup experimentation led to a 24-hour (day-after) recall test with aided recall to the product class level. (Doc Smelser was a friend of Claude Robinson, then Mr. Gallup's partner at Gallup & Robinson.)

About the same time, Compton Advertising, one of P&G's oldest agencies, started work on a similar system called CSMI (Compton Sales Message Index). Recalls Howard Kuhn, then manager of research at Compton, "We tested the recall on commercials 12, 24, 48 and 72 hours after exposure and finally settled on 24 hours—an arbitrary decision—where there was still enough recognition of copy ideas to evaluate impact."

P&G's MRD had been doing some research of its own along similar lines. When P&G was sold on the technique, all of its advertising agencies were urged to use it, and a long relationship with the research company now known as Burke Marketing Services, a unit of SAMI/Burke, began. Cincinnati-based Burke did the DAR field work for P&G, conducting the first effort in 1952 in Bloomington, Ind. It was based on door-to-door interviews with viewers of the "Loretta Young Show."

According to Donald L. Miller, president of Burke at the time, "P&G was very secretive about the technique, and they regarded it like one of their product formulations. They felt they had a considerable advantage over the competition." P&G's horse-sense attitude toward such matters is exemplified by this statement in 1972 by John D. Henry (who succeeded Doc Smelser as manager of MRD in 1959): "We do on-air testing, and we talk to consumers following exposure without ever having recruited them to look at the advertising. In our judgment, this is the way one should look at advertising. This is the way one should measure communication, as it has to take place in the real world—fighting for attention and memory and reaction against all the advertising that competes for a share of the consumer's mind. That's doing it the hard way, I guess, but that's how it is in the real world as we see it."

Of course, when word got out that P&G had endorsed the DAR technique, it became the thing to do, resulting in a business boom for Burke. It's not surprising that all through the years P&G's MRD has given its outside suppliers strict instructions not to discuss their relationship with P&G or the exact nature of the work they do. But, well aware of the mystique connected with being associated with work on cutting-edge research for P&G, some of those companies—through the years and continuing still today—find ways to let it slip that P&G is a client.

MRD goes overseas

The last big MRD push under the Smelser regime started in 1950, when he assigned a long-time member of his staff, Raymond S. Croop, to set up MRD staffs in the operating subsidiaries outside the U.S. It was difficult because, as Mr. Croop said recently, "There were no jets in those days; we traveled by propeller [airplane], and it took a long time to get around." Also, there were 26 countries involved, and Mr. Croop's project lasted until 1961. (Mr. Croop's wife, Marge, worked as an investigator in MRD's field operation.) But this work led to the addition of possible overseas duty to the MRD staff-development procedure in Cincinnati.

One of Mr. Croop's stories about those days describes how he was supervising a coincidental radio-audience survey door to door in Caracas, Venezuela, in the 1950s. The idea was to observe quickly, home by home, if the radio was on and to what station it was tuned. But how would P&G effectively cover the many homes needed for 15-minute time-span reads? The answer, produced by a P&G field supervisor, was to hire bullfighters

or would-be bullfighters, who would have the speed and stamina to run down the street as required. It worked. The point is that through such studies, P&G's MRD often knew more about the audience size of some stations than the stations did, and, hence, had the know-how to buy advertising time at bargain prices. This sort of emphasis on media and audiences has made MRD a key player in the planning of media buys at P&G.

A new manager

In 1959, Doc Smelser retired and moved to Arizona, where he later died in an accidental fire. His replacement was John D. "Jack" Henry, who had joined P&G in 1945, having been recruited out of the University of Delaware. Like others of his era, Mr. Henry had gone through the investigator-training program and spent his first year or so at P&G conducting interviews. Under the Henry regime (which lasted until his retirement in 1984), the focus of P&G interviewing shifted from door-to-door to telephone interviewing from a central facility in Cincinnati. By the early 1970s, MRD was conducting about 1.5 million interviews a year, either via phone or mail.

The famous "Habits & Practices" studies, conducted on a much larger scale today via mail panels, originally involved sending field investigators into about 300 households. Their job was to observe closely how housewives actually went about specific housekeeping chores, such as washing dishes or scrubbing floors. Every detail of product usage was observed. Obviously, one of the goals was to look for new product openings or line extensions of existing products.

The famous ex-chairman of P&G, Neil McElroy, is quoted as saying, "Find out what the consumers want and give it to them." The marketing research department started in 1925 has, to all outward appearances, certainly fulfilled the "find out" part of that mission.

Dawn of the Computer Age

Exploding technologies give P&G the means to probe consumer behavior like never before.

JOHN D. "JACK" HENRY, RETIRING AFTER 25 years as manager of Procter & Gamble's market research department, hosted a luncheon on Dec. 19, 1984 to introduce his successor. The guests, who gathered in a private dining room at Cincinnati's Westin Hotel, were from research companies that had worked closely with Procter & Gamble's MRD through the years. Top executives came from Burke Marketing Services; Walker Research; Information Resources Inc.; Burgoyne Information Services; NFO Research; The NPD Group; The Data Group; and Market Facts. Selling-Areas Marketing Inc. and the Marketing Research Group USA of A. C. Nielsen Co. sent client service executives. Curiosity was high. For many in the room, P&G was their single largest and most demanding client.

Instead of greeting a well-known MRD staffer who was moving up, as might have been expected, Mr. Henry's guests discovered that the new head of one of the country's largest marketing/advertising research staffs—and budgets—was unknown to them. Robert J. Herbold, then 42, was coming from the post of advertising manager in P&G's packaged soap and detergent division—one of the top marketing jobs in the company. Previously, he had held the same post in the beauty care division. Perhaps more significant was the fact Mr. Herbold, who had joined P&G in 1968, had a Ph.D. in computer science from Case Western Reserve University. Earlier in his career at P&G, he had been manager-management sciences in the company's management systems division, and later, in the same division, manager of the operations staff (field staff, telecommunications staff and corporate data center).

Some luncheon guests got the point immediately: MRD was shifting gears. Others, it turned out, didn't catch on right away; it took future developments to awaken them to the supplier consequences of the changes in the department. From here on there would be more emphasis on computer technology, information systems and database management. The high-tech era had arrived at MRD.

Since that luncheon in 1984, there have been significant changes in the way P&G's MRD does things:

■ P&G gave MRD approval to increase its staff. It now numbers about 250, of whom about 160 are professional-level employees.

■ In times past, MRD, which hires and trains its own people, had fulfilled most of its needs from direct applicants, most of whom were college graduates. Currently the majority of new hires come from campus recruiting at Purdue University, the University of Michigan, Michigan State University, Indiana University, Vanderbilt University and Miami (Ohio) University.

The reasons for selection of these institutions, according to Mr. Herbold, are the very high success rate with previous hires; a high retention rate; a preference for students familiar with the Midwest; and a work ethic that seems to prevail among students at these schools. The most-sought traits among potential hires are "good quantitative instincts; a high energy level; and a clear interest in consumer research," Mr. Herbold says. All take an MRD test that is "closely aligned to the marketing brand manager test," a longtime standard at P&G.

■ New hires are immediately assigned to assist a seasoned brand research supervisor so "they'll feel they are participating and that they have a real job." In due course, they still pass through an in-house training program—a formal set of modules—that has been traditional at MRD. As they move up to MRD, the new staffers may get a research assignment at one of P&G's overseas subsidiaries.

MRD, through its own research operation (field, tabulation of hard copy, electronic data processing), used to do as many as 80% of its custom projects in-house. Now it's less than 10%. The size of the in-house staff has remained about the same, but there is much more volume. Particularly confidential or difficult studies are conducted in-house.

■ Traditionally, in the area of custom ad hoc survey research projects, MRD had used outside companies for field work only; the questionnaires were sent to MRD for processing, printing of a final tabular report, and analysis. Now, six survey companies are "qualified" to print reports, but analysis stays in-house. According to Mr. Herbold, this added capacity means that finished reports are being produced in less than half the time previously.

■ P&G acquired a part interest in Metaphor Computer Systems, a Mountain View, Calif.-based company specializing in sophisticated data-interpretation software and hardware. One reason for this was "the obvious MRD applications." MRD is now well-populated with CRT [cathode ray tube] stations manufactured by Metaphor.

■ In contrast to the tight-lipped past, P&G's MRD personnel today feel more comfortable discussing their activities, although discussion doesn't extend much beyond what is fairly well known in the trade anyway.

MRD's organization

The organization of P&G's market research department reveals how various data sources are integrated into P&G's decision-making process.

The consumer research group consists of research brand staffers assigned to each of P&G's operating divisions: paper products, food products, health and personal care, beverage, et al. Most of their work pertains to custom ad hoc survey support for marketing brand managers.

About three years ago, a second major group, market measures, was organized. Its staffers also were assigned to operating divisions. The reason for this, says Mr. Herbold, was that "technologies were exploding" in the area of syndicated market measures and test marketing. "The intent was to digest [the new developments], figure out how to use them, build the new systems that enable us to take maximum advantage of the new tools. Now that we've got that perfected," says Mr. Herbold, "we're beginning to think about the evolutionary step of equipping the research brand supervisors not only to run consumer research for their divisions, but also to do the market measures."

Most users of single-source test-marketing facilities like BehaviorScan, ERIM, or AdTel take reports from suppliers. MRD, however, takes delivery of the whole database for analysis—and education.

Backing up the research brand staffs are specialty groups Mr. Herbold calls "technique oriented." One such group is advertising/media research. "We view copy testing as a very serious business," he says, "and we want to make sure that we've got ironclad standards on how to test copy." Given this, one MRD staff unit specializes in new TV copy-testing technique development and manages a normative database of all P&G copy-testing results. (All P&G copy testing is fielded through one outside supplier, Research Systems Corp., Evansville, Ind.)

Other specialty groups include market modeling (pre-test market testing and forecasting), package testing, concept testing, qualitative research and marketing information systems. "There is a lot of R&D inherent in these activities," says Mr.

Herbold. "When we see an important business is-sue for the future, [we approach it by organizing] around it—to try to invent, from a research standpoint—to come up with a contribution we can quantify, validate and then spin off." Some of the work of MRD's specialty staffs is used in non-marketing areas such as the public relations de-partment (for which it conducts surveys), person-nel, packaging design, etc.

The field and data-processing units within MRD have the additional function of conducting periodic appraisal reviews with outside research companies. "We talk with them about those aspects of their work we like, those aspects we'd like to improve and new capabilities we would like for them to con-sider for development," says Mr. Herbold.

The MRD field manager and data-processing managers are deeply involved, too. They have a group of supplier representatives who often visit outside research companies "to make sure the work is being done in a way that satisfies our stan-dards," Mr. Herbold says. I personally view the whole thing [MRD] as an independent company. R&D develops our products; field and data pro-cessing is our manufacturing, and so on, he says." Mr. Herbold and MRD report to the VP-advertising at P&G.

The new era

In an interview just before his promotion to the newly created position of manager-information services—with both the market research depart-ment and management systems division reporting to him—Mr. Herbold spoke about the rapidly changing U.S. research industry and the impact innovation is having on all package-goods market-ers. "Over the past five years, new ways of read-ing consumer behavior have emerged, and most are electronic; that will continue. That provides people who study consumer behavior an im-mense, rich, new database. The skills that are needed in a market research department today to tap and exploit that information are much differ-ent than before that information was available. Now, you have to understand how to boil down those data and to determine what measures you want to select and study in terms of their impor-tance.

"So, today most market research departments need a lot more EDP, quantitative, analytical re-sources for data reduction, and systems people who are up to date—and, hopefully, ahead of the pack. Then you can take a database and turn it into a learning experience. But it takes a lot of money and lot of people." Obviously, P&G has both.

CHAPTER TWENTY ONE

Dealing with No. 1 —
The Supermarket Trade

Recognizing the need to upgrade its image with the supermarket trade, P&G responds with "We hear you."

D ON CUNNINGHAM SHUDDERS WHEN HE RE-members Procter & Gamble Co.'s relationship with the supermarket trade. As a trainee in brand management in 1948, the young Northwestern University graduate was sent by P&G on his first sales call to a Chicago supermarket. "Hi, I'm from Procter & Gamble," Mr. Cunningham, now senior VP at Cochrane Chase, Livingston & Co., Los Angeles, recalls saying to a supermarket buyer. The buyer, brandishing a meat cleaver and shouting obscenities, chased young Mr. Cunningham out of the store.

Fred Clay, now marketing manager-consumer sales division, Presto Foods, City of Industry, Calif., remembers a trip to a New Hampshire supermarket. During his stint as a P&G brand assistant in the early 1970s he arrived at the store with a local P&G representative. "No sooner had the rep introduced me as an executive from Cincinnati, the retailer tore him [the rep] up one side and down the other," recalls Mr. Clay. After enduring the tirade, the shaken Mr. Clay asked the rep if the retailer would still buy from him. "Every day," was the rep's reply.

Call it stormy. Call it a love-hate relationship. Procter & Gamble's relations with the supermarket industry have always been controversial. "They'd come in with their wing-tip shoes and tell buyers the products they needed on their shelves," explains Jim Lewis, buyer-merchandiser at Safeway Stores' Phoenix division. "They didn't care what the retailers wanted or needed."

P&G's seeming arrogance nurtured deep resentment among the retail trade. While it always maintained uniform policies toward the trade and its sales personnel were among the best prepared, P&G was without peer when it came to getting its way. Some contend P&G's sales force wasn't beyond subtle threats. "Retailers were under intense pressure to try what the [P&G] salesman was recommending," recalls Mr. Clay. "If not, there was some suggestion your allocation [of P&G prod-ucts] wouldn't come through."

In the past, P&G's position as the nation's largest advertiser gave it the muscle to rule the trade. Retailers had to put up with what some considered shabby treatment because P&G's products were in such high consumer demand. Then, in 1979–80, P&G's fortunes changed, as unit sales declined in key areas and competition accelerated. P&G's problems coincided with dramatic changes in the retail landscape. Once viewed by P&G as mere middlemen, retailers gained clout in the marketplace as they grew through business consolidations and mergers. With the advent of sophisticated computer-scanning sales data, they also had become more savvy. P&G could no longer control every aspect of its business. It had to share power with its customers.

"It [the company] learned it can't strong-arm the trade anymore. Retailers won't accept anything thrown down to them," says Bob Hughes, senior editor of *Supermarket Business*, New York. Responding to the changing marketplace, P&G loosened some of its promotional policies, realigning its payment terms to bring them in line with standard business practices. In addition to altering the language of its contracts to make them more understandable, it began offering extended credit and raised coupon-handling fees. It began offering retailers more flexibility in the timing and brands associated with P&G-funded promotions. (Competitors responded by offering more liberal promotional packages to the trade.)

N. Duane Stauffer, a San Francisco-based P&G district sales manager in its bar soap and household-cleaning products division, maintains P&G never actually changed its policies toward retailers. He acknowledges P&G had an image problem but insists its policies and objectives have remained constant. Today, however, P&G is better at communicating its point of view to the industry, he argues.

In a major public relations campaign begun in

the early '80s, that consisted of print ads regularly placed in trade publications like *Supermarket News* and *Progressive Grocer,* P&G set out to upgrade its image with retailers. The intent was to "tell them of our mutual opportunities and challenges," Mr. Stauffer says. In 1982 it dispatched then Chairman Owen B. "Brad" Butler to a convention of the Food Marketing Institute, the Washington-based trade organization.

"It is this basic attitude—the desire to do business within a framework of integrity—that governs many of our decisions, some of which I know are unpopular with some of you," Mr. Butler told the assembly. "I know there are times when we seem rigid in our policy. I know there are times when it seems to some of you that we are not willing to listen. I hope we can reverse that feeling because we are at least as anxious to listen to you as we are to obviously in our interest to offer the kinds of merchandising programs for our brands which you like and want."

FMI acknowledged Mr. Butler's efforts by giving him its highest honor, the William H. Albers Trade Relations Award. When it presented the award, Stephen D'Agostino, then-chairman of FMI, noted that, "Under his guidance, P&G has taken leadership roles in developing equitable programs for the industry in such matters as coupon-handling allowances and the development of legally approved and non-discriminatory backhaul programs [programs allowing wholesalers and retailers to haul manufactured goods to retail outlets themselves]."

Coinciding with the PR offensive, P&G changed its ads aimed at the trade to address the problem. "We hear you," early executions said. Today, ads outline P&G's contribution to retail profits and the technological innovations it has fostered. Current ads feature testimonials from significant players in the supermarket trade, including Don Smith, Safeway Stores' group VP-director of marketing.

"P&G recognized that to succeed it had to work with the trade," explains Richard Frederick, VP-management supervisor, Saatchi & Saatchi Compton, New York, which handles the campaign. "You can't benefit with all the elements of the business unless you're working side-by-side."

In recent years, P&G also has named key executives to act as liaisons with key customers like Dayton Hudson Corp., K mart Corp., Kroger Co. and Safeway.

"One of the challenges we have is that [our customers] often see several different P&G sales organizations," explains Mr. Stauffer. "Many times there were issues that particular departments weren't equipped to handle because they were corporate rather than departmental issues." P&G has tried to smooth relations by sharing with the trade some of its research relating to displays, pricing and advertising. Most recently, it began a Direct Profitability Program that allows retailers to gauge the cost of handling a product from warehouse to consumer sale through a computer model. It is also using a Uniform Communication Standard system that allows customers' computers to talk to P&G's computers for automatic ordering. "We're trying to give the retailers flexibility," says Mr. Stauffer.

In a major change, P&G last year began testing the use of food brokers—traditionally more loyal to the trade than to manufacturers—to supplement its sales force. After nearly 70 years of using its sales force exclusively, P&G is using 12 full-service brokers to sell Always and Puffs paper products in 40% of the U.S. It also has been using brokers in southern California for Duncan Hines cookies and Pringle's potato chips and in Florida and Texas for other P&G brands.

How has P&G's new attitude affected its image? Most supermarket buyers say P&G has improved over days past, but there are still complaints. "I'd like them to get in touch with the real world," says Safeway's Mr. Lewis, who insists P&G

should offer "slotting allowances" or additional funds to offset the cost to retailers of storing and selling manufacturers' goods. P&G doesn't offer such allowances, although it does offer a variety of other trade deals. Mr. Lewis also complains that he rarely sees executives from P&G headquarters.

Competitors acknowledge the PR blitz has helped enhance P&G's image, but question whether much has really changed. "They [P&G] were able to get out there and sell a lot of sizzle, but they still don't throw lots of dollars to the trade," says Bill Robertson, a former VP-marketing for Phoenix-based Dial Corp.'s laundry and household products division. "[Yet] they still control almost every aisle."

CHAPTER TWENTY TWO

Tenuous Partnership
P&G and Its Ad Agencies

❧

Working for the country's top package-goods marketer evokes mixed feelings. For some agencies, it's a case of knowing P&G "wants and appreciates good advertising and has the money to spend on it." Others, however, claim the company is arrogant and vindictive.

PROCTOR & GAMBLE'S WEIGHTY IMPACT ON the advertising agency business goes far beyond its size or reputation as a package-goods marketer. That it is the No. 1 U.S. advertiser only partly helps to explain why, if such things could be measured, it would also be the No. 1 influence on the agency business.

Why does it seem to matter so much when P&G reassigns brands, or why it smiles on one agency and frowns on another? The answer seems to be the consistency of its character and principles regarding agency relations and its belief that the brand-franchise building nature of advertising genuinely affects the success of its business. The history of P&G's agency relations is striking because of how much that history repeats itself. Ever

since Harley Procter, a son of one founder, was inspired in 1879 to rename P&G's White Soap as Ivory, this company has believed in the promise of a brand, its relationship with the consumer—which is what advertising is about.

P&G has loomed large in pivotal developments in the agency business in the 1980s, whether it was its negative reaction to Saatchi & Saatchi Co.'s 1986 acquisition binge or Young & Rubicam's dramatic 1983 resignation of $60 million in P&G business to take on rival Colgate-Palmolive's $120 million in billings. The latter was a move that essentially declared the primacy of worldwide account growth.

But for every recent development, there's a historical parallel. P&G's conflict policy figured prominently in the Saatchi and Y&R events, as it did 25 years ago when Gardner Advertising became the first agency to resign P&G because it saw limitations to its growth in the P&G policy. A phrase used 26 years ago to begin an ADVERTISING AGE story about a P&G agency switch—"Procter & Gamble, the company that remains loyal to its agencies and moves an account only as a last resort"—is still valid.

Moreover, despite some views that P&G is a recent convert to the values of creativity in advertising, the company in the late 1960s and early 1970s was assigning brands to several of the hottest agencies during the era of advertising's creative revolution: Papert, Koenig, Lois; Lells, Rich, Greene; and Doyle Dane Bernbach.

Even the descriptions of P&G from its agencies, although glowing as one would expect from any agency even about its worst client, explain why P&G is different. It's quite simple and basic: "They believe in advertising, they truly believe in what you provide," says Robert Jordan, vice chairman of Saatchi & Saatchi DFS Compton, New York, who has worked on the P&G account for almost 30 years at forerunner Compton Advertising. "A lot of clients question why they should advertise at all. That's a battle you don't really have to fight."

The company is an "advertising dream," says Neil Kreisberg, an exec VP who oversees Grey Advertising's P&G business. He has worked on the account at that New York agency for 20 years. "They come with a good product, they want and appreciate good advertising and they have the money to spend on it."

"They're one of the best clients an agency can have," says Patrick McGrath, president of Jordan, Case, Taylor & McGrath, New York, who previously had worked on P&G business in the 1960s for seven years at Benton & Bowles (now D'Arcy Masius Benton & Bowles), and was able to attract P&G as a client to his current agency in

1985. "I think they have a greater appreciation of what an agency can do for you. They really do believe in the power of advertising." Not everyone would agree that P&G is the best thing since white soap, however. They're tough, as even their own agency fans agree. "Pussycats they're not," says Mr. Kreisberg. Mr. McGrath notes, "There are some violent battles and hand-to-hand combat." But while both agency executives follow those comments with paeans to P&G's fairness and ultimate reasonableness, others say the flip side of the company's principles are arrogance and vindictiveness. One agency executive, who previously had worked closely with P&G and wishes to remain anonymous, laughs scornfully at the word "partnership" describing P&G's agency-client relations. "If they make a change, they'll do it with a snarl," he says, and holds one hand high and the other low to describe P&G's idea of partnership. "One's up here and one's down there," he says.

Certainly, P&G's advertising has received enough vocal creative criticism over the years to raise questions about what in advertising the company is committed to. But P&G is not a static, unchanging, monolithic entity, as it is so often portrayed. It has made significant changes in how it works with its agencies and develops creatively engaging advertising. Certainly the current P&G reel shows much more variety than P&G generally is given credit for.

The willingness to be more open creatively is what the P&G agencies point to as the significant shift in recent years. "They're less insulated," says Mr. McGrath. "Their biggest change is the acknowledgment or interest in outside circumstances. They're more interested in what other people are doing and how they're using other techniques." However, he adds, "They don't change unless they're absolutely sure that changing something is the best thing to do, but they are more apt to be modifying things."

Ed Meyer, the chairman-CEO of Grey Advertising who has been involved with P&G business ever since his first job in advertising in the early 1950s at the now-defunct Biow Co., believes the client's expansion into new business areas has contributed to its change. "In the last five years in particular, they have been much more inclined to try a broader range of techniques. Their palette has expanded considerably," he says, explaining that foods, coffees, beverages, etc., have become more important in the product mix, and when there is "a wider range of products you market, you come up against more vocabulary." What makes that relevant, says Mr. Meyer, is that "one of the remarkable things about Procter & Gamble is that they work at trying to learn from experience." If somebody learns something on one brand, "they try to distribute the learning across the entire company . . ."

That there has been a formal change in P&G's agency relationships is confirmed by the company. But it is continuity and change relevant to the advertising development process that make P&G such a force on the agency business.

Robert Goldstein, P&G's VP-advertising, describes what led to the current changes and how they affect the process by which P&G and its agencies develop advertising. He feels P&G has become better at working with its agencies, and traces the change back some three years to complaints from Leo Burnett Co., Chicago. "I think we've gotten a lot more sensitive to the issue in the last several years," he says. "Part of this was when we asked each of the agencies to send their top management in to talk to us specifically about . . . how they rated the work they were doing for us relative to their other clients, and to talk to us about what we could do to be a better client and, as a result, get better advertising. And [we wanted to know] what they could do, in turn, to be a better agency for us."

Those meetings came about, says Mr. Goldstein, as "an outgrowth of a discussion with Leo Burnett, one of our more outspoken and independent agencies. [The agency] had commented to one or more of our senior executives about the relationships that characterized some of the clients with whom they worked very well and very successfully—the Philip Morrises and the United Airlines, the Charlie the Tuna people at StarKist. . . . That sparked the idea.

"The other piece of the process was that we began to step back and look at our own advertising relative to our competition and ask ourselves, what is it that leads to really successful advertising? How much of what we have is really successful? How much of it is okay? How much of it is bad? We became aware that, apart from the advertising itself, there's a process that goes into creating it. We began to separate the end result from how you got there. We began to realize that sometimes the most effective way to affect the end result was to work on the process rather than simply to say, what we need is better advertising. In fact, there are very few cases in which simply saying [that] gets you better advertising. Nobody's out there putting advertising on the air that they don't think is any good." The result was that P&G began to "delve a lot more deeply" into how better to bring out "the integrity of independent thought."

"The Procter & Gamble ethos is one of a democracy of ideas, where everybody can have an opinion and we hash them out," Mr. Goldstein says. "We debate them, we make a decision; then we all put our shoulder to the wheel. And that's important with the agencies, too. We've always talked that way, but in practice, the relationship has not always been as two-sided as it ought to be. I think we've come to recognize the need to [encourage] a hard-hitting, two-way democracy [between P&G and its agencies] and not a situation in which we have the upper hand."

Accomplishing these changes has included working on the attitude of P&G brand and advertising executives. "What you basically do is remind them copy is important and make it clear that they have a responsibility for helping generate outstanding advertising, and that they are going to be judged and rewarded on that. [We let them] talk with the agencies, the agencies with them, and then with each other."

In addition to copy training, "Today we have meetings that are a series of programs for associate advertising managers and even advertising managers. We have it across division teams. They address issues like, 'How come, Charlie, you're getting this great copy there and we're not getting it over here?' They talk about what they do and how, and there's cross-pollination as well as formal training. We've always had some [interdivision discussions] but we've organized more of it. We redirected the attention, the time, that was devoted to this subject. Brand managers in today's environment have a lot of responsibility and a tremendous range of demands on their time. So we took some things to reduce the distraction from [what] we thought was really important [in order] to get more time on copy and creative marketing, generally, but particularly advertising."

Mr. Goldstein explains further that competitive advertising also influenced the changes. "There were some instances in which we were feeling that competitive advertising had gotten better than ours, or at least that we didn't have an advantage." But it also was something the company had known it had to explore. "I found a note I wrote in 1980 that said, 'Hey, look, part of what we ought to be thinking about in the agencies is the process that we're working on.' It took us two or three years, but I think that everybody today in the company is a lot more sensitive to both structural changes and psychological and organizational change."

In terms of specific changes, Mr. Goldstein says, "There have been a number of what I think are improvements in training and sensitizing our own people; streamlining the decision-making

process to get advertising to the ultimate decision makers much more quickly; encouraging the agencies to speak up when there are differences of opinion." When such differences arise, "Rather than continuing to debate it, [we now try] to resolve it by appealing within this hierarchy of what I call the democracy of ideas.

"One of the ways you find out that you can make improvements is by comparing what you're doing in the best operations and the not-so-good operations. So all of these things existed at some places at some time [within P&G]. What we tried to do was start an epidemic of it. More than anything else," he adds, "it was simply saying, 'Recognize that this relationship needs cultivation, recognize that the copy in advertising is important, recognize that you're responsible for getting great advertising out of the agencies, not that the agencies are responsible for bringing you great advertising while you sit like a bump on a log.'

"More of a partnership developed, and I think we gave the agency more support, more breathing room. I think they gave us better results." P&G even instituted in 1986 a creative award, which it called the World Class Copy Awards, for its agencies. The advertising campaigns that grew out of that process include the Folgers' "Wakin' up" campaign and efforts such as Always' "Wings," Bounce's "Jump," Jif's "Jiference," White Cloud's "Little Clouds" and Zest's "Zestfully." Some of those campaigns are somewhat different from [the 'formula' advertising] people have accused us of having in the past. And some of it can fit very comfortably within those formulas," says Mr. Goldstein.

"Our great marketing successes of the last year are the Tide, Crest and Pampers relaunches. In the case of Tide, the advertising that we are using is slice-of-life. In the case of Crest, it is a stand-up presenter. In the case of Pampers, it is a testimonial. Gee whiz, aren't those the same old formats that have been associated with the company? The answer is, yes, they are. And you know what? They built an awful lot of business last year and they are every bit as important a part of the company today as they ever were.''

Mr. Goldstein disputes the idea there was any less risk-taking in the past than now. The stereotype of P&G as method-driven and unable to make a decision without a pre-test go-ahead ''was nonsense when I was a young brand manager and it's still nonsense.'' He offers the Scope ''Medicine breath'' campaign as an example. ''It was an outgrowth of [an idea of a] brand manager who went beyond giving facts and figures to the agency. When he was sitting there trying to figure out why people wouldn't use his product—which tasted better than Listerine and was just as effective—he was sniffing the bottle [of Listerine] and he said, 'My God, this stuff smells like medicine. I don't know why anybody would use it.' [That idea] led to a campaign called medicine breath that rocketed the Scope share from what I guess started out at 15% to 25%. It's that kind of

digging and going beyond simply name, rank, and serial number that is one of the responsibilities of a brand manager—the client—in this type of relationship.''

Mr. Goldstein also gives an example of advertising risk-taking from his own brand days at P&G. ''In 1967, I believe, we ran a spread in *Life* showing a toothbrush with some Crest on it. The headline was 'Now Crest is only 26 flavors behind Howard Johnson's.' That was when we introduced mint flavor, our second Crest flavor. I don't think anybody can characterize that as formula advertising.

''Many of the techniques that today are associated with [our products] in many cases were forms we invented and had to ourselves for a long time. Then everybody else started copying them. I think the continuing-presenter format is a widely copied version. Some of the best testimonials on television today are culled from the people who stop your headaches at Tylenol. And goodness knows, in the mid-'60s we were running 'a sock in

P&G's current U.S. advertising agencies

Agency	Year retained	Agency	Year retained
1. Saatchi & Saatchi Compton (formerly Blackman Co. and then Compton Advertising.)*	1922 to date	9. Glick & Lorwin Group (subsidiary of WCRS Group-North America)	1965 to date
2. DFS Dorland Worldwide (formerly Blackett Sample Hummert and then Dancer Fitzgerald Sample.)*	1933 to date	10. Wells, Rich, Green	1968 to date
		11. Medicus Intercon International (Partner Company of D'Arcy Masius Benton & Bowles)	1972 to date
3. D'Arcy Masius Benton & Bowles (formerly Benton & Bowles)	1941 to date	12. Klemtner Advertising	1977 to date
4. Leo Burnett Co.	1951 to date	13. Ketchum/Mandabach & Sims	1980 to date
5. Grey Advertising	1956 to date	14. Lally, McFarland & Pantello	1982 to date
6. Tatham-Laird & Kudner (formerly Tatham-Laird	1956 to date	15. Burrell Advertising	1983 to date
		16. Dimensional Marketing (DMI)	1985 to date
7. N W Ayer, Inc. (account from Cunningham & Walsh, acquired by N W Ayer, January, 1987)	1963 to date	17. Jordan, Manning, Case, Taylor & McGrath	1985 to date
		18. FCB/Lever Katz Partners	1985 to date
8. Northlich, Stolley, Inc.	1965 to date	19. Peter Rogers Associates	1985 to date
		20. Slater, Hanft, Martin	1985 to date

*Agencies merged June 1987 to form Saatchi & Saatchi DFS Compton.

a sock in a pocket' Tide testimonials. The presenters take different forms. Some of them are real; some of them are animated. The ones that failed you've forgotten about; the ones that continue [to air] every night on TV are . . . still on because it still works.

"The vignette or slice-of-life commercial, which is one of the earliest of ours, today is a much smaller percentage of our advertising—probably under 15%. But a lot of people make very successful use of them.

"The other thing you have to understand . . . is that the nature of the product line of Procter & Gamble has changed dramatically in my career," Mr. Goldstein continues. "When I went to work here there were a couple of brands in the food division, a couple of brands in the toilet goods division, and the soap business—the soap business was 99% of it. Today those products, with a few exceptions like Prell, tend to be pretty functional.

"We're looking for advertising that builds the business, that increases the brands' position," he says, "but . . . we're looking for advertising that creates an enduring equity value. It's the kind of things that the Jolly Green Giant has done or the 'Friendly skies of United,' " he says. "It's the kind of thing we've done with purity and mildness in '99 44/100' with Ivory, and Dawn's grease-handling story, or Scope's 'medicine breath' or 'squeezably soft' Charmin. Sometimes it's called personality. Sometimes it's expressed as brand character," Mr. Goldstein says.

"They hunger for world-class advertising. They know what works, what really works," says Stuart Upson, chairman and co-CEO of Saatchi & Saatchi Advertising. His father was a VP at P&G; he first became associated with the P&G account in 1946. Mr. Upson was one of those who felt P&G's creative thrust was often misunderstood and under-appreciated. "A lot of their products are huge tonnage. They're trying to change habits from some very major brands, and [consumers]

need something to be convinced, not with gentle music, or big guffaws . . . many of their products [face competition] in areas that are big on private labels or no labels. You have to have a product that is better—and better enough on important points that it is advertisably better. They don't blow smoke," says Mr. Upson, noting that he thought P&G was misunderstood. "I think people think they work to a formula which can be imitated. They don't, and it can't."

John Bowen, chairman-CEO of D'Arcy Masius Benton & Bowles, New York, who started on P&G's sales force in 1949, also feels P&G's creative commitment was misunderstood. "If you're a copywriter and you have an idea and the strategic base is right, you have enough leeway to have that idea produced. You can . . . try it out until there is consensus in one form or another. The Bounce 'Jump' advertising was sold as an idea, tested as an idea and run as an idea," he says.

These two top agency executives are attesting to P&G's belief in partnership with its agencies and its integrity in dealing with its agencies. "They follow the principles of fairness and honesty," says Mr. Bowen. "When P&G withdrew Rely tampons from the market, they went to DMB&B, their agency, and said, 'We realize it's a hardship.' They said they didn't want anybody to be let go and offered compensation," he adds. Although he refused the offer, noting, "We are very healthy on your other business, don't think this is warranted and take our lumps along with you," P&G insisted that the agency take a check. "They meant it to be a generous gesture, although we weren't planning to let people go anyway," he says.

"Part of it is that you are a partner," says Mr. Upson. "There's nothing you can't know about your brands. You have the right to make advertising you believe in even if you can't sell it to them [P&G]. You can produce it and they'll pay for it. They'll make the advertising and test it. That's pretty unique." Mr. Upson notes that there is an absence of arbitrary personal decisions. "I haven't seen more than two or three decisions in all these years where somebody just wants to do it his way. When you go down in flames, usually the brand manager goes with you."

In the same vein, Mr. Upson says about the Encaprin introduction—one of P&G's more visible failures in which DFS was a partner—"We mutually made some mistakes. But you really do work together so much that there's very little finger pointing. They're as demanding of us as they are of themselves." Grey's Mr. Kreisberg observes, "They're the kind of client that really views their agency as partners. They've been willing to discuss everything from how many meetings there should be to who approves copy to how much will be spent on advertising."

When Saatchi bought DFS and Compton, P&G did not waver in its conflict policy and longtime P&G shop DFS suffered. "We were disappointed and chagrined, but we were not surprised," says Mr. Upson, who was CEO of DFS. "It was part of their honesty in sticking to their principles and sticking to their policies. We didn't like it a damn bit. It was very painful, emotionally and financially, but we couldn't get mad at them upfront. We always hoped they would bend but we didn't expect them to," he says.

"The long pull is the way you operate with these people," says Mr. Bowen. "The relationships with agency people are decades long. If you understand how they operate and you operate that way over the years, they'll stick with you through thick and thin."

That is true in products, as Mr. Jordan can remember. In 1969, he was involved in P&G's attempt to launch Tag, a liquid laundry detergent. The product never made it. "They got to an Era and a Liquid Tide eventually," he notes. "They are good at long-term thinking." At P&G, "the great well-founded idea will eventually win the day."

P&G, although reluctant to make agency changes, felt it had no alternative in the Saatchi & Saatchi case where agencies within the holding company handled competitive brands. "We thought about it as a point of principle," says Mr. Goldstein. "We made the decision right away we weren't going to change the conflict policy. We sat down and said, 'What do we get for it; what does it cost; how reasonable is it?' I turned to my favorite advertising mentor, a man named David Ogilvy, and he said, 'A lawyer may represent a client he knows to be guilty of murder, and a surgeon may operate on a client he dislikes, but professional detachment doesn't work in advertising.' We looked at our relationships with the agencies [and concluded] there was simply no practical way that we felt we could abandon a good sound policy because of what it was going to cost us. It cost us dearly and I didn't like it. It made my year miserable, and it certainly didn't help our business in the short term. But the decision was made swiftly and clearly because it was a question of principle. Do we want to have agencies organizing themselves around a conflict policy by incorporating different names on different floors or different buildings or in different cities?

"And we said, if we do that we might as well have basically no conflict policy. At the heart of it is conflict of interest," says Mr. Goldstein. "The security issue is a real and specific manifestation of that." Asked why it took so long to act if the decision was made right away, Mr. Goldstein says, "There was some pleading [by the agencies] going on, but it didn't really take that long. The Bates [Saatchi's acquisition of Ted Bates Worldwide] thing tipped it off, really. The Dancer acquisition was the first one that raised an issue and we did have some discussions about it. It took them awhile to consummate that and it was structured in a very unique way. . . . The decision was made and then it took us a couple of months to actually figure out what to do with the business. Once the

Bates acquisition was made, I think it was clear that was the way we had to resolve it. There was no choice in the matter.''

Rival Colgate-Palmolive's presence at Bates was not an issue. "Colgate was gone in a matter of weeks. That was clear from the day they bought it. They said they would be breaking up with Colgate.''

Also, P&G's initial impression was that the acquisitions might have no impact. "We were told last summer that it would have no impact, that all of these things would be totally independent, right?'' Mr. Goldstein says, noting that was Saatchi's public statement.'' We're not anti-merger,'' he says, noting he was "fully supportive'' of N W Ayer's acquisition of Cunningham & Walsh as well as the merger that created D'Arcy Masius Benton & Bowles. Because P&G expressed itself by moving business, the key question is how it evaluates agencies for new assignments or for adding an agency to the family.

"We have been very reluctant to change agencies,'' says Mr. Goldstein. "The reasoning behind it is that all of our agencies can write good, even great copy. And the process of changing agencies is very upsetting. It's a total disruption of the business and the relationships. It takes a while to get around to establishing them. You might as well count on losing a year. Although we don't have a lot of experience doing it, the experience we do have is that it seldom fixes the long-run problem. There are a few cases where an agency has been a catalyst for basic change, but when we've got a long-run problem or something doesn't work and the business is going to hell, it's seldom as simple as [resolving the problem with] a new advertising campaign. When we can track the brands that have moved and have been fixed, as in the case with Pringle's or Bold, usually they got fixed in part because we made a fundamental strategic change involving the product and not just the advertising. Once in a while you get something

that's totally advertising, but it's a minority of the cases. It's a bad-odds bet. It doesn't mean you shouldn't do it, but it's no panacea,'' he says.

P&G's history with agencies is filled with changes. "The first recorded agency that we've turned up any record of is Procter & Collier, which we started working with before 1900 and apparently continued with until 1921. Compton, which formerly was under the name Blackman Co., started with us in 1922,'' Mr. Goldstein says.

"But it isn't a question of adding or not adding. We have agencies that have been appointed going back to 1912 and then for one reason or another—I don't know why—we broke up. We have agencies we've been with for 65 years. We have agencies we've brought in as a result of acquisitions of other companies, like Cunningham & Walsh, now a part of Ayer, but we broke in with the Folgers coffee business and we stayed with them and built up a broader and broader relationship. We have other agencies that have come with acquisitions where we parted company, both I think a long time ago and more recently. Said another way, I don't think this is a static phenomenon. It isn't that we have a policy that says we only have so many agencies and they have to be so big or so little. They range in size ... from Northlich Stolley here in Cincinnati or Slater Hanft Martin in New York, which are relatively small shops, to agencies like Saatchi, which, at least within its holding company configuration, is $7 billion in billings worldwide.

"Adding or subtracting really isn't the issue,'' Mr. Goldstein continues. "It isn't a philosophy and there aren't any rules.'' And there aren't really any specific guidelines, either. "This thing is really not like the Internal Revenue Service,'' says Mr. Goldstein, combating the image of P&G as the staid master of method. "You do not come in and whip out a form and check off a bunch of things.''

CHAPTER TWENTY THREE

How Keeping in Touch Pays Off for Potential P&G Shops

Making the trip to the "major leagues."

How does P&G make its decisions about agencies? A recent illustration is the selection in 1985 of Jordan, Case, Taylor & McGrath for the Zest brand. (The agency also was awarded the Bounty account last year.)

Becoming a P&G agency does confer a certain status, conceded Pat McGrath, JCT&M's president. "Suddenly we were in the major leagues," he says. "It helped us solidify a position we felt we had already achieved. Everybody knows how careful and serious P&G is about agencies and advertising."

Mr. McGrath, who had worked on Zest, Crest, Scope, Pampers and Prell when he was at Benton & Bowles in the 1960s, has "always had a long-range vision to work on that business again. I realized I could not work on it until we [the agency] were capable of it. I just kept in touch and kept them aware of our fledgling operation, Case & McGrath." After that shop merged with James Jordan's agency in 1980 and reached $80 million in billings, Mr. McGrath thought he could begin thinking about making his wish come true.

"I think that we made a presentation in late 1983," recalls Mr. McGrath. "Never did we have a conversation about P&G products. We resisted the temptation, though it popped up now and then, to go to them with solutions on problems with brands they have," he says. "We never talked about their products, but our ability to solve problems day in and day out. We shared work we had done for other clients and work James Jordan had done."

When the presentation was made in the Cincinnati office of P&G VP-Advertising Robert Goldstein, Chairman John Smale popped in just to say hello. "I hadn't seen him for 15 years, but he did not participate in the meeting. And after that we had no meeting for a year," says Mr. McGrath. "I kept sending information on what we were doing. I would also send cassettes of our work to other people who worked in P&G's advertising area," says Mr. McGrath, noting it was like any long-term selling job. In the first few months of 1985 it "became evident something was going on. There was more interest in having us show our latest reel," Mr. McGrath says, noting that two people who worked for Mr. Goldstein paid a visit to hear the same presentation given a year earlier.

JCT&M also was busy studying P&G's latest commercials, taping spots off the air "so we were ready to have an intelligent conversation about campaigns," says Mr. McGrath. "We never had any conversations about any particular products unless I initiated it," says Mr. McGrath, adding that P&G's questions focused on existing JCT&M work and "Why did you do this and not that?" Finally, he got a call requesting that he and Mr. Jordan, the agency's chairman, fly to Cincinnati, where it was announced they would be awarded Zest, previously handled by D'Arcy Masius Benton & Bowles.

From the P&G side of the story, the search also focused on general capability and not on specific products. After Young & Rubicam dropped P&G in 1983 and Doyle Dane Bernbach did the same in 1984, the company knew it had to find another agency. "We went out and we interviewed six or seven major agencies that would have been available to work with several of our divisions, but with some specific brands and parts of the business in mind," says Mr. Goldstein. P&G criteria for selecting an agency "starts with a view of 'What's advertising for?'" The answer, in P&G's case, is advertising "that sells the product without drawing attention to itself. And so we look at people, at agencies' feelings about advertising, what they want to get out of advertising. And it starts with advertising that sells as an end result.

"We look at businesses. How successful has the agency been in building businesses, selling products and services, particularly packaged goods?

We look for the advertising reel which shows humanity and something special and that really became a cutting edge," Mr. Goldstein says.

In the case of JCT&M, "They had a reel of advertising that had not only proven very successful for a wide variety of products, but it had some values in it which were less evident, a little bit different from those we had in Procter's stable of agencies before that. I think the same is probably true of Wells, Rich, Greene when we went to work with them in 1968. Those were the days of Benson & Hedges and Alka-Seltzer and the vignette copy, which was their hallmark. If you looked at that reel you'd say, 'You don't really see some of the humanity they were capturing in that reel in every piece of advertising that every agency writes.' And so that became the key issue.

"We look for basic business skills, good solid people who understand advertising, who have solid, strategic thinking skills, who have a track record of being able to deal with our kinds of business problems. You never know how well you're going to get along with an agency until you do it. You try to reduce the guesswork by looking at the experience the agency has, the copy the agency has, getting to know the people as well as you can."

Speculative presentations weren't requested or considered desirable. "No way, no sir," says Mr. Goldstein. "We basically looked at the agencies as developing a relationship, not as, 'Can you come up with what might be a great idea with a minimum of information at great expense to yourself?' I don't believe we've ever had a speculative presentation, and if an agency offered one, I wouldn't want to do it," says Mr. Goldstein. It's "just a waste of their money. Their presentation is the stuff they've got out there for their clients right now. That's the test of their abilities.

"There are P&G agencies, but there's no such thing as a set of criteria or type of copy or advertising that we want, or a size of agency or a location of the agency," he says.

But doesn't making an agency search that way force a prospective agency to reveal confidential information about existing clients? "We start off and say, 'Look, I'd like to talk to you about the results of this. If it's a brand that's competitive, or business that's competitive, or anything that you feel is sensitive, don't give it to us. We don't want it.' Now . . . let's talk about what's publicly available information," Mr. Goldstein says, noting that P&G has the same syndicated sales information as other marketers. "And usually, of course, there's such a breadth of brands on the reel, many of them aren't competitive at all. So I get a chance to learn some interesting things about the toy business, or the retail clothing business, or some areas I otherwise might not know about.

"The other point I'd offer is that, like a family relationship or getting married, a lot of this depends on the character, the ethics, the values and principles of the agency. They set the standards, the tone. They express the values usually of what they're planning to do. It's very important that the client be comfortable with that, and it's very important that the client be comfortable with what they agency wants to stand for. The marketplace is the ultimate test of advertising," says Mr. Goldstein, "but there's still some judgment in picking an agency, just as there is in deciding what campaign to go with.

"I don't care what the category is. If you're selling airline services, and if the airline develops a reputation as a result of the advertising where it celebrates performance attributes, and their share of market goes up . . . then that's the ultimate evaluation of it. The humanity issue, whether it's got some particularly sharp edge, is a guess at what makes it effective, and there's room for disagreement among even professionals as to what the edge is. But my sense is that, other than market sales, there's no objective way to measure the effectiveness of advertising."

CHAPTER TWENTY FOUR

Advertising in the '80s

Vivid images, creative copy and contemporary twists on traditional themes are hallmarks of much of P&G's print and TV advertising today.

Pampers

D'Arcy Masius
Benton & Bowles

Secret

Leo Burnett Co.

Era

Leo Burnett Co.

Oxydol   DFS Dorland Worldwide

Comet   Saatchi & Saatchi DFS Compton

Crisco   Saatchi & Saatchi DFS Compton

Citrus Hill   Cunningham & Walsh

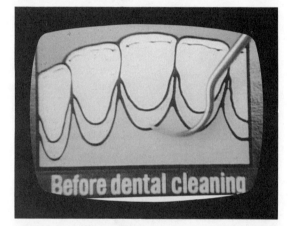

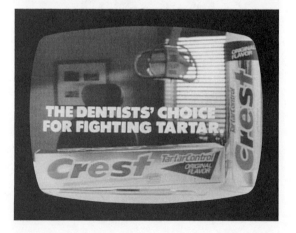

Vidal Sassoon
Peter Rogers Associates

Tartar Control Crest
D'Arcy Masius Benton & Bowles

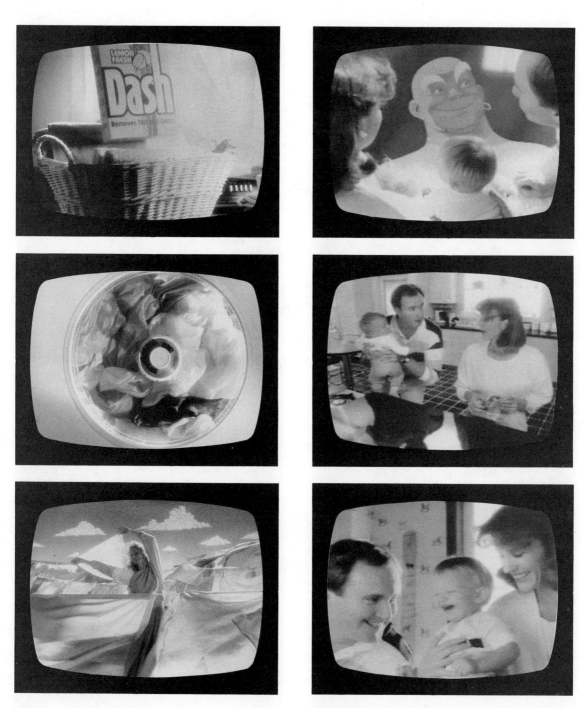

Dash

D'Arcy Masius Benton & Bowles

Mr. Clean

Tatham-Laird & Kudner

Head & Shoulders   Tatham-Laird & Kudner

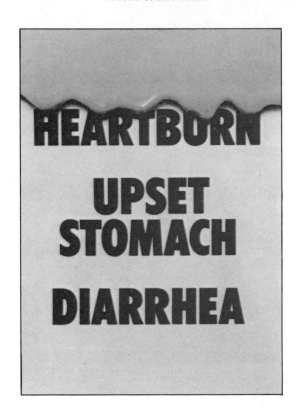

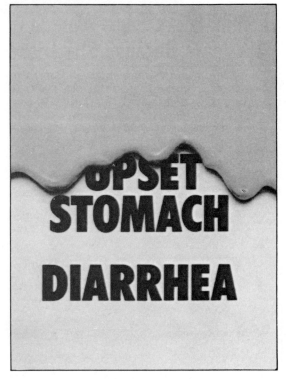

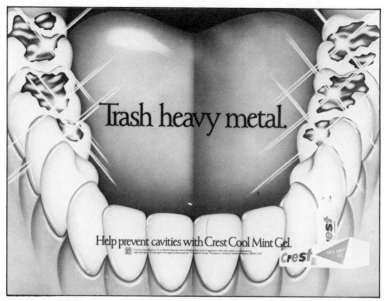

Crest   D'Arcy Masius Benton & Bowles

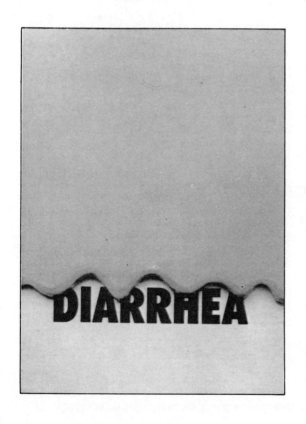

Pepto Bismol   Leo Burnett Co.

CHAPTER TWENTY FIVE

Where Those Ad Dollars Go

Competitors grudgingly acknowledge P&G's thoroughness and objectivity in media placement. While Crest, Tide and other big sellers get major TV support, the company is seeking greater efficiency, mainly through syndication. As dollars swing between national and spot TV, broad-based spending in other media buys constant weight in key categories.

P&G brands by ten-year spending

Product/brand	Media total	Magazine	Newspaper supplmnts	Network TV	Spot TV	Network radio	Outdoor
1. Crest	318,207.9	33,442.5	499.6	233,817.4	46,307.1	3,782.8	358.5
2. Folgers	297,891.3	1,104.1	627.8	151,109.1	141,398.5	3,651.8	0.0
3. Duncan Hines	265,312.0	39,794.9	525.8	163,554.1	61,437.2	0.0	0.0
4. Tide	230,155.5	27,665.1	3.6	134,108.8	68,288.3	0.0	89.7
5. Crisco	229,858.9	37,073.7	17.1	135,021.1	57,747.0	0.0	0.0
6. Pampers	209,419.2	15,578.2	51.8	137,499.6	56,285.7	0.0	3.9
7. Downy	164,815.7	6,816.5	46.1	115,709.8	42,243.3	0.0	0.0
8. Head & Shoulders	162,093.6	17,397.0	786.9	100,474.0	43,225.2	210.5	0.0
9. Ivory Bar Soap & Shampoo	157,773.9	5,700.4	0.0	107,199.0	44,362.1	512.4	0.0
10. Ivory Liquid & Snow	146,518.7	7,822.7	0.0	108,344.0	30,352.0	0.0	0.0
11. Luvs	144,736.9	14,251.7	0.0	63,822.5	66,458.6	0.0	204.1
12. Secret	141,607.5	15,992.9	99.4	93,544.5	31,961.1	0.0	9.6
13. Sure	138,968.5	11,470.0	193.0	101,447.6	22,391.3	3,466.6	0.0
14. Cheer	138,634.6	7,564.9	122.2	82,754.3	48,193.2	0.0	0.0
15. Bounce	136,883.4	9,775.5	0.0	90,765.5	36,342.4	0.0	0.0
16. Cascade	136,289.1	26,133.3	0.0	82,009.9	28,145.9	0.0	0.0
17. Era	135,857.4	4,458.5	190.0	78,545.3	52,663.6	0.0	0.0
18. Scope	120,554.5	9,739.2	47.6	83,874.0	26,870.4	0.0	23.3
19. Dawn	117,006.1	7,890.0	0.0	87,587.9	21,528.2	0.0	0.0
20. Prell	108,442.5	8,698.4	156.6	75,235.0	23,635.2	717.3	0.0
21. Bold	104,399.7	874.9	0.0	61,647.0	41,877.8	0.0	0.0
22. Joy Liquid Detergent	103,744.8	4,253.9	0.0	76,428.9	23,062.0	0.0	0.0
23. Coast	100,690.7	2,312.2	0.0	63,631.6	29,036.6	5,710.3	0.0
24. Bounty	99,444.3	5,214.6	81.8	50,312.1	43,796.7	0.0	39.1
25. Pringle's Potato Chips	98,880.4	127.8	273.8	68,378.8	30,046.2	53.8	0.0

NOTE: Dollars are in thousands.
Source: Leading National Advertisers, editions 1977 to 1987, including magazine and newspaper spending as reported by Publishers Information Bureau; network and spot tv and network radio spending as reported by Broadcast Advertisers Reports;and outdoor spending as reported by Institute of Outdoor Advertising and Outdoor Advertising Assn. of America.

THERE IS NO MYSTIQUE ABOUT PROCTER & Gamble Co. media spending. It tends to be as basic and pervasive as Lava soap planted by mothers in shower stalls of high school football teams across the U.S. At risk of oversimplifying matters, because P&G is a creative user of media to reach any audience, its measured media spending is TV and more TV.

A retrospective of P&G measured media totals for the past 10 years shows the company is no niche player but is after market dominance. Its top 25 products read like "Who's Who" in market brands, from No. 1 Crest toothpaste supported by $318.2 million in the decade to P&G's No. 25 spender, Pringle's potato chips, $98.9 million. Market leaders like Crest, Tide laundry detergent, Crisco shortening, Head & Shoulders shampoo, and Pampers and Luvs disposable diapers are kept in the public eye through heavy TV spending. In 1986, P&G maintained its No. 1 rank as the nation's biggest network TV advertiser, with expenditures of $456.3 million. It was a close second to PepsiCo in spot TV with $233.9 million, according to Leading National Advertisers. Within P&G, of the $6.05 billion spent the past 10 years in measured media, 60% went to network TV and 31% to spot TV.

Such 10-year summaries disguise more recent movements by P&G to bring greater efficiency to its TV buys. Faced with continued higher rates and declining audiences in the medium, P&G has moved increasingly into first-run syndication, syndicated movie packages for independent TV stations and production of made-for-TV movies. It also continues to produce daytime soap operas, although the number of productions has dropped to three from six in the early 1980s. It has added greater clout to spot TV buying by assigning agencies multi-brand buying in select markets as opposed to single-brand coverage across markets.

Media summaries for the 10 years also minimize P&G's surge begun in 1984 in network radio. It is now the ninth-ranked network radio advertiser, spending $13.9 million in 1986 (it was fifth in

1985 with a smaller expenditure). Also not included in the 10-year retrospective is network cable TV advertising because monitoring of that medium by LNA, the source for the 10-year data, only began in 1985. P&G, one of the first supporters of cable advertising, ranked the No. 1 advertiser in the medium with $27.7 million in spending in 1986. Totals for network and spot TV fluctuate as a percentage of total P&G media spending. Network has ranged from a high of 69% in 1982 to 55% in 1985; spot TV from a high of 35% in 1978 to a low of 25% in 1982. Spot and network also play teeter-totter: When one rises, the other falls as a percentage of the total.

This TV teeter-totter affect generally reflects heavy new-product support in regional markets (spot TV) followed by national TV bursts in support of national distribution. Undergirding spending swings between national and spot is broad-based spending in other media that buys constant weight in marketing categories.

A veteran of marketing battles often pitted against P&G says the P&G catechism for supporting products is essentially thoroughness, objectivity and the ability to read every shred of intelligence in the marketplace, adding that in typical P&G fashion, products are built up by needs of consumers.

The battle for greater ad play within P&G is intense within the segments for more dollars and greater efficiency. The personal-care segment among P&G's three leading segments has clearly emerged as the leader. Products in the segment have outspent those in P&G's other two major segments—laundry & cleaning products and food & beverages—dramatically since 1982. P&G has an "other" segment that largely involves industrial products. Personal care includes bar soaps, toothpastes, mouthwash, deodorants, haircare, skincare, paper tissue products, disposable diapers, cough/cold remedies and other pharmaceuticals.

P&G's major acquisitions in the past few years also are supporting this segment, or at least the healthcare subsegment within personal care. Norwich-Eaton Pharmaceuticals (Pepto-Bismol, Chloraseptic) was bought from Morton-Norwich Products in June 1982, Richardson-Vicks (Nyquil, Formula 44D cough syrup, Sinex, VapoRub, Oil of Olay, Clearasil, Vidal Sassoon haircare products) in November 1985, and several brands from G.D. Searle & Co. (Metamucil, Dramamine and Icy Hot) in December 1985.

Since 1982, personal care has claimed 44.2% of measured spending, followed by laundry & cleaning with 34.5% and food & beverages, 21.2%. Worldwide sales of the personal care segment have risen from 37% of total worldwide sales in 1982 to 42% in 1986. P&G reports in its 10-K worldwide ad costs of $1.297 billion in 1986, up 230% from 1977. Connecting this to worldwide sales, which grew from $7.28 billion to $15.44 billion during the period, the overall ad-to-sales ratio has grown from 6% to 8%.

An ad-to-sales ratio for U.S. segment operations can only be estimated. P&G, which had domestic sales of $5.32 billion in 1977 that grew to $11.21 billion in 1986, does not break out domestic sales or advertising by segment. The domestic ad-to-sales percentage in the divisions probably ranges from about 8% to 13% during the period, according to analysts. This estimate may be on low for several reasons. First of all, 73% of worldwide sales consistently have come from the U.S. in the 10-year period, and there is more availability of ad media in the U.S. than abroad, and media costs in the U.S., particularly TV, are high. A 10-year review of media spending within the three major P&G divisions follows. (U.S. media-spending data used for the review are for six media tracked over the period by LNA: network TV, spot TV, magazines, newspaper supplements, outdoor and network radio. P&G spends more on advertising than this six-media measured total, which is estimated by AD AGE as representing 70% of P&G's

total U.S. advertising in 1986, down from an estimated 81% in 1977—reflecting a shift toward "unmeasured" advertising support such as direct marketing, sampling, refund offers, price-off and on-pack premiums, point of sale, and promotions.

Personal care

P&G's worldwide segment sales of personal-care products have grown from $2.24 billion in 1977, or 31% of worldwide sales, to $6.45 billion, or 42% in 1986, giving this segment bragging rights over laundry & cleaning—P&G's leading segment until the 1980s.

Measured advertising in the six media reflects a similar movement, growing from $144.9 million in 1977 to $371.4 million in 1986, or from 38.9% to 47% respectively, of total P&G measured advertising.

Unlike other P&G segments, personal care has been influenced heavily by acquisitions, particularly the Richardson-Vicks buyout. LNA identifies 34 advertised items in 1977, which grew to 50 by 1984 before exploding to 115 at the end of

1985, the entry year for R-V on the LNA list. Personal care has been dominated in the 1980s by sales of disposable diapers. In 1980, disposable-diaper sales of $1.5 billion accounted for 41.7% of personal-care sales worldwide. The diapers, represented by Pampers and Luvs, grew to $2.5 billion in sales, or 38.8% of segment sales in 1986.

Measured advertising for disposable diapers expanded from $37.1 million in 1980, the first year Luvs began to move into national markets, to $40.7 million in 1986. Pampers has been on the market since 1961. Unmeasured advertising activity in some years has dwarfed measured media expenditures. For every dollar spent on measured advertising in 1980, disposable diapers generated $40 in sales in the marketplace, rising to $61 by 1986. But two years in that period broke consecutive-year growth patterns for diaper sales—1984 and 1985. After hitting $2.12 billion in sales in 1983, Pampers and Luvs stalled at $2.07 billion in 1984 and $2.04 billion in 1985. These years were marked by a shift from national to spot TV.

A switch back to national TV in 1986 put dis-

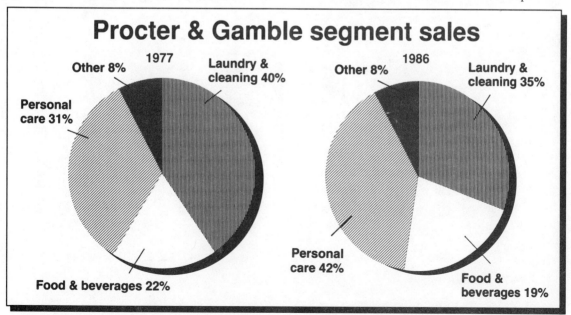

Procter & Gamble segment sales

1977
Other 8%
Laundry & cleaning 40%
Personal care 31%
Food & beverages 22%

1986
Other 8%
Laundry & cleaning 35%
Personal care 42%
Food & beverages 19%

posable diapers back on the growth track, but it left spot TV claiming only 22% of the segment's six measured-media total, down from 30% in 1985, as network TV jumped from 55% to 62% of the total. Magazines claimed 13% in 1986, up from 12% the prior year, and network radio stayed even at 3%. Cable, not included in the six-media total in this report, entered the picture for the first time with a respectable $15.2 million expenditure, supporting 25 products with at least $200,000 each.

P&G cut down on the six measured media during calendar 1986. The year opened six months after P&G recorded a 29% drop in worldwide net income for fiscal 1985 (ending June 30), the first

drop in years. Subtracting measured totals for R-V products for 1985 and 1986 of $93.2 million and $104.2 million, P&G measured spending on existing brands in the personal-care segment—the segment affected totally by R-V—showed a 7.6% increase in calendar 1985 to $317.6 million, before plunging 15.8% to $267.2 million in calendar 1986.

Measured advertising declines were recorded in the other two segments as well, while P&G reported worldwide growth in advertising costs of 20% to $1.29 billion in fiscal 1986 from 1985. This 1986 worldwide figure, which includes a half year's worth of spending for R-V and the Searle brands (minor spenders), indicates P&G either

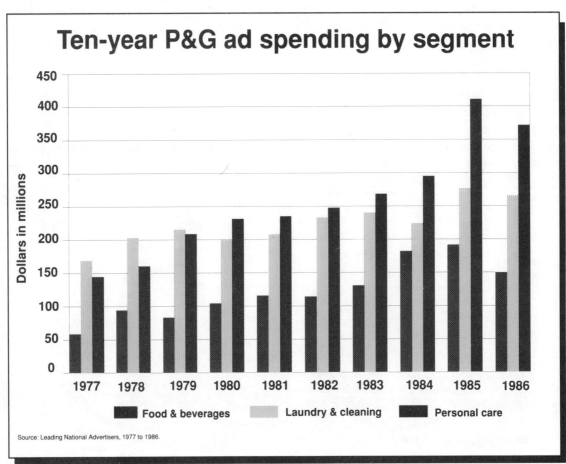

Ten-year P&G ad spending by segment

Source: Leading National Advertisers, 1977 to 1986.

spent a lot more in advertising abroad, or shifted to unmeasured media. The latter is more likely the scenario. Over the 10-year-period, network TV took 63% of total spending in six media, spot TV, 26% and magazines, 9%.

Laundry & cleaning

Although worldwide segment sales of laundry & cleaning products have grown, their percentage of the P&G total has diminished as personal care has taken off. L&C segment sales were $2.89 billion in 1977, or 40% of worldwide sales, and $5.35 billion, or 35% of sales, in 1986. Measured advertising for the segment followed a similar pattern, rising from $168.7 million to $264.8 million, although as a percentage of total P&G measured spending, it dropped from 45% to 33.5%.

This segment has shown little growth in the number of products advertised in the 10-year period. LNA records 36 items in 1977 and 39 in 1986. New-product introductions have not been strong in the mature laundry detergents market category except for the more recent phenomenon involving the introduction of liquid varieties of brands previously marketed only in powder form. The large number of players in the field are dominated by P&G and its Tide franchise. Tide measured media expenditures the past 10 years of $230.2 million rank it No. 4 among P&G advertised brands.

Market share data from Kidder, Peabody & Co., New York, comparing fall 1986 with fall 1985, indicate how P&G competes against itself. Liquid Tide, which burst on the market in 1985 with measured spending of $19.7 million, claimed a remarkable market share of 7.8% that grew to 10.2% a year later. All P&G detergents, which took a 51.7% share in fall 1985, however, grew to only 53.1% a year later—and part of that growth was Bold 3 liquid, claiming a 2.5% share in 1986 in its first full year on the market. Tide powder itself

dropped from an 18.6% share to 17.3%.

Most of the other litany of P&G products were cannibalized, and major competitors Colgate-Palmolive and Lever Bros. showed slight market-share gains from stepped-up marketing activity of traditional brands to new-product introductions.

In any comparison of P&G segments, laundry & cleaning has the disadvantage of being more narrowcast than the other two major segments in which products are not in as much head-to-head competition with each other. But it is in this segment that P&G has shown itself an innovator in segmenting a market and building new brands within it. While some company brands compete with one another, P&G mostly targets each into market segments and pushes them to leadership positions. A quick read of the brands in this segment—Biz, Bold, Bounce, Bounty, Cascade, Cheer, Comet, Dash, Dawn, Downy, Era, Gain, Ivory, Joy, Mr. Clean, Oxydol, Solo, Tide, etc.—indicates P&G is a firm believer in virtually limitless product life cycle.

The three dominant media in the six measured media over the 10-year period for the segment are network TV, 59%; spot TV, 35%; and magazines, 5%.

Food & beverages

Worldwide segment sales of food & beverages have grown from $1.59 billion in 1977 to $2.92 billion in 1986, although as a percentage of total sales, the segment has dropped from 22% to 19% in the 10-year period. The segment's measured advertising was charted at $58.5 million in 1977 and $149.7 million in 1986, although the latter tally was down from the spending high of $191.4 million in 1985.

Dominant advertising media for this segment among the six monitored by LNA over the past 10 years are network TV, 57%, spot TV, 34%, and magazines, 7%.

As a percentage of total P&G measured spending, food & beverages climbed from 15.7% to 19% during the 10-year period, reflecting the number of product introductions and line extensions to mark continually changing food trends.

In the number of products advertised from 1977 to 1986, the segment has grown from 18 to 45 advertised products. This matches the internal growth of the personal-care segment without its R-V or Searle contributions. This is characteristic of the food market in general, which is becoming more and more driven by health-related concerns. Part of that growth came through the acquisition in July 1980 of Crush International's U.S. operations, which produce Crush, Hires and Sun Drop soft drink brands. Measured spending on the brands in a field of heavy hitters has been largely in spot TV and as a result, nominal (a high of $5.2 million in 1982 on Crush beverages).

The Citrus Hill orange juice brand is characteristic of the swings in media spending involved in developing a brand "chestnut" like Crisco or Folgers. Citrus Hill frozen and ready-to-serve orange juice charged into the market with $8.6 million in spending in 1983, split between network and spot TV. That ballooned to $12.3 million in 1984 as the network share took command, before dwindling to $3.9 million in 1985 and virtually nothing in 1986.

Meanwhile, the franchise was being carried forth by Citrus Hill Select frozen and ready-to-serve orange juice that broke onto the market with $10.5 million in 1985, split between network and spot TV, and building to $13.7 million in 1986 as network spending grew. A new Citrus Hill line extension now has entered the picture— Citrus Hill Plus Calcium. J.A. Folger & Co., bought in 1963, was P&G's entry into the coffee market. Folgers is the No. 2 ranked brand among P&G products the past 10 years in measured spending with $297.9 million. Its other coffee brand, High Point decaffeinated, is a declining brand. Developed in 1975 to meet the growing decaffeinated market that accounted for 30% of consumption at the time, the High Point brand ranks No. 26 in measured spending with $91.9 million over the past 10 years. There currently is only a trace of measured media support for High Point.

A review of measured spending of the two brands demonstrates how High Point basically has served as point man for the venerable Folgers in the coffee marketing wars. High Point decaffeinated, which reached national distribution in 1980, peaked in measured spending of $9.4 million in 1982 before slipping back to $8.7 million in 1983, its last year on the measured charts. But as it dropped from the charts, Folgers came out with its still viable decaffeinated flanker.

A similar pattern developed in P&G's introduction of decaffeinated instant coffee. High Point led off, reaching national distribution in 1983 at a measured spending level of $23.7 million, but its measured spending level plunged to only $190,000 by 1984. That was the year Folgers decaffeinated instant was launched with a $6.4 million expenditure in measured media. Spending has grown ever since.

Internal growth has produced new brands like Puritan Oil, heavily tested in the late 1970s before hitting the national market in 1979, drawing $10 million in media support. Spending, mostly in network and spot TV, tapered to $5.6 million by 1983 before ballooning back to $10.9 million in 1986 to support reformulated Puritan. Old standby Crisco also expanded its vegetable-base line with Crisco Corn Oil in 1986.

P&G's competitiveness and opportunism are reflected in the support shown for Crisco, especially in 1983. Crisco spending levels traditionally stay just ahead of outlays by BCI (formerly Beatrice Cos.) for its Wesson Oil and CPC International for Mazola Corn Oil, Crisco's two major competitors, but in 1983 Crisco spending thundered to $22 million from $11.1 million the previous year. This peak in Crisco spending also matched the valley in Puritan measured spending.

What was happening in 1983 to have justified such a seismic spending leap? The country was in recession. Marketers were tightening their budgets. At CPC, worldwide sales continued to tailspin; Mazola Corn Oil measured spending fell 31% from 1982. Changes were just beginning for Esmark, then the marketer of Wesson Oil. Esmark had just bought Norton Simon and was soon to be bought by Beatrice. Sunlite Sunflower Oil marketed in 1982 became Wesson Sunlite Sunflower Seed Oil in 1983, and together with Wesson Oil, drew the same expenditure ($10 million) as in 1982. Conditions were ripe for a surge in market share.

Duncan Hines, the most multifarious brand in the lineup and the third largest spender the past 10 years among P&G brands with $265.3 million, has traditionally funneled most of its ad dollars into cake mixes, with strong support for brownie, muffin and cookie mixes, frostings, and more recently, ready-to-serve cookies. The brand's diversity allows it to be on the cutting edge on new tastes. For example, no fad pushed DH into the production of such "in" finger foods as consumers' hunger for brownies and muffins, which have been around for years. Fads influence line extensions of these products and greater advertising.

Expenditures on brownies have moved steadily upward from $1.8 million in 1977 to $6.3 million in 1985 before dipping back to $5.2 million in 1986. Muffin advertising has grown from $622,100 in 1977 to $4.6 million in 1985 before dropping back to $3.5 million in 1986 in measured media—which is network and spot TV for both brownies and muffins, and some magazine spending for the latter.

Being positioned for a trend is not the case with the soft ready-to-eat cookies, which broke into the market with $13.9 million in spending in 1984, mostly on a regional basis, before exploding to $22.1 million on a national level in 1985. That lone expenditure propelled total measured spending on Duncan Hines products to $56 million in 1985, the largest for any P&G brand in a single year.

However, measured media advertising for the soft-cookie line dropped back to $10.5 million in 1986. Similar drops were recorded by other soft-cookie marketers—Keebler, Frito-Lay and Sunshine. These companies had jumped into the fray in 1983–1984 as reports from test markets surfaced that soft cookies would quickly become 30% to 35% of the market. Analysts later viewed this overwhelming initial response to the cookies as being colored by excessive spot media buying and media coverage. Continuing the national spending levels could not be justified when the soft-cookie market failed to build more than a 10% share. Virtually all soft cookie marketers got snookered. Layoffs and plant closings have since occurred because of overcapacity caused by reduced demand.

This drop in advertising for soft cookies was the largest contributor to the food & beverages segment's overall decline in measured media of 21.8% to $149.7 million in 1986 as total advertising for P&G in the six measured media dropped 10.4% to $789.9 million in 1986—a painful scrub-down to traditional media, not unlike the effect of Lava on a grass burn.

This is the first decline in the food & beverages segment since 1982 when it slipped 1.5% from 1981, the only year-to-year loss by P&G over the 10-year stretch. P&G also reduced measured spending on laundry & cleaning products by 4.1% and on personal care products by 9.6% for the year. But P&G rebounded from the 1982 decline in food & beverages segment spending with annual increases until 1986, so there is reason to believe the budget cleansing of 1986 can be the foundation for increased spending in traditional media in subsequent years.

CHAPTER TWENTY SIX

Genesis of the "Soaps"

When P&G discovered the radio serial in 1933, it knew it had a winner. As the potential of TV was recognized, the company began to experiment and during the '50s had as many as 13 serials on the air. But times changed and P&G's daytime media bargains may be no more.

Procter & Gamble's "Oxydol's Own Ma Perkins" radio serial created the phenomenon of the "soap operas."

FIFTY-FOUR YEARS AGO, A GROUP OF ACTORS surrounded a microphone in Cincinnati and performed scenes from something called "Ma Perkins," America's first radio serial. While this initial 1933 broadcast attracted few listeners, the leaders of Procter & Gamble, which had previously produced radio shows like "Crisco Cooking Talks" and "Sisters of the Skillet," knew they had something special.

They were right. When the show moved to Chicago and joined the National Broadcasting Company's radio network, it became known as "Oxydol's Own Ma Perkins" and spawned an American phenomenon known as "soap operas"—or "washboard weepers"—because of the soap manufacturer's sponsorship and the serial's daily heart-wrenching plots. Most important, it helped move merchandise—in this case Oxydol laundry detergent—off the store shelves.

"P&G's management at the time saw that the kind of loyalty and dedication listeners developed for the characters could be transferred to P&G brands," says New York-based Ed Trach, P&G's manager-daytime programming. Thus began a string of P&G-produced radio serials, each designed to help sell a P&G product. "The Road of Life" pushed mild Ivory soap. "Young Doctor Malone" plugged Joy liquid dishwashing detergent. Oxydol and "Ma Perkins" became synonymous as did Duz and "The Guiding Light," Tide and "Life Can Be Beautiful" and Cheer and "Backstage Wife."

"We had a gold mine where products were burgeoning and growing," says Mr. Trach. "But then the specter of television [in the late 1940s] loomed on the horizon. The question was: Would women sit and watch television during the day? It was almost a decadent implication that we were taking housewives away from their work and families," he says. But P&G recognized the advertising and marketing potential of the new medium and decided to experiment. The company made a TV pilot in the late 1940s of "Ma Perkins," produced by Dancer Fitzgerald Sample, but it didn't work. After more than 15 years on the radio, loyal fans had their own images of the serial's characters and wouldn't accept the TV version.

So P&G tried to create made-for-TV soaps. One, called "The First Hundred Years," didn't even last nine months after it debuted sometime in the early 1950s.

In 1951, a 15-minute serial produced by Leo Burnett Co. called "Search for Tomorrow" finally struck a chord with TV viewers. P&G was on its way to creating what has become the longest-running and most successful media strategy in U.S. advertising history. As viewers began to accept TV soaps "The Guiding Light," which celebrates its 50th year of broadcasting during P&G's sesquicentennial, followed in 1952 as the first radio serial to succeed on TV. But to avoid alienating fans who didn't have TV sets, Compton Advertising produced both a TV and radio version of the show until P&G started phasing out its radio serials in 1955.

By concentrating on TV, particularly daytime soap operas, P&G discovered a niche—as both the biggest program supplier and in which it could command cost efficiencies for its brands as great as 75% less than some competitors.

"Advertising value is why we got into the production business initially and why we are in it today," explains Robert Wehling, P&G associate general advertising manager. "When we can produce successful programming and reach a large and appropriate audience, we can use the combination of programming and media deals to develop advantageous cost-per-thousands for our brands." Indeed. By the early 1970s, the soap opera had matured to become a formidable power on daytime TV and was firmly entrenched as P&G's star performer. The majority of viewers were female, and in 1971, the cost to reach women aged 18–49 in daytime averaged between $3.50 to $4.15 per thousand compared with the $9.50 or more it cost to reach the same female audience in prime time. "Somerset," a show produced by Young & Rubicam for P&G, reportedly gave the company a cost per thousand of $1.60, the lowest of any daytime show (AA, May 31, 1971).

"[Media efficiency] is the driving motivation for us," adds Mr. Wehling. "We're in the production business for advertising. Other major producers of both daytime and nighttime programming are in it strictly for profit." But times have changed and P&G's media bargains, at least in daytime, may be no more. Just as the rise in production costs and increased prices for ad time forced sponsors to abandon prime-time shows like "Texaco Star Theater," "The Kraft Music Hall" and "The U.S. Steel Hour," increased competition for women viewers, lower ratings and the

One of P&G's remaining TV serials, "As The World Turns," is one of the top 10 daytime network shows.

cheap commercial inventory on daytime network TV today have eroded the advertising value of P&G's soap operas.

"The economies have changed as have the demographics," says one media buyer. "P&G used to spend a few million dollars and command an hour of daytime with a low, low cost-per-thousand. They can't do it anymore and they have to answer the question of what to do instead."

The company, which had as many as 13 serials on the air in the mid-1950s, has canceled "Edge of Night," "Texas" and "Search for Tomorrow" within the last five years. "Another World," once P&G's top-rated soap, now finishes third in its 2 p.m. (E.T.) NBC time slot and is in danger of cancellation. "As The World Turns" and "The Guiding Light," P&G's two other serials, earn high enough ratings to be in the top 10 among daytime network shows, but both finish second in their respective time periods.

No longer the dominant force in daytime and caught in a squeeze between higher production costs and network pressure on producers to spend more—despite keeping a lid on license fees nets pay—P&G may look for other ways to reach its customers and could conceivably discontinue or sell the soaps.

Several suitors apparently have approached P&G about its three serials, but the company maintains it has no intention of selling its properties. Mr. Wehling emphasizes P&G's commitment to reach a large female audience through its daytime soap operas and would not predict the future. "It's a matter of economics," he says. "We can compare the advertising value on our programs versus what we're able to buy out there. If there's ever an imbalance where it's not worthwhile to be the producer of our own programming, we would obviously re-evaluate our position. If it is ultimately advantageous to our brands, we're going to be there. If it is not, we're not going to do it as a hobby.

"The other crucial element is reaching the right audience," he adds. "The bulk of our brands are [targeted to] women . . . the primary purchasers of our brands. So the better the chance a program will reach and appeal to a large female audience, the greater the chances we will be associated with it, be it in daytime, prime time, syndication, cable or radio. We want an investment . . . in each medium commensurate with where the audience is. If 60% of all viewing is on the networks, roughly 60% of our media dollars will go to the networks. Likewise with cable, print and radio. . . . If we can get a better deal for the brands by doing more first-run, more cable or something else, we will do it," he says.

In fact, as the audience delivery of the serials started to deteriorate in the late 1970s, P&G quickly expanded into other areas of TV and eventually reopened its West Coast office after a 12-year absence from Hollywood (AA, Aug. 15, 1983). The results have been sometimes spectacular, sometimes disappointing. Critics and viewers have raved about P&G-produced miniseries like "A.D." and "Marco Polo" and TV movies such as "The Corn is Green," "Wilma" and "Sunrise." Syndicated first-run TV shows such as "Sha Na Na" and "Throb" (produced in association with Los Angeles-based Taft Entertainment) and cable TV series "Down to Earth" and "The Catlins" for Superstation WTBS reach targeted audiences to P&G's satisfaction.

The "Miss Universe," "Miss USA" and "Miss Teen USA" beauty pageants also serve a specific purpose. "What better vehicle for our beauty care and cosmetic brands?" asks Mr. Wehling.

But since the P&G-produced comedy "Shirley" aired briefly on NBC in prime time in 1979, the company has yet to get a series on any of the networks' prime-time schedules. CBS rejected four pilots this year, but P&G will continue to pursue prime-time development, both on its own and in various production partnerships, including one with Culver City, Calif.-based MGM/UA Communications Co. "We had the property and the people, they had the track record," says David Gerber, president of MGM/UA Television, "We have hopes 'Changing Patterns' will get picked up by CBS as a midseason replacement, but we're also working on first-run shows for syndication and more. We hope we're building to the future for a strong relationship. It certainly isn't bad to be backed by P&G."

Mr. Wehling also explains P&G's expansion into prime time, first-run syndication and cable TV as "a hedge against an uncertain future. We see a lot of viewer fragmentation." Mr. Wehling also says the company remains in the production business for the "opportunity to provide a good environment for our commercials to air in."

But the company no longer commands the same degree of control it once had in the 1950s, 1960s and 1970s. NBC, in particular, now has story approval in key creative areas of "Another World." "When I broke into daytime TV in 1979, P&G would just deliver its shows," says Brian Frons, VP-daytime for NBC Entertainment, Burbank, Calif. "But P&G is a bit more obstinate in defending . . . opinions. They are a bit slower to change." Mr. Frons' observation is surprising, especially considering P&G's history of innovation. After the company transferred the soap opera genre to TV, it was the first to produce half-hour serials—"Another World" and "Edge of Night" in 1956—and the first to expand to an hour with "Another World" in 1975.

As the original purveyor of serials, P&G always seemed to be one step ahead of the competition in terms of production value and story lines. But eventually P&G producers and writers such as William Bell and Gloria Monty left P&G to work for competing serials. Without any P&G guidelines or restrictions, they added "spice" and sex to the plots of shows like "General Hospital" and "Young and the Restless." The racy glitz and glamor attracted younger and large audiences, leaving the P&G soaps reeling in the late 1970s.

The company reluctantly followed the provocative trend, but without as much success. "We adapted somewhat, but our viewers didn't seem to want the fantasy storylines. They were accustomed to real characterizations," says Mr. Trach. "We do fantasy. We do adventure, a lot of romance and action sequences, but we try to do it in a manner that will fit our shows, our characters and our materials," he says.

Three serials—"Edge of Night," "Texas" and "Search for Tomorrow"—lost their followings and never recovered. But P&G blames the network for changing their time periods. "Edge of

Night," for example, was moved from 4:30 to 4 p.m., and then to 2:30 p.m. and lost audience share. P&G then moved the show to ABC to get back its 4 p.m. time slot. But ABC couldn't convince enough affiliates to air it, the ratings dropped and it was canceled.

"Texas," a P&G offering created in the 1970s, lasted five years. Mr. Trach admits the show had creative problems but blamed its failure on the 3 p.m. time period and the overpowering popularity of its competition—"General Hospital."

"Search for Tomorrow" moved from 12:30 p.m. to 2:30 p.m. on CBS. The show survived the change and rebuilt its audience share. But when CBS wanted to move it to 4 p.m., P&G balked, remembering the 4 p.m. experience of "Edge of Night." The company then moved the show to NBC because it would air at 12:30 p.m., but "Search" never caught on again. By November 1986 the ratings fell below 3.0 with a 9 share.

At those depths, even P&G brands wanted out of the show. "We had to cancel it then," says Mr. Frons. "How can you keep a show on the line if the producer has no faith in it? By pulling its spots, P&G essentially canceled the show, but it was a mutual decision."

The same fate may await "Another World," which also airs on NBC. "It's not like we're saying 'Another World' is gone. What we're saying is let's not let this go the way of 'Search for Tomorrow.' NBC will add a significant amount to the budget this summer to try and get it off the dime. We're saying let's fix this thing. But this is the last time we're going to say that," Mr. Frons says. "I think the problem is we've all been chasing the same 18–49 urban woman. That makes it harder and more difficult to do something different. We all tried to be funny, to have adventure, to have a love story. Now the form is looking for the next breakthrough concept. Maybe P&G has a surprise in store for us."

50 years later, "Light" glows on

ACH WEEKDAY AT 3 P.M. (ET), "THE GUID-
ing Light" sets a new record as the longest-
running program of any type on any
medium.

For 50 years, radio listeners and then TV viewers
have traced the fictional trials and tribulations of
the Bauer, Lewis and Spaulding families in
Springfield, Ill., through more than 10,000 epi-
sodes. Even if CBS-TV and Procter & Gamble Co.,
which owns the show, decided to cancel it tomorrow, its longevity record would stand for at least 15
years. "This may never happen again. It's certainly
a historical milestone," says Ed Trach, P&G's
manager-daytime programming in New York.

Hundreds of actors have lived through the vari-
ous maladies afflicting the soap opera's characters.
Kevin Bacon, Sandy Dennis, JoBeth Williams,
Cicely Tyson, Joseph Campanella, Christopher
Walken, Chris Sarandon, James Earl Jones, Billy
Dee Williams, Blythe Danner and Ruby Dee can
all list "Guiding Light" on resumes.

It all began 50 years ago when P&G and Compton Advertising asked Irna Phillips to come up
with a new show to add to the soap company's
growing stable of radio dramas.

Ms. Phillips, known to many as the "mother of
soap operas," created the mythical town of Five
Points, Ill. (its original fictional home), and its char-
ismatic town leader, Rev. Dr. John Ruthledge.
Both P&G and Compton, the company's supervising producer for many of its serials, were delighted.
On Jan. 25, 1937, the first 15-minute episode was
broadcast on NBC's Red Network.

The impassioned sermons of Rev. Ruthledge
and his resolve to lead his congregation through
fictional traumas gained an immediate following.
As part of the plot, Rev. Ruthledge always kept
his reading lamp visible at his window to let the
townspeople know he was there. He was, so to
speak, keeper of the "guiding light." The character became so popular in the 1940s that a hard-
cover anthology of his speeches sold 300,000 copies. But circumstances changed. P&G switched
the serial to CBS Radio in 1946 and moved the
show from Chicago to Hollywood. It settled in
New York in 1949.

About the same time, the Bauer family was introduced with Papa Bauer, Meta Bauer and eventually Bert Bauer, portrayed by one actress until
her death in 1985. The name of the actress, coin-
cidentally, was Charita Bauer.

On June 30, 1952, "The Guiding Light" aired
on national network TV for the first time. While
it quickly became the first radio soap opera to succeed on TV, its radio version remained the top-
rated serial of the 19 radio dramas during the mid-
1950s. The cast and crew worked on both
versions and many were thankful when P&G canceled the radio show in August 1956 to concentrate on TV.

Ms. Phillips, the show's creator, left in 1958,
but her replacement, Agnes Nixon, kept the show
at or near the top of the ratings. It remains among
the top 10-rated daytime series and shows no sign
of losing viewers.

"We once made a TV show called "The First
Hundred Years,' " says Mr. Trach. "It only lasted
nine months, but we fully expected it to last 100
years. Maybe 'The Guiding Light' will."

V

P&G's
Global
Marketing

CHAPTER TWENTY SEVEN

A Global Comeback

There have been some false starts and outright flops along the way, but P&G's global marketing efforts finally show signs of paying off. These accomplishments are taking place in a tough international marketplace, where profit margins generally are lower than in the U.S., distribution is a challenge, and consumer habits are, in a word, foreign.

THREE YEARS AGO PROCTER & GAMBLE CO. Vice Chairman Edwin Artzt, who also is president of P&G International, was admiring a painting of a Japanese tea ceremony in the office of Chairman-CEO John Smale. The two executives were discussing P&G's increasing losses in Japan, when Mr. Smale surprised his international chief. If you can turn a profit in Japan, he said, the painting is yours.

Now Mr. Artzt can start making room on his wall. This fiscal year, for the first time since P&G entered Japan in 1973, the company is making a profit on its established brands in Japan, excluding new products. "I'll get the painting next year," Mr. Artzt promises.

Japan is leading an international surge at P&G. Observers expect international sales to reach $5.6 billion in 1986–87, or 31% of P&G's worldwide sales, and 24% over 1985–86 international sales of $4.5 billion.

Of P&G's worldwide corporate profits, 27% comes from outside the U.S., up from 22% during the last fiscal year and from 12% just three years ago. Only a third of this increase is explained by the weak dollar. Last year's goal of getting international up to 25% of worldwide profits by 1990 already has been eclipsed. These accomplishments are taking place in a tough international marketplace, where profit margins generally are lower than in the U.S. As a result, P&G must grow faster outside the U.S. than domestically just to keep up.

Even Hercules Segalas, senior VP at Drexel Burnham Lambert, and a past critic of P&G's international strategy, is impressed. "International is looking more positive than at any time in the last decade," he says. "The combination of acquiring Richardson-Vicks and the weak dollar has helped."

In the non-U.S. arena P&G faces enormous pressures it does not face here. In most developed markets, excess capacity holds down prices. Many foreign countries have price controls. Europe tends to have more competitors because shipping products across borders is easy. In France, for example, P&G competes against Swedish, Danish and Italian companies in many categories.

Also, commercial TV time is limited worldwide, making new-product introductions expensive and hazardous—given that TV is the most efficient means to spread knowledge quickly about a new product. Innovative, below-the-line marketing techniques also are restricted (in Japan, for example, the value of premiums and prizes is controlled). Powerful non-U.S. competitors, such as Anglo-Dutch Unilever and Germany's Henkel, are entrenched, and used to lower returns to shareholders than P&G finds acceptable.

"International markets have tended to be rapid growth markets; therefore, you get an enormous amount of price competition and people willing to sacrifice in order to build share in a market," Mr. Artzt says. P&G has an added burden: Competitors are automatically tipped off to P&G's new products and strategy by watching what the marketer does in the U.S.

P&G's primary international problem is profits, not sales. To build profit margins, P&G has been cutting costs and getting efficient—making the same product lines at fewer facilities. The company also is building market share in high-margin segments, such as cough/cold products and skin creams, which P&G added to its product list when it acquired Richardson-Vicks in 1985. The company is actively trying to use the R-V acquisition to boost revenues and margins on the international side.

In May 1987, the company began "Procterizing" its R-V holdings outside the U.S. by consolidating $75 million to $100 million in R-V advertising at D'Arcy Masius Benton & Bowles, Leo Burnett Co. and other agencies it favors. P&G executives want R-V to work with agencies the way P&G does—on a brand basis, rather than by category, and on a pan-European basis, rather than market by market.

"Sometimes we'll have two brands in a category at different agencies," Mr. Artzt says. "We think that provides better strategic delineation between brands overall. If we have two brands in the same category competing with one another, we shouldn't have somebody saying, 'Well, I'm going to give this one my child and this one my dog.' You need real competition within your businesses like you have outside your businesses."

P&G executives also want to use R-V's strong organizations in countries where P&G is weak—such as Australia, India, Indonesia, Thailand, and all over Latin America—to help boost sales of P&G products. R-V and P&G businesses internationally remain separate profit centers in big markets, but in smaller markets the two organizations are being integrated. In many countries like Hong Kong, Singapore and Malaysia, P&G people run the show. In Australia, R-V people are in charge.

P&G already is gaining some market efficiencies with media, for example. By combining operations with R-V, the new organization is qualifying for media discounts. But most important, P&G

wants to position R-V's over-the-counter drug products at the forefront of a strong marketing push for high-margin otc drugs in foreign countries. R-V's cough/cold products and skin creams are lower volume, less competitive and command higher profit margins everywhere in the world, compared with the profit margins of P&G's detergents and diapers.

To further "Procter-ize" R-V, executives are stressing product "initiatives," with a strong commitment to research and development. Mr. Artzt says P&G is stressing "database market analysis" or "getting the numbers to support what you think is going on in the business. We used to look at the international business and say, 'By God, we've grown faster than the rest of the company, and we've grown in importance to where we're nearly a third of the company's business, but in the same breath we were always embarrassed to talk about our profits," Mr. Artzt says.

As U.S. market growth gets tough, the pressure on P&G to grow in new, international markets has intensified. This has brought significant changes in P&G's global strategy over the years. After World War II, P&G's strategy was to take core U.S. businesses—now defined as soap, toothpaste, diapers and shampoo—and export them to the rest of the world. An "export operations division," which still exists, was set up in Geneva in 1953 to market products to most of the world, excluding Latin America. For 13 years P&G built its non-U.S. business this way all over the world.

However, P&G's philosophy was not just to export, but to build demand in countries through exports, then follow that up with in-country organizations, once the infrastructure was available for providing packaging material, processed chemicals and skilled labor. Continuing through the 1960s, P&G drew on its root technology for product advantage and then moved closer to consumers by setting up local businesses. This avoided the expense of building plants until demand had grown through exports.

As Mr. Artzt points out, protectionist tariffs force U.S. companies to set up local businesses to keep those brands competitive "because of the amount of innovation in product and packaging in all parts of the world."

Even now, "old" products such as Camay soap, Head & Shoulders shampoo and Pampers disposable diapers are marketed similarly everywhere. But while those products were not launched with global distribution in mind, new products are. Mr. Artzt says if P&G were introducing Pampers today, it would aim to get the product into world markets in five years or less. In fact, it took P&G 15 years to get Pampers into 70 countries. Now P&G tries to introduce products on a worldwide scale early in their development, not after they have been established in one market and competitors can react. This is true not only in the healthcare area, but for soaps and household cleaning products as well.

For this reason Mr. Artzt says global marketing is a "technology-based issue, not a brand-based issue," New tartar control ingredients in Crest, for example, can be applied globally, even in non-Crest brands that P&G markets in individual countries. In fact, P&G sometimes approaches foreign markets more as a regional than global marketer.

Many of its products—even the "core" ones—are changed to suit different markets. The smell of Camay, flavor of Crest and formula of Head & Shoulders varies from region to region, as does the company's marketing strategy.

For example, P&G's Always sanitary napkin is based on new technology involving an absorbent material wrapped in a perforated polyethylene film. The product has rolled out in 13 countries over the past two years, but "women in different parts of world have different habits during their menstrual cycle," Mr. Artzt says. In Japan, women wear "menstrual pants" to keep their silhouette attractive under clothes. So the Japanese sanitary napkin, called Whisper, is a thinner version of Always. "The idea of moving quickly by taking a piece of technology and implementing it to fit the habits of local markets has taken hold and is leading our operation," Mr. Artzt says.

He also says there is a reluctance to fix something that isn't broke—i.e., to alter a product or marketing strategy that has been successful in one country because it doesn't fit the global pattern.

P&G has had to modify other global strategies over its history. First, it has had to downplay its original policy of setting up only wholly owned subsidiaries, and accept joint ventures—usually 50-50. Countries such as Mexico and Malaysia limit foreign ownership by law. Second, P&G has changed its thinking about primary lines of business. Instead of taking a product everywhere, the marketer now looks more closely at individual markets and may hold off introducing a product if there are compelling reasons to stay out. New brands are still planned globally, but each market is examined to see if it is an exception to the rule. But the biggest change is in speeding up the export-first philosophy. Because competitors are watching P&G's moves in the U.S., "We have to move quickly around the world to exploit innovations," Mr. Artzt says.

To exploit its perceived edge in sanitary napkins, P&G moved Always into six countries—including Canada, Singapore, France and Saudi Arabia—within nine months of the start of its test in the U.S. Because of modifications to the Japanese product, it is in only 20% of that country since its September 1986 rollout. P&G also recently moved the product into Greece.

And there have been product failures, some stemming from lack of sufficient market research because of the emphasis on speed. Others result from a perception that P&G executives in Cincinnati have not always paid close enough attention to individual market differences around the world.

Walter Lingle, P&G's first VP in charge of overseas operations, said many years ago: "We have decided that the best way to succeed in other countries is to build in each one an exact replica of the U.S. Procter & Gamble organization. . . . We believe that exactly the same policies and procedures which have given our company success in the U.S. will be equally successful overseas." That philosophy caused P&G some problems over the years. U.K. observers point to P&G's recent launch of Crest Tartar Control Formula in the U.K.—in a silver box. Two months later, Colgate-Palmolive Co. launched its tartar-control toothpaste—but in a gold box. Some sheepish P&G officials—who agreed that C-P's choice of the gold color was better than P&G's silver—said the silver box was required because that is how it is packaged in the U.S.

P&G's biggest international flop—from which it later recovered—is the marketer's experience with Vizir in Europe. (The name was chosen because it is memorable and P&G had the trademark.) Based on new liquid detergent technology (which is also the basis of Liquid Tide), Vizir was rolled out in Europe in the early 1980s. What P&G failed to take into account was that European washing machines were at that time equipped to accept powder detergents but not liquids. When liquid detergent was added to a powder dispenser, as much as 20% of the liquid was "lost" at a collecting point at the bottom of the machine. As a result, so far "the brand was a failure," says Mr. Artzt flatly.

P&G afterward convinced washing machine manufacturers in Europe to design liquid dispensers, but this had little impact on a market where the average machine is replaced once every 15 years. So P&G developed what it called a "retrofit" system—a plastic device that fit into existing powder dispensers and kept the liquid from leaking, while dispensing it at the same time. The device would be mailed to consumers, free of charge. A neat idea, P&G executives thought. But it didn't work. "Most European machines are bolted to the wall," Mr. Artzt explains. "When

Procter & Gamble

PRINCIPAL SUBSIDIARY	HEADQUARTERS	KEY BRANDS	AD AGENCY
Richardson-Vicks Pty. Ltd.	Melbourne, Victoria Australia	**Oil of Olay Lotion** **Napisan (sterilizer)** **Vicks Vaporub**	B&B TB B&B
Procter & Gamble **Vertriebsgesellschaft m.b.h.**	Vienna, Austria	**Pampers** **Ariel** **Dash**	S&S S&S LB
Procter & Gamble Benelux	Brussels, Belgium	**Pampers** **Dash** **Ariel**	S&S LB S&S
Procter & Gamble Inc.	Toronto, Ontario Canada	**Tide** **Pampers** **Bounce**	S&S B&B B&B
Laboratorio Geka S.A.	Santiago, Chile	**Odontine** **Crest** **Camay**	LB LB GRY
Procter & Gamble GmbH	Schwalbach am Tanus, Germany	**Lenor** **Ariel** **Pampers**	GRY S&S S&S
Procter & Gamble OY	Helsinki, Finland	**Fairy Liquid** **Ariel** **Tag**	GRY TUR TUR
Procter & Gamble France	Neuilly Sur Seine Cedex, France	**Ariel** **Dash** **Vizir**	S&S LB GRY
Procter & Gamble **Hellas A.E.**	Nea Smyrmi, Athens, Greece	**Tide** **Jet** **Ariel**	LB S&S S&S
Richardson-Hindustan **Limited**	Bombay, India	**Vicks Inhaler** **Vicks Vaporub** **Clearasil Cream**	B&B B&B B&B
Procter & Gamble **Italia, SpA**	Rome, Italy	**Dash** **Ace** **Ariel**	LB GRY S&S
Procter & Gamble **Far East, Inc.**	Osaka, Japan	**Cheer** **Pampers** **Bonus**	GRY GRY LB
Procter & Gamble Manufacturing **Co. of Lebanon, S.A.T.**	Beirut, Lebanon	**Yes** **Ariel**	S&S S&S
Procter & Gamble **de Mexico, S.A. de C.V.**	Lomas de Vista Hermosa, Mexico	**Ariel** **Salvo** **Rapido**	NOB NOB LB
Moroccan Modern **Industries**	Casablanca, Morocco	**Tide** **Camay** **Ariel**	HAV HAV HAV
Procter & Gamble **Benelux**	Rotterdam The Netherlands	**Pampers** **Dash** **Ariel**	S&S LB S&S
Deterperu, S.A.	Lima, Peru	**Ariel** **Camay** **Crest**	GRY GRY S&S

Agency abbreviations—**B&B**–D'Arcy Masius Benton & Bowles; **GRY**–Grey Advertising; **LB**–Leo Burnett; **M–E**–McCann-Erickson; **NOB**–Noble (B&B);

International

PRINCIPAL SUBSIDIARY	HEADQUARTERS	KEY BRANDS	AD AGENCY
Procter & Gamble Philippine Manufacturing Corporation	Manila, Philippines	Tide (laundry bar)	LB
		Mr. Clean (laundry bar)	S&S
		Tide (granual)	S&S
The Procter & Gamble Commercial Company	San Juan, Puerto Rico	Pampers	WIN
		Ariel	LB
		Charmin	S&S
Modern Industries Company	Dammam, Saudi Arabia	Tide	LB
		Ariel	S&S
		Fairy Liquid	S&S
Procter & Gamble Espana, S.A.	Madrid, Spain	Ariel Automatic	S&S
		Dash	LB
		Fairy Liquid	GRY
Procter & Gamble Actiebolag	Stockholm, Sweden	Ariel	S&S
		Jor	GRY
		Pampers	S&S
Procter & Gamble A.G.	Geneva, Switzerland	Ariel	S&S
		Vizir	GRY
		Pampers	S&S
Modern Home Products Limited	Taipei, Taiwan	Easy	LB
		Safe & Free	LB
		Zing	LB
Procter & Gamble Limited	Newcastle upon Tyne, England	Fairy Liquid	GRY
		Ariel Automatic	S&S
		Bold	GRY
Procter & Gamble de Venezuela	Caracas, Venezuela	Ariel	GRY
		Ace	B&B
		Crest	B&B
Richardson GmbH	Gross-Gereau Germany	Oil of Olay	S&S
		Clearasil Lotion	B&B
		Vicks Medinite Cold Medicine	B&B
Vick Internationale RV-France	Paris, France	Petrole Hahn Lotion	S&S
		Vicks Cough Syrup	S&S
		Oil of Olay	S&S
Richardson-Vicks Europe	Egham, England	Head & Shoulders	B&B
		Crest	B&B
		Oil of Olan	S&S
Vick International SpA	Milan, Italy	AZ toothpaste	B&B
		Pantene Shampoo	GRY
		Oil of Olay	S&S
Nippon Vicks KK	Osaka, Japan	Colac laxative tablets	M-E
		Pantene Shampoo	LB
		Vicks cough drops	M-E
Richardson-Vicks S.A. de C.V.	Mexico City, Mexico	Choco Milk Vitamin Supplement	GRY
		Vicks Inhaler	B&B
		Pepto Bismol	B&B

Agency abbreviations—**S&S**—Saatchi & Saatchi Compton; **TB**—Ted Bates (S&SC); **TUR**—Turkama (B&B); **HAV**—Havas; **WIN**—West Indies Advertising.

we called these women and said we want to provide you with a retrofit dispenser free of charge, just tell us the model number, they said, 'I don't know, the machine is bolted to the wall. I can't see it.' "

There was some panic at P&G—not known for panicking. "We had a major barn on fire . . ." Mr. Artzt admits. The solution finally appeared when P&G invented what it called the Vizirette reusable dispensing ball. The key to the ball's effectiveness is that it sits on top of the clothes and dispenses after the machine fills up. Now Vizir is the third-largest selling detergent in France and doing respectably after relaunches last year in Germany, Belgium, Holland, Switzerland and Austria. "I think this will go down in history as one of the great all-time rescue jobs," Mr. Artzt says.

One unexpected spinoff: Arielette, a reusable plastic ball placed inside washing machines for Ariel liquid. P&G intends to sell the Arielette plastic ball to consumers.

The Vizir experience has caused P&G international executives to focus more attention on product packaging, which "can play a functional role in the success of a product," Mr. Artzt says. He also says the experience "reinforces the importance of local initiatives in this whole process of what we call global market planning." The key to a product's success overseas is the "ability of a local organization to know the difference between what makes a piece of Always technology right for the Japanese consumer, whereas the Europeans might not buy it or like it," he says. "In putting together world technology, this is the core, with all these groups of people around the world knowing their markets and their business and their consumers."

To criticism that P&G barks out orders and imposes them on its international managers, Mr. Artzt concedes that there have been times where that criticism has been "fair." Partly to get around that problem, P&G's international arm is now run by country "core" teams in Europe. These teams "get together and map out a testing program or development program for product improvements and new brands," Mr. Artzt says. "They will tell you that *they* are the ones making the difference in the success or failure of each brand."

This idea stems from a change in the mid-1970s, when P&G adopted a "Euro-market" concept and began thinking about the region as one market, but encouraged local execution. That idea has now expanded worldwide and P&G's strategy is to make global plans, then replan for each region, and execute locally. P&G executives believe that, ultimately, local differences will diminish, and that may have an impact on P&G's future approach.

The core team approach works this way: Each team might suggest a product "initiative"—taking a product and adapting it to a market in an inventive way, such as Tartar Control Crest, which was introduced in the U.S. To get it into world markets fast, P&G now is dealing quickly with questions about flavor, packaging and regulations that in the past took many years to answer.

Using these core groups, Crest tartar control technology was rolled out into 25 countries in 12 months. Even more impressive, it was quickly adopted even in countries like Italy, where there is no Crest toothpaste, but another, local brand. Those countries even adopted the P&G advertising approach of showing people scratching tartar off their teeth. "Nobody thought that anything was being imposed on them," Mr. Artzt says. "They all wanted to beat the competition into the market."

The core groups, and the feeling of autonomy and control they have, are the key. "There is no way the company can impose a direction on them," he says. "We can challenge them, but it's their ideas that make or break these brands," Mr. Artzt says. The core groups share ideas and try them out all at once, rather than waiting for each idea to work in an individual market, and then studying to see if it could be applied elsewhere.

Now even the core team concept is evolving. This year P&G created a new Asia/Pacific division, and a new functional division at P&G's European Technical Center in Brussels to look after disposables and beverages. This functional division is the first one to go beyond geography and focus on product categories. The reason for the move is to increase the marketer's focus on its main lines of business, and to simplify the P&G organization, i.e., one ad manager for Europe instead of nine.

P&G overseas also is pushing for promotion from within, and low turnover, similar to its personnel policies in the U.S. This means a greater expense for "recruitment, training and development of people as a way of surviving as a company," he says.

One international trend helping P&G is the deregulation of media throughout Europe, which is creating new, private channels and more options to advertise new products. "There just isn't enough media advertising to go around and for a long time that was having a real effect on brand planning," says Mr. Artzt. "Now you'll see more innovative products moving into the European market faster."

Internationally, P&G's core products are not as strong as in the U.S. Camay, a "beauty" soap, is a trouble spot and getting a lot of P&G attention. Camay is an old brand in 140 countries that is trying to gain shares of a market fragmented by hundreds of new soap varieties positioned in countless ways—for cleaning and deodorizing, for example.

P&G is working on the "next generation" of Camay products to keep the brand strong in a majority of markets. "Camay must continue to modernize itself because that is its appeal," Mr. Artzt

says. To do that, "We're trying to examine what's working and not working" in different countries. Japan, France and Venezuela are strong Camay markets, for example, and those markets are being analyzed closely. One problem is the Camay perfume, which is different from country to country. "It doesn't do you a whole lot of good to have 25 different perfumes if the majority of them are not superior," Mr. Artzt says.

Another "core" product, Head & Shoulders dandruff shampoo, is the subject of many P&G "product initiatives," in packaging, for example, as well as line extensions—such as a conditioner in parts of Asia and in test market in the U.K. The product "generates a lot of volume and works on a worldwide basis," Mr. Artzt says.

A fourth core product, diapers, is down but "coming back" outside the U.S. The original Pampers diaper "went down the tubes" in Japan and lost its market-leading position in the U.S., admits Mr. Artzt. He says P&G is reversing that trend by rapidly introducing thin, super-absorbent diapers everywhere in the world and "our business is looking very strong."

Fabric softeners are turning into an active area for P&G internationally. Lenor, which is like Downy in the U.S., has just entered Canada and is strong in Europe. P&G's core teams are now working on the smell and concentration levels of the product for different parts of the world. In Germany, P&G just introduced Lenor dryer sheets, like Bounce sheets in the U.S. On the horizon is an expansion of Lenor sheets, which has been held back outside the U.S. because they did not work well in old-fashioned European dryers.

"Lenor is a strong brand name," says Mr. Artzt. "Soon every fabric softener will have to have dryer sheets line extensions to keep the brand strong."

CHAPTER TWENTY EIGHT

In Japan, It's "Learn the Hard Way"

Massive losses resulted from critical mistakes.

THE SUN HAS NOT OFTEN SHONE ON PROCTER & Gamble Co. in Japan. Since 1973, when P&G entered the country, it has lost an estimated $250 million, and it's been painful.

Huge initial successes with Cheer detergent and Pampers diapers abruptly soured because of poor distribution, faulty advertising and tough competitors that clobbered P&G with superior products.

Now for the first time, P&G may be turning the corner in Japan. In 1986–87, the company cut its losses to the "modest" level and actually was in the black for established brands, according to P&G Vice Chairman Edwin Artzt. P&G executives expect to move the Japanese operation into the black next year. P&G accomplished the turnaround by loosening the company's rigid marketing policies, listening more closely to its managers in Japan, modifying products and tuning in more closely to the Japanese consumers. "We had to

learn the hard way," says one P&G executive in Japan.

First, P&G had to overcome its own history. To enter Japan with Cheer laundry detergent, P&G purchased a faltering Japanese soap company, Nippon Sunhome, partly to buy its way into the country's complex distribution system, which effectively blocks entry to foreigners.

In a move many consider a tactical mistake, P&G tried to boost Cheer's sales by undercutting the price of its competitors' products, which enraged rivals Kao and Lion. The two companies responded by marking down the price of their detergents, triggering a price war that continues to be a problem. "Our core laundry business is priced at a loss," Mr. Artzt admits. And there is no sign it will improve. Cheer now has 5% of the market and is the No. 4 detergent. P&G has only 200 salesmen compared with Kao's 2,500 and Lion's

1,000. Below-the-line marketing is tightly regulated in Japan, making it impossible for P&G to make up for its lack of distribution power. For example, Japan regulates the value of premiums based on the price of the item being promoted. Relatively low-price products like P&G's are restricted from big-ticket promotions.

P&G also has made mistakes on the advertising side. To promote Cheer, P&G initially used slice-of-life commercials that ranked among the most hated in Japanese consumer polls. Spots from agency Grey Daiko now show a side-by-side demonstration of cold-water Cheer's cleaning superiority. Similarly, Grey's ads for Camay beauty soap initially portrayed men approaching women and telling them how lovely they look. In a country where male appreciation of women doesn't take that form, the advertising went over so poorly that Camay's market share has never gone above 2%.

The commercials have since been replaced by others that play up the image of European-based soap. "We have developed a far greater sympathy for the Japanese culture," says Durk Jager, VP-Japan.

Overall, P&G has radically increased the number of commercials it produced in Japan, from 20 a year to more than 100, Mr. Jager says. To improve profitability, the company also is introducing more in extensions and products in new, profitable areas.

Diapers are a key area for line extensions. Before P&G's introduction of Pampers into Japan in 1977, the only available disposable diapers were made of cheap paper. P&G initially ran away with 90% of that business, until it stumbled. Because Pampers' success in the U.S. is keyed to housewives who do laundry at most once or twice a week, P&G overlooked the fact that Japanese housewives do laundry every day. So P&G found Pampers were being used only at night, and cloth diapers still reigned during the day.

Then along came a new domestic competitor, Moony, which improved on the P&G product by making some parts of the diaper reusable—a strong selling point for the thrifty Japanese. Under pressure, P&G's market share slipped to less than 10%.

There are signs P&G is coming back. Last April, the company introduced New Pampers, a smaller, thinner diaper geared to the Japanese market. "To the Japanese, thickness is not relevant," says Mr. Jager. "They know that if you have the right 'ingredients,' thickness makes no difference." Sources at P&G in Japan claim the new diaper is the market leader with more than 20% of the $700 million retail market.

To P&G, the most important reason to be in Japan is to gain a technology edge. Mr. Artzt describes Japan as the "spawning ground of many new products we'll be seeing in the U.S. and Europe for many years to come." For example, the super-absorbers used in Pampers worldwide are a Japanese invention.

P&G also is on a new-product binge in Japan. Besides New Pampers and Whisper, the marketer has introduced or relaunched other products in the past year, including Ariel powder and concentrated, premium-priced liquid detergent; Attendo, a diaper for adult incontinence; Monogen Baby, a detergent specially formulated for babies' clothes; Muse, a medicated soap (its sales already exceed Camay); and Monogen Uni, a fine-fabric detergent.

The pessimists point out that P&G is in for a rough ride in Japan. A report in *Business Week* quotes analysts predicting a diaper price war, which could cripple P&G's diaper comeback.

But Mr. Artzt says, "I'm optimistic about Japan because we've become a good Japanese company. We understand the Japanese consumer, we're developing products for the Japanese market that are winners in Japan, and we have the product edge in detergents, diapers and sanitary napkins. It's taken us 15 years, but we've learned how to get street smart in Japan."

CHAPTER TWENTY NINE

Foreign Shores Tough Even for P&G

How America's package-goods giant was stung by Unilever and the locals.

P ROCTER & GAMBLE CO. DOES NOT COMMAND the same respect—or fear—outside the U.S. that it does domestically. An informal AD-VERTISING AGE survey of major world markets seems to indicate that outside the U.S., P&G has had a rough time. Often it is beaten to the market—sometimes with superior products—by tough competitors like Unilever, which have no fear of America's premier consumer-marketing giant.

As a result, P&G has strong brands, but relatively few market-leading ones around the world. In Europe, most of P&G's brands rank second, third or fourth in their categories. In Latin America, P&G has very few brands at all, and in Asia, the marketer is just starting to break into many markets.

In the huge U.K. market, P&G has the No. 2 detergent (Ariel powder), disposable diaper (Pampers) and fabric softener (Lenor), and the No. 4 bar soap (Camay). Fairy liquid dishwashing detergent, Head & Shoulders shampoo and Flash, a Spic and Span clone, are No. 1.

"P&G puts 99% of its emphasis on the U.S.," says an ex-P&G executive turned management consultant. "P&G is comfortable only in advanced societies. In places like India and Africa, Unilever for a long time could knock the socks off P&G."

But even in developed markets, P&G has taken some hits. In Japan, local disposable diaper marketers took market share from P&G by coming out with disposable diapers with reusable parts—a superior product for that market.

But less well-known are P&G's diaper problems elsewhere. For example, the battle with French disposable diaper giant Peaudouce is as vigorous as anything in Japan. That battle intensified in 1984 after Pampers lost its U.K. market lead to Peaudouce—a lead it has not since regained. Last month, Peaudouce sought an injunction in France against P&G's commercial for new ultra-thin Pampers, charging that the spot's super-absorbency claims are misleading advertising.

In the spot, water is poured on a new Pampers diaper and on another disposable diaper. Then both diapers are squeezed, showing that the ultra-thin Pampers is leak-proof, but brand X isn't. Peaudouce alleges that the new Pampers only passes this test when distilled water is used; when used by a real baby, the diaper isn't as leak proof. The court case is important because P&G is launching ultra-thin Pampers in the U.K., too, and would like to use the same spot.

P&G concedes that the diaper market worldwide is getting tougher. Edwin Artzt, P&G's vice chairman, says, "It was the original rectangular diaper that went down the tubes in Japan and also was outpaced by the French diaper in the U.K. We've since replaced that with our thin, super-absorber diaper."

In some cases, U.S. competitors have beaten P&G in foreign markets. In the U.K., for example, Crest trails Colgate-Palmolive Co.'s toothpaste.

But more often, foreign competitors have hurt P&G. In the U.K., where European competition is perhaps fiercest, the Anglo-Dutch Unilever pits its Wisk liquid laundry detergent against P&G's new Ariel liquid in a $600 million market. Unilever took great delight in beating P&G to market last year by three months—and both products appear to have gained around 10% of the business. That story is repeated throughout Europe, with the added problem that P&G has been slow off the mark.

In Spain, P&G has the No. 4 detergent, trailing German-based Henkel and Unilever. Crest, Head & Shoulders and Pampers are still in test markets there. "By the time P&G came to Spain many of its products were being copied by local competitors," says one source in Spain.

In Sweden, P&G is losing money, and Connie Karlsson, P&G's country manager-Scandinavia, says, "We are a late entry with strong, entrenched competitors."

In France, where P&G has the leading laundry

detergent and all-purpose cleaner, Pampers is the No. 3 diaper and Lenor the No. 4 fabric softener. P&G has been cutting back media spending, and sources in France believe it's because of the company's increased profitability drive.

One problem P&G has is obtaining retail shelf space, particularly for new products. Another problem is French regulations that prohibit most Richardson-Vicks products, like cough/cold remedies, from being sold anywhere but in drugstores.

Six years ago, P&G went on a spending spree in Europe to gain market share fast. Ad budgets soared, test marketing was cut back and new product introductions spread like wildfire. In the U.K., ad expenditures rose from $19.2 million in 1978–79 to $79.5 million in 1982, and P&G introduced more new products than all its competitors combined. Partly because of that spending binge, profitability suffered in some markets. In the past, that has been the case in West Germany, where P&G recently invested heavily in Pampers and fruit juices. Its Pampers market share there has dropped from 60% several years ago to 40% today.

In the past two years P&G has been on a new-product binge in Germany. Some products have done well, but not all. A P&G laundry "booster" sheet, Top Job, introduced in 1985, was attacked by environmentalists and flopped, sources say.

P&G this month agreed to buy Blendax-Group, a leading West German toiletries products maker, which should strengthen P&G's position in European personal-care.

P&G's strategy is completely different in the less-developed markets of Latin America and Asia/Pacific, where the R-V acquisition is playing a big role because that company is more entrenched in those markets than P&G. In many markets both the R-V and P&G operations are being integrated.

The company has found its experiences in Latin America humbling, for example. It was chased out of Argentina, unable to enter Brazil and forced to abandon Chile—all mainly for political reasons. Most of its consumer products are unknown in the region.

For several years, P&G has struggled in Latin America with its faltering Orange Crush soft drink, once a strong brand in the region, but which sunk into insignificance. In Brazil, Merrill-Dow Pharmaceutical has a wholly owned subsidiary that manufactures such R-V products as VapoRub and Vicks Cough Drops. R-V is considering similar agreements in Argentina and has an operating agreement in Venezuela and a joint venture in Colombia.

In Mexico, R-V's largest Latin America operation, the company markets a chocolate milk additive and candies in addition to its traditional brands. One problem with expanding P&G's consumer products in Latin America is political instability. Another is finding the right partner. For example, P&G has been scouting for a Brazilian partner for years, sources say, but with no luck.

P&G has targeted the huge Asia/Pacific market for expansion. The first stop is Australia. In the early 1950s P&G entered Australia, using its export operation based in Geneva. "One assumes that Australia got a little lost, being so far from Geneva, and that is why P&G never succeeded in developing brands out here," says R-V Australia Managing Director Geoffrey C. Leonard. R-V has been in Australia since 1926 and ranks among the top three brands in healthcare, toiletries and suncare products.

Last January, P&G formed a new division in the Asia/Pacific region to focus on growth there, and, unusual for P&G, R-V executives were given a dominant role. "Our No. 1 priority is to keep R-V's business growing," says Mr. Leonard. That business includes the Vicks brand of cough and cold products, Oil of Olay and Clearasil.

Disposable diapers and detergents will be rolled out in many Far East markets, Mr. Leonard says. "Obviously, we are doing a lot of homework on category opportunities from the great smorgasbord of P&G offerings," he says.

VI

A
LAST LOOK

CHAPTER THIRTY

Patience and Perspective

In an interview with Advertising Age's editor in chief, Rance Crain, and editor, Fred Danzig, John Smale reviews the company's 150-year history, its human values and how it can compete in the future.

John Smale on community involvement: "I think the people would be involved . . . because of the kind of people they are. It just flows naturally, and we are heavily involved."

RANCE CRAIN: WHAT SPECIAL SIGNIFICANCE does your 150th anniversary have, not only to your company, but to your employees, the U.S. business community and consumers?

John Smale: It's a testimony to the approach developed by the founders of this company and perpetuated by successive generations of managers dealing with people. Dealing with the fundamental aspect of human relationships as related to, in this case, a business enterprise.

Businesses and other institutions often get hung up in thinking about what's happening today. At Procter & Gamble, what's happening today is directly related to the concept that the company has grown because of its relationship with people, with employees.

I guess it's not unique in American industry, but it is relatively distinctive. If you think back 150 years, there were dozens of soap companies in Cincinnati alone. Why has one lasted and the others are no longer here? Again, I think it is rooted in the fundamental concept of human relationships, of the belief in the values that are important to people and the willingness to run an enterprise in a fashion that's consistent with those values. I think the other institutions in this nation that have lasted decades and centuries through all kinds of change have lasted for the same basic reasons: Because they were sound in concept. Somehow, the successive managers, or the people who have been responsible for these institutions, have been able to maintain the basic values of the institution.

The essential strength of this company is its people, and the values that the company has, and the values that the employees in the company embrace. Those values haven't changed.

Mr. Crain: We've read a lot lately—and I know you're very interested in this topic—about U.S. business losing its basic competitiveness. Do you think that regaining these basic human values that you talked about are part of the formula for U.S. business to reestablish its competitive position in the world?

Mr. Smale: No question. I think it's got to be the foundation of it. But we have to be careful we don't paint with too broad a brush.

This company and our competitors in the consumer goods field have been competitive because we've been operating around the world. So I don't think there has been any reduction in the degree of competitiveness of U.S. consumer goods companies broadly.

But certainly there are broad areas of U.S. industry that have not been competitive, and there are, perhaps, a number of reasons for that, having to do with the value of currencies, and changes in costs of energy, and so forth.

At the root of it, I think, is what you're suggesting: Our ability to compete is based on people. It's based on their education. How well are we educating young people vs. other countries with whom we compete? It's based on the relationships within the organization between people, between hourly employees and management. There have been major steps toward improving these human relationships in American industry, and American industry is getting more competitive.

Fred Danzig: You've articulated the values and the standards by which Procter & Gamble grew. Is there a way of defining the way this company manages to adhere to those principles in the people that it brings in and, yet, stays ahead of everything?

There is this feeling that P&G demands hard-charging, aggressive initiatives in order to stay in its leadership role. How the management of this company manages to keep that edge is of interest to us.

Mr. Smale: We do it imperfectly, but I think one of the principal challenges that the management of the company has is to be able to communicate the values of the company, to be sure that managers understand those values and live by them.

We have enormous help in this process because of our promotion-from-within policy. The people who are managers in the company basically have spent their entire career with the company. When you're a young person in an organization, you watch what the managers do. You watch how they make decisions. What are the principles they use when they make a decision? Through that process, you communicate. But it is a major challenge as the company gets larger, and we try to spend a lot of time at it.

Now, maintaining the company's competitiveness is a challenge we face, and it's not dissimilar from the challenges that other consumer goods companies face.

I do think that in this question of values, again, that we have an advantage. When people are at work in the Procter & Gamble Co., they don't have to worry about whether or not the company is putting out safe products, or somehow polluting, or whether the management of the company is operating in a totally ethical fashion. I don't want to hold us up as a paragon of virtue in American business, because there are a lot of fine companies in the United States. But I also believe what I'm talking about is real, that it's possible for young people to go to work in business situations—both large or small businesses—in which that isn't always the case. Those values are not always there, and it can be distracting.

Mr. Crain: In many cases, what you're describing sounds a lot like what Japanese companies have been successful in doing, sort of a management by consensus, having everyone throughout the organization understand exactly where the company is going, on the one hand, and on the other hand, not having that wide chasm between top management and the workers. Do you see any similarities?

Mr. Smale: Yes. We've made that analogy from time to time. This is not a Japanese-like company, certainly, in a total sense, because Americans don't operate like Japanese as a society. They're much more of a homogeneous society than we are.

Absolutely, the foundation of our ability to be successful is to be able to embrace the talents of every person working in the company, to really get everything they've got to give, to contribute.

Mr. Danzig: Procter & Gamble gets involved with local development, with civic programs. I'd like to hear your comments about the role of

Procter & Gamble in the society immediately surrounding it, and why that's important.

Mr. Smale: Well, again, in this community, lots of businesses are involved in its cultural and civic activities. This company and its managers, its people, have been involved in Cincinnati activities I guess as long as we've been around.

Some of this can be easily defended on the basis of the value to the company of having a pleasant community in which to attract managers, because we hire managers from all over the world. But even if you took that away, I think the people would be involved in the activities of the community because of the kind of people they are. It just flows naturally, and we are heavily involved.

We try to be a good corporate citizen in all of the areas in which we operate across this country, and in other countries as well.

Mr. Crain: The human values that you hold so dear at Procter & Gamble seem to extend naturally to the way you think about marketing: Having respect for the customer and trying to find out what the customer really wants rather than what you want to sell the customer. Do you see any analogy there?

Mr. Smale: Sure. Our business is based on understanding the consumer and providing the kind of products that the consumer wants. We place enormous emphasis on our product development area and our marketing area, and on our people knowing the consumer.

If they're responsible for laundry products, they need to know how people get dirty clothes clean. They do it in a whole variety of ways using a whole variety of standards. Our people have to know that like the palm of their hand. Perhaps one manifestation of that is the 800 line. We have something like 110 operators at those phones 10 hours a day answering questions. Some people

call to complain about this or that—and we want that, too—but the vast majority of the calls are for information.

They want to know nutritional information about food products, or they want to know how to bake a cake at an altitude of 5,000 feet. They may call and say, "I'm giving my neighbor a Lilt home permanent and I'm stuck on this part of the directions. What do I do?"

I get a cassette about once a month, and I play it in the car, and listen to people who call. All of this is reported monthly and broken out by brands. It's a statistical report that is circulated.

And at the ground level, where we're dealing with individual products, our people go through focus-group interviews. They sit and listen to people by the hour.

Mr. Crain: In the next 150 years, Procter & Gamble seems to be poised to enter a very exciting new era. You have olestra, your new calorie and cholesterol-free fat substitute. You seem to be having a new interest in healthcare with your Richardson-Vicks acquisition, your G.D. Searle acquisition, your prescription-drug thrust. Can you describe, in general terms, how you see Procter & Gamble evolving in years ahead?

Mr. Smale: Well, let me try to put it in historical terms. The company came out of World War II basically as a soap and detergent company. It had already, however, started to branch into some other areas. Crisco has been around since 1911.

Then there was a period in the late '40s through the early '50s when the company was growing dramatically as a result of new products like Tide. There were new washing habits, automatic washing machines, which changed consumption patterns, increased consumption. And, at that point, we were starting to expand internationally.

Then, beginning about the mid-50s, and roughly for about a decade, the company diversified from a product-line standpoint. At the same time, there was important growth being generated in what we then called the toilet goods division of the company.

Then there was a period from roughly the mid-'60s through the late '70s, in which the company was back doing what it had done in one of these earlier periods, which was consolidating its position in these new fields.

Toward the late '70s, we again began a process of moving into new categories of business, and that process has embraced part of what you referred to in relation to the Richardson-Vicks and the Searle brands. Before that, we bought Orange Crush and, for Citrus Hill, the Ben Hill Griffin production facility. We acquired Norwich, a pharmaceutical and otc drug business, now part of our health and personal care division.

It's hard for me to predict the future, partly because it's inappropriate, partly because I can't, literally. But I think we expect to spend the next few years doing what we've done in the past, and that is consolidating our position in these new fields we've entered, trying to achieve share leadership where we can. Again, I want to be careful not to try to suggest that we wouldn't enter another field if an opportunity came along that we felt was important. There is relevance through all of this from a marketing standpoint. These products are sold in outlets with which we're familiar; that is, basically, grocery stores, mass merchandisers, drug stores. With the exception of the pharmaceutical business, we've entered businesses with which we're familiar.

Mr. Crain: Can you talk about this new calorie and cholesterol-free substitute, olestra? How is that linked to what you've been doing?

Mr. Smale: We got into Crisco because cottonseed oil was related to laundry products and now we're by far the largest producer of shortening and oil in the country. We've done a lot and are doing a lot of research in fat technology, and this broad interest brought forth this thing. You can think of it as a Shmoo [a reference to Al Capp's friendly, all-purpose food supplier of cartoon strip fame]. It's very clear that Americans are interested in healthy foods, and foods made with olestra are going to be healthier.

Mr. Danzig: This evolutionary description you've given us of the brands and the business categories that you've gotten into post-World War II—can you superimpose over that the way the brand-management system has helped bring that development along, and what kind of changes were made in that system to adjust to the changes?

Mr. Smale: The brand-management system basically hasn't changed importantly. I wasn't here when it was put together in the early 1930s, but the concept is the same now, that you make one group of people responsible for a business. Each of our brands has a brand manager and a brand group that's responsible for it. It's a management technique. It's a way of managing a business that has become increasingly diverse. It's certainly, today, not unique to Procter & Gamble.

The changes that go on in the environment that surround the brand—in media and in consumer interest—don't really require a change in the way of managing the brand.

Mr. Crain: Some people have suggested that one way the brand-management system might change is that we might be evolving to something like segment marketing, in which a man or a woman might be responsible for marketing several products to the older segment of consumers, and, perhaps, pulling out other important segments as well. Would anything like that ever work at this company?

Mr. Smale: Oh, I suppose it could. I don't think that we would reorganize along those lines. I think that having a brand manager or a brand group be totally knowledgeable about the brand and the use of the category involved is probably more relevant to running the business than having them be total experts against a slice of society—older people or working mothers, or what have you—and have multiple brand responsibility within that slice.

Think about Tide. In the 1950s, it came in about four sizes. Today, there is Liquid Tide, Tide unscented, and in test market there is Tide Multi-Action Sheets, a totally new approach in bleaching and softening in the laundry process. Those changes are in response to consumer interest, and yet, they can be managed by the same basic techniques that were used in the '50s to manage Tide.

Mr. Danzig: Dos it get any more difficult for you to reach consumers on TV these days given the programming problems and pricing problems?

Mr. Smale: It's more difficult, in fact, because the networks don't reach as many people as they did, regardless of how much it costs to do it. On the other hand, I've got to say that network television is still by far the most efficient way to reach 60% or 70% of the homes.

There has been a clear segmentation of media, and that's responsive, again, to changes in society—the number of specialty kinds of magazines, as an example. And I assume that that kind of trend will continue on into the future.

Mr. Crain: Is it now becoming harder for a mass marketer like Procter & Gamble to reach the consumer in an effective way?

Mr. Smale: It's becoming different. If you define harder on the basis that you can't reach as many people through network television as you could 10 or 20 years ago, then, yes, it's harder. But you can still reach those people, and we do.

I suspect if you go back into the last century, it was much more difficult for the company to reach consumers, because that predated mass media. But the company operated with that kind of a challenge, and it will operate in the future with the kind of challenge represented by the diversity of people P&G wants to reach. We'll have to make adjustments to one degree or another, but it doesn't stand in our way of being able to grow in the future.

Mr. Crain: And you will continue to bring out products with mass appeal and not just products with more of a direct appeal to certain consumers?

Mr. Smale: Yes. You can look at a brand like Secret and find that deodorant in three different scents, in cream form, in aerosol, in anti-perspirants, in roll-on, in stick—but we're selling Secret. While the number of forms has changed because of consumer interests, we don't run 16 different commercials on Secret. We're selling Secret for what Secret is. That's true, basically, on all of our brands.

Mr. Danzig: Could we turn to the agency situation? I think what's coming through here is you have a patient and evolutionary view of Procter & Gamble's history in the marketplace, and you adjust to changes while always remaining true to your main businesses and the nature of the products.

With all the changes going on in advertising agencies today, how do you assess this vis-a-vis Procter & Gamble's requirements?

Mr. Smale: Our attitude or our relationships with our agencies really hasn't changed. We see our advertising agencies as close partners in the venture, which is the product or the brand. Certainly there have been changes, mergers and so forth in the agency field, but that really hasn't affected our attitude about that relationship.

Mr. Crain: Do you think it's inevitable that as companies acquire other companies and get bigger, that's going to happen on a parallel basis in the agency world?

Mr. Smale: I really don't know. In the final analysis, acquisitions and mergers have got to be justified on the basis of their efficiency, and the marketplace, eventually, will determine whether a given consolidation has produced greater efficiency. We don't see that larger is necessarily better in relation to agencies. We don't believe that, by the very nature of what they do, there is a lot of added efficiency in the merger of major agencies from the standpoint of the client, or the advertiser, or the manufacturer.

The agencies, individually, run their businesses according to their own self-interest and the self-interest of their employees, as they should. I'm not trying to suggest that we would try to interfere with that process. I'm simply saying that, from our standpoint, the kind of service they provide is a very personal thing. The creation of outstanding advertising is what they're all about, and we don't think that having a huge agency is necessarily any more productive in that area than having smaller agencies.

Mr. Danzig: Are you generally satisfied with the level of creativity that you're getting today? Do you see it as being better or on par with what you've had in the past?

Mr. Smale: I think on par. I'm not sure we'll ever be satisfied that we've got as many very strong campaigns as we ought to have, given our number of brands. But I think that the kind of service we're getting from our agencies today is, by and large, as strong as it's been in the past.

Mr. Crain: Do you think because of your strong thrust into new areas such as healthcare, it's going to be harder to maintain the standard that you have with agencies as far as your conflict policy is concerned?

Mr. Smale: I don't think so. But, again, it depends on what kind of future we're talking about, how far you can see in the future. We have seen nothing, at least in the current situation, that suggests that we're not being well served by our conflict policy, and that we can't continue to operate quite successfully in agency relationships with that policy.

Mr. Danzig: Do you consider P&G to be a global marketer in the sense of promoting a brand globally in one uniform way?

Mr. Smale: I think of us as a global marketer, but I wouldn't define it quite the way you have. We're a global marketer in the sense that we bring basic technology, basic innovation to as many markets as we think we can be successful.

Pampers is an illustration of that. We don't market the same Pampers product all over the world, and we don't market it with the same advertising copy all over the world. No, we're not global, but the consumer isn't global, either. Consumers are different, even in what would seem to be as straightforward a proposition as a baby diaper. Babies aren't built the same everywhere in the world and consumer habits and practices vary.

Mr. Danzig: How do you, as a manager, stay on top of this far-flung operation?

Mr. Crain: Even the 83 brands in the U.S. is quite a task.

Mr. Smale: It isn't as complicated as it might seem. I could ask you the same kind of question: How can you keep track of all your different departments?

Mr. Crain: I've got a brother.

Mr. Smale: Well, I've got several brothers. But there are techniques. We have reviews with each of the divisions, and we have reviews at our international subsidiaries. I get reports of one nature or another about shares and volume and profits, etc. It really is not quite as complicated as it might seem.

I don't really get involved in the day-to-day operations of these brands. I spend much more of my time dealing with the future; that is, the strategic issues that we think we're dealing with in one category or another. Much of what goes on on a day-to-day basis I learn about after the fact.

Mr. Crain: On your watch as chief executive, what has been your personal greatest satisfaction and your biggest disappointment?

Mr. Smale: I think my greatest satisfaction has been the crystallization of my realization of the character and strength of the Procter & Gamble organization.

That's not something that started on the 5th of January of 1981, when I became CEO—not necessarily an accomplishment of mine. But in these intervening years, from the standpoint of personal satisfaction, it has been, I think, the most significant change. . . .

I don't think I've had any major disappointments. Certainly, Rely was a disappointment, the fact that we were unable to persuade the authorities, the Food & Drug Administration, that our product was not peculiarly involved in toxic shock syndrome. There's also the fact that it has taken us longer than one would have wished to become successful in Japan, but we think we're well on our way there now. Those things, I think, are part of being in business, and I suspect that 20 years from now, somebody else will be answering the question the same way, because there are going to be other disappointments.

There will be successes and, hopefully, the successes will outmatch the disappointments; certainly, that's been the case so far.

Mr. Crain: It occurred to me that the significance of your 150th anniversary is that it teaches you to have patience.

Mr. Smale: Patience and perspective. We've got to be careful about ancestor worship; we've still got to run this business. It's a highly competitive business, and 150 years doesn't move the needle one inch in relation to volume and profit growth in the next fiscal year, but it does give you a perspective.

I don't know how you measure the value of that, but it's very real, not just to the chief executive officer, but to everyone in the organization. It gives the organization, importantly, a sense of stability.

CHAPTER THIRTY ONE

Tribute from a Friend

Few if any American advertising executives have had as long or as intimate a relationship with Procter & Gamble as Bart Cummings, who joined Compton Advertising in New York in 1947, eventually became supervisor of all P&G business at Compton (now Saatchi & Saatchi DFS Compton) and was named president of the agency in January 1955. He became chairman of the executive committee in 1971 and chairman emeritus in 1979.

THERE IS NO DOUBT IN MY MIND THAT Procter & Gamble Co. is one of the wonders of the world—certainly the world of manufacturing, marketing and advertising. I spent the greater part of my life working with and observing the operations of this unique and amazing company. In my judgment, it sets standards and practices that all companies should strive to emulate if they too wish to reach the pinnacle of business success.

It has been my privilege to see P&G's annual sales volume grow from approximately $800 million to $17 billion, with diversification from basically a soap and detergent manufacturer to a producer and marketer of paper products, food products, toiletries and proprietary drugs. Most of P&G's brands are No. 1 or No. 2 in their categories, and in many cases the company has the No. 1, 2 and 3 brand in certain product categories. In tandem with growth in sales, of course, the advertising budget has grown just as spectacularly, from about $40 million annually to well over $1.5 billion annually.

People have wondered how P&G has managed to achieve such a great track record over the past several decades? The answer, in a word, is *people*. The company takes its recruitment of new personnel very seriously, and it is able to seek out and find the kinds of people it can train and build into leading experts in all areas of a large manufacturing concern: product development and evaluation; engineering; sales research; marketing; advertising; promotion; and analysis.

These areas encompass virtually every skill and talent that one can think of that is required to build and administer an outstanding organization. P&G believes in finding and hiring the very best and paying top dollar for this great talent. I was lucky enough to have worked with some of P&G's best. My relationship with P&G began in fall 1949 when Bob Holbrook, Compton Advertising's president-CEO, called me into his office and said, "I have decided that I am going to put you on the Procter & Gamble business." Frankly, this piece of news sent a chill down my spine. ME on P&G? I had been at Compton for about two years and had heard a good deal about the company from some of my peers. I really did not know all that much about it, except that, from all reports, they expected account executives on their brands to be slide-rule artists with the ability to analyze numbers, put together all kinds of reports and recommendations—with everything in writing. It somehow sounded like a numbers game, and not very appealing.

Being a former copywriter, my great interest still was in creating advertising. I said to Mr. Holbrook, "I think you may be making a big mistake putting me on P&G; I'm not an expert in marketing. I just don't feel right about it." But he didn't give me much choice. And believe me, I had to work hard—very hard. I'd stay in the office or take work home almost every night, and it wasn't unusual for me to work weekends as well. But I had to learn, and I had good instruction from the people I worked with at Compton.

The people at P&G were extremely patient with me, particularly Tom Harrington, group promotion manager on Duz—the brand to which I was assigned—and other brands under his jurisdiction. My P&G counterpart was brand manager Frank Zeaman and the brand assistant was Tom Carroll (who later became president of Lever Bros.)

My brand, Duz, was the leading package laundry soap in the U.S. by a good margin, but P&G had a new heavy-duty laundry detergent in test market—Tide. It was looking very strong in hard-water areas. It really scared the hell out of all of us who had anything to do with Duz.

After about a year, P&G moved Mr. Zeaman to another brand and replaced him with Ed Harness. He had been a brand assistant on Ivory bar soap, which also was being handled by Compton. Ed was one of the most intelligent, brilliant men I ever worked with. Our relationship ripened into a lifelong friendship I will cherish as long as I live.

When Tide started its expansion in hard-water areas, it really made strides. Duz, a soap product, was not particularly effective in hard water.

I will never forget the struggle Mr. Harness and I had with his back-up associates and mine at the agency. We were trying to defend our position against this breakthrough product, which had so much money and top P&G management support behind it. To make a long story short, Duz began to decline, and it became a great joke in P&G and Compton circles that Ed Harness and Bart Cummings rode to great success in the business by taking the No. 1 laundry brand down to minor-league status.

After two years Mr. Holbrook made me an account supervisor and gave me another P&G brand, Ivory Soap Flakes. William Gurganus, who later became president of P&G International, was the brand manager. Chester Dudley was Compton's account executive. Ivory Soap Flakes also was on a downhill slide because of the introduction of light-duty detergents. It's obvious to see what was happening: We were sliding with our soap brands and we didn't have a detergent brand with which we could grow. Mr. Harness and I agitated for P&G to develop a low-sudsing detergent to compete with the very successful high sudsers like Tide. Ultimately P&G did develop such a product. It was Dash, and it was assigned to Compton.

By this time Mr. Harness had become a group promotion manager in charge of several brands, among them Dash. He and I, Bill Wichman, Dash's brand manager, and Ed Artzt, brand assistant (and now vice chairman and president of P&G International), and John Hise, Compton's account man, worked together to develop Dash's test-market and introduction strategy. We worked closely with Ivorydale's technical people in the development of Dash. We watched it being

tested in the lab's washing machines and then in consumers' homes around the country.

This helped to measure consumer response and aided in the development of advertising, marketing, promotion and a media plan for the brand. Dash went into test market in 1953, then expanded across the country and became a national brand in 1955.

One of the axioms by which P&G lives is "Every brand must stand on its own feet." I was able to see that put in practice several times while working on the Dash account. One incident also provided insight into what can happen behind the scenes when an agency works with P&G.

A special sales film for Dash, written and produced by an independent studio under the supervision of P&G technical staff, the brand group and Compton had been created to stimulate enthusiasm for Dash among the sales staff. It explained the advantages of low-sudsing Dash vs. the high sudsers, particularly in smaller front-loading washing machines. Lab comparisons showed front-loading washers' superior cleaning abilities.

The first presentation was made before a small group of P&G top brass: T.J. Wood, VP-sales; Mark Upson, sales manager; W.R. Chase, VP-advertising; E.A. "Bill" Snow, group promotion manager; Mr. Harness, Dash brand promotion manager; Mr. Wichman, brand manager; Mr. Artzt, assistant brand manager; and yours truly, agency account supervisor. When the lights finally came up, T.J. Wood let out such a torrent of expletives I thought he was having a fit. Essentially he said, "The film is a lie and it will never be shown again." Mr. Chase agreed 100%. Mr. Upson, who had read the script and had edited some of it, said he couldn't believe it was a film of the script he had approved. (It was.) Mr. Snow, who also had approved the script, said he had never seen it; he, too, agreed with Mr. Wood.

Mr. Harness and I were speechless at this reaction to a film that had been so painstakingly written and produced. When we finally got our bearings and started to counter their objections, we were told the film could wreck P&G's biggest profit maker, Tide. Mr. Harness and I were unhappy and shocked at how Mr. Upson and Mr. Snow had let us down, how they had rolled over after Mr. Woods' blasts about the film. Mr. Harness decided he couldn't work for a company run by men like that; he decided to quit.

I urged him to calm down, to think it over. We agreed later to talk to Howard Morgens, then P&G's exec VP, show him the film, and see what he could—or would—do about it. Mr. Morgens watched the film, realized its implications, and commiserated with Mr. Harness. He didn't say it was a "lie," but he counseled Mr. Harness on the damage it could do in its present form. He suggested that perhaps some changes and deletions could be made to soften the blow on Tide. Mr. Harness was placated by Mr. Morgens' skillful handling of the matter, and life went on.

The film, which cost about $100,000 to produce, was never revised or used. The lesson I learned was, "*Not* every brand is allowed to stand on its feet." It depends.

As I look back on it today, T.J. Wood had been right in his decision not to let us use the film. The company's mistake had been to let us, in our youthful enthusiasm, get the script written and the film produced in the first place.

As time went on, I gradually took over the supervision of all the Compton-handled P&G business. I became Compton's president in 1955 when Bob Holbrook became board chairman. At the same time, Ed Harness moved up the P&G ladder, becoming an advertising manager of the soap division, exec VP, president, CEO and finally chairman-CEO.

P&G's past executives were brilliant. They are equally so today. The leadership at the very top of Procter & Gamble has come from a relatively few, starting with R.R. Deupree in the 1920s, '30s and into the '40s; Neil McElroy in the '40s and '50s; Howard Morgens in the '50s, '60s and '70s; Edward Harness in the '70s and '80s; and P&G's current Chairman-CEO John Smale.

The personalities of these great leaders have differed widely, but their methods and their standards were and are much the same—first class.

It is little wonder that P&G has been selected year after year as one of the best-managed companies in the world. And it is little wonder that the company, time and again, has been innovative in its approach to marketing, perfecting brand and sales analysis, media selection, product and consumer research, product development and testing, test marketing, consumer attitude and appraisal, copy testing, trade development and trade relations, sales promotion and merchandising methodology.

In my judgment, given its wealth of talent and dedicated people, P&G has a head start on its next 150 years of prosperity.

Index

Dial Corp., 157

DiCamillo, Gary, 86, 87

Direct Profitability Program, 156

Direct to retailers policy, 16

Dividend Day, first, 12, 39

Dixie Terminal, 63

Doornick, Ron, 113, 119–21

Downing, Maggie, 147

Downy, 29, 69, 181, 199

Doyle Dane Bernbach, 159, 167

Drake Hospital campaign, 50

Dramamine, 25, 46, 178

Dreft, 19, 23, 29, 42, 104

Drene liquid shampoo, 19, 24, 43, 77

Drexel Burnham Lambert, 26, 34, 193

Dudley, Chester, 218

Duncan Hines, 27, 29, 35, 44, 59, 68–69, 74, 94, 139, 156, 183

Duncan Hines Institute, 27

Duttenhofer Building, 63

Duz, 23, 29, 77, 185, 217

E

Eberle, Charles, 32

Economic research department, 18

"Edge of Night," 186, 188

Edison, Thomas Alva, 8–9, 37

Edler, Richard, 85–86

Eight-hour workday, 13, 40

800 toll-free number, 68–69

Eisenhower, Dwight D., 27, 44

Encaprin, 59, 164

Environmental protection interests, 54–55

Environment pressures, 30–31

Era, 24, 170, 181

ERIM, 152

Esmark, 183

"Euro-market" concept, 198

Executive development, 90–99

"Eyes on Tomorrow," 11, 13, 15, 18, 20, 21, 25, 26, 32, 146–47

F

Fab, 23

Fairy liquid dishwashing liquid, 203

Federal Trade Commission regulations, 31–32

Federation of Organized Labor Trades and Labor Unions, 12

Fels-Naphtha, 14

Ferguson, James, 92–93

Fink, Steven, 69

"First Hundred Years," 185